T0205967

Lecture Notes in Business Information Processing 424

More information about this series at http://www.springer.com/series/7911

Selmin Nurcan · Axel Korthaus (Eds.)

Intelligent Information Systems

CAiSE Forum 2021
Melbourne, VIC, Australia, June 28 – July 2, 2021
Proceedings

 Springer

Editors
Selmin Nurcan 🆔
University of Paris 1 Panthéon-Sorbonne
Paris, France

Axel Korthaus 🆔
Swinburne University of Technology
Melbourne, VIC, Australia

ISSN 1865-1348   ISSN 1865-1356 (electronic)
Lecture Notes in Business Information Processing
ISBN 978-3-030-79107-0   ISBN 978-3-030-79108-7 (eBook)
https://doi.org/10.1007/978-3-030-79108-7

This Springer imprint is published by the registered company Springer Nature Switzerland AG
The registered company address is: Gewerbestrasse 11, 6330 Cham, Switzerland

Preface

The CAiSE Forum is a place within the International Conference on Advanced Information Systems Engineering (CAiSE) for presenting and discussing new ideas and tools related to information systems engineering. Intended to serve as an interactive platform, the Forum aims at the presentation of emerging new topics and controversial positions, as well as demonstration of innovative systems, tools, and applications. The Forum sessions at CAiSE facilitate the interaction, discussion, and exchange of ideas among presenters and participants.

Two types of submissions are invited to the Forum:

(1) Visionary papers that present innovative research projects, which are still at a relatively early stage and do not necessarily include a full-scale validation. Visionary papers are usually presented as posters.
(2) Demo papers describing innovative tools and prototypes that implement the results of research efforts. The tools and prototypes are presented as demos at the Forum.

This year, the CAiSE conference, originally planned to be held in Melbourne, Australia, took a virtual form due to the COVID-19 pandemic.

Contributions to the CAiSE 2021 Forum addressed many of the CAiSE 2021 conference topics and in particular this year's theme: *Intelligent Information Systems.*

The 18 papers presented in this volume were carefully reviewed and selected. The management of paper submission and reviews was supported by the EasyChair conference system in a double loop. Selecting the papers to be accepted has been a worthwhile effort.

The CAiSE Program Board recommended 14 visionary papers, submitted as short papers to the main conference, which were among the top 30% of the submissions to CAiSE 2021 in terms quality and innovation. The four demo papers were directly submitted to the CAiSE forum and were accepted for their high potential. All papers received three reviews from the members of the forum Program Committee and the Program Board, and were presented in the cyber space of CAiSE 2021 during the forum session.

As the CAISE 2021 Forum chairs, we would like to express again our gratitude to the Forum Program Committee and also to the CAiSE Program Board for their efforts in providing very thorough evaluations of the submitted papers. We also wish to thank all authors who submitted papers to the CAISE 2021 Forum for having shared their work with us.

Last but not least, we thank the organizers of CAiSE 2021 for their help with the organization of the event, particularly adjusting to the changing circumstances during the global COVID-19 crisis and facilitating the transformation to a virtual event. We would have liked to meet in person in the lovely city of Melbourne. We wish to thank the CAiSE 2021 Program Committee Chairs and the Organisation Committee for their support. We also thank Springer, and in particular Ralf Gerstner and Christine Reiss, for their assistance during the production of the proceedings.

May 2021   Selmin Nurcan
                                                                                              Axel Korthaus

Organization

Chairs

Selmin Nurcan   Université Paris 1 Panthéon-Sorbonne, France
Axel Korthaus   Swinburne University of Technology, Australia

Program Committee Members

Said Assar   Telecom Ecole de Management, France
Renata Guizzardi   Federal University of Espírito Santo, Brazil
Massimo Mecella   Sapienza University of Rome, Italy
Michalis Pavlidis   University of Brighton, UK
Jolita Ralyté   University of Geneva, Switzerland
Janis Stirna   University of Stockholm, Sweden
Arnon Sturm   Ben-Gurion University, Israel
Moe Thandar Wynn   Queensland University of Technology, Australia

Contents

Innovative Tools and Prototypes

Visionary Papers

Evolution of an Adaptive Information System for Precision Medicine

Ana León$^{(\boxtimes)}$, Alberto García S., Mireia Costa, Andrea Vañó Ribelles, and Oscar Pastor

PROS Research Center, Universitat Politècnica de València,
Camí de Vera, s/n, 46022 València, Spain
{aleon,algarsi3,opastor}@pros.upv.es,
{micossan,anvari}@etsii.upv.es

Abstract. Precision Medicine has emerged as a computational approach to provide a personalized diagnosis, based on the individual variability in genes, environment, and lifestyle. Success in such aim requires
extensible, adaptive, and ontologically well-grounded Information Systems to store, manage, and analyze the large amounts of data generated by the scientific community. Using an existing adaptive information system (Delfos platform) supported by a conceptual schema and
an AI algorithm, the contribution of this work is to describe how the
system has been improved to address specific challenges regarding the
clinical significance of DNA variants. To do so, the following topics are
addressed: i) provide an ontologically-consistent representation of the
problem domain; ii) improve the management of clinical significance
conflicts; iii) ease the addition of new data sources; and iv) provide a
scalable environment more aligned with the data analysis requirements
in a clinical context. The aim of the work has been achieved by using a
Model-Driven Engineering approach.

Keywords: MDE · Conceptual modeling · Information Systems ·
Precision Medicine

1 Introduction

Precision Medicine (PM) has emerged as a computational approach to interpret
omics (e.g., proteomics, genomics, and metabolomics), facilitating their application to healthcare provision [2]. One of the pillars of the PM approach is the
genetic diagnosis, that is based on determining the practical importance of each
DNA variant according to its role in the development of disease (known as clinical
significance). There are different public databases that provide interpretations
of the clinical significance of variants (i.e. variant interpretations) such as Clin-
Var (www.ncbi.nlm.nih.gov/clinvar/), Ensembl (www.ensembl.org/index.html),
ClinGen (www.clinicalgenome.org) and CIViC (www.civicdb.org/home).

Even though the mentioned databases are an excellent source of information,
the interpretation of the clinical significance that they provide is a challenging

© Springer Nature Switzerland AG 2021
S. Nurcan and A. Korthaus (Eds.): CAiSE Forum 2021, LNBIP 424, pp. 3–10, 2021.
https://doi.org/10.1007/978-3-030-79108-7_1

process that may significantly affect diagnosis and clinical care recommendations [4]. Our experience with these repositories has allowed us to identify two main problems: i) lack of a clear representation of the clinical significance at phenotype level; and ii) a generic and sometimes not very precise identification of conflicts between interpretations. The consequence of these problems are explained in detail in Sect. 2.

Adaptive Information Systems (AIS) are key to overcome these challenges, by extending and adapting their functionality to the dynamism of the domain, presenting the available evidence with a well-grounded ontological basis, and providing automated algorithms to properly handle conflicts. The contribution of this work is to describe how using a Model Driven Engineering (MDE) approach, the above mentioned problems can be solved to improve an existing genomic platform, Delfos platform, to: i) consistently represent what a variant interpretation is; ii) allow the efficient management of conflicts between interpretations; and iii) provide a consistent environment for the precise evaluation of the clinical significance of DNA variants in the context of an efficient genomic data management.

To this aim, the work is organized as follows: Sect. 2, describes in detail the problem and the consequences from an information Systems Engineering perspective. Section 3 presents our proposed solution. Finally, Sect. 4 concludes and discusses future research directions.

2   Clinical Significance and Conflict Management

2.1   The Clinical Significance

The clinical significance is the practical importance of a variant effect (e.g., benign, pathogenic, or uncertain significance). The clinical significance of each variant is interpreted by experts, after the review and evaluation of the available evidence that supports the association of the variant with a phenotype (trait or disease). Different public and nonpublic databases provide interpretations of the clinical significance of variants, as introduced in Sect. 1.

A DNA variant can be interpreted multiple times by different experts and for different phenotypes. To help experts assess the clinical interest of a variant, an aggregate clinical significance is usually provided by these databases, which is useful to determine if the different interpretations are concordant or discordant. For example, the variant c.986A > C has been interpreted in ClinVar by 13 experts for different phenotypes (e.g. glycogen storage disease, GBE1-Related disorders, and polyglucosan body disease) [1]. As all the experts consider the variant as pathogenic in all the interpretations, and for all the phenotypes, the aggregate clinical significance is pathogenic.

Nevertheless, the complexity of human disease implies that the effect of a variant may be different for different phenotypes. In such cases, the databases do not compute a precise aggregate, and the user must review and analyse each of the experts' interpretations to identify the correct role of the variant for each phenotype. This frequently conforms a tedious, manual, and prone-to-error working process that diminishes the added value of Information Systems for the development of an efficient PM. Nevertheless, the higher impact of this approach occurs when conflicts between interpretations are analyzed.

2.2 Conflicting Interpretations

The conflicts between interpretations arise when experts disagree about the role of a variant in the development of disease. In general, interpretations have a high degree of concordance [7]. However, as knowledge about the mechanisms of disease evolves, the existence of conflicts in the interpretation of variants over time is not uncommon [6].

As mentioned, the different interpretations of a variant are typically aggregated into a "global" clinical significance. As a consequence, a variant that has been interpreted as disease causing for a given phenotype, and as not disease causing or uncertain for another, could be considered as having conflicting interpretations. These variants are more likely to be discarded from genetic diagnosis since they are considered as conflicting, although their exclusion could lead to missing important information.

Thus, the precise analysis and treatment of the conflicts is a key feature of any information system that integrates data from different sources.

3 Extending an AIS by Adding the Clinical Actionability

In the PROS Research Center (http://www.pros.webs.upv.es/), we have developed an AIS, called the Delfos platform, ontologically supported by the Conceptual Schema of the Human Genome (CSHG). [3,5] and a deterministic classification AI algorithm.

The aim of Delfos is to ease the management of the genetic data with clinical purposes. Thanks to the ontological support of the CSHG, Delfos can be extended to include new functionality, and consequently can be adapted to any change in the domain.

Initially, the CSHG modeled variants so that they can be associated with multiple clinical interpretations (see Fig. 1). Each variant (Variation class) may have multiple clinical interpretations provided by the scientific community (Significance class) for each Phenotype. Interpretations are described by the "ClinicalSignificance" and the "levelOfCertainty" attributes. The "ClinicalSignificance" determines the practical importance of the variant. The "levelOfCertainty" represents the relevance of the evidence used by each expert to assess that importance.

Nevertheless, in the context of an advanced genomic management platform, the aggregate clinical significance approach, followed by most of the genomic sources, is not useful because of the problems and uncertainties mentioned in Sect. 2. This led to the need of providing a better solution.

To this aim, we have followed a MDE approach with the following steps: i) an ontological characterization of the main concepts, ii) an extension of the CSHG

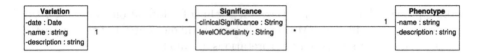

Variation		Significance		Phenotype
-date : Date	*	-clinicalSignificance : String	1	-name : string
-name : string	1	-levelOfCertainty : String	*	-description : string
-description : string				

Fig. 1. Clinical Significance in the CSHG

to represent the new knowledge, and iii) an application of changes to make a new version of the Delfos platform. MDE promotes the systematic use of models in order to raise the level of abstraction at which software is specified, increasing the level of automation in software development, what we consider to be the most appropriate approach according to the context and aim of this work.

3.1   Ontological Characterization

As mentioned in Sect. 2.1, the clinical significance is the practical importance of a variant effect, commonly associated with a phenotype. The impact of this effect is characterized according to terms such as Pathogenic (variants that cause a disorder), Protective (variants that decrease the risk of a disorder) and Uncertain significance (variants with insufficient or conflicting evidence about their role in disease).

To help assess the degree of concordance between interpretations, databases compute an aggregate clinical significance, but without specifying which one corresponds to each phenotype. This means that the treatment of conflicts are reduced to a limited number of terms, excluding potentially relevant combinations.

3.2   Evolution of the Conceptual Schema

The different types of clinical significances can be grouped according to their likelihood of being the cause of a potentially damaging phenotype, or providing protection against one. Clinical significances related to drug or treatment responses are special cases since their definition does not specify if the effect is positive or negative.

Using this approach as basis, we propose to create an aggregate value for each phenotype associated to a variant, by grouping the different interpretations into a new conceptual entity that we have called "clinical actionability". Therefore, instead of having a general term for each variant (an approach whose limitations have been stated in Sect. 2), the information system would provide a set of terms that allows a more precise assessment of a variant effect, according to the different phenotypes that have been studied. This approach is more aligned with the data analysis requirements in the context of a clinical practice. To represent this new knowledge, and provide the Delfos platform with the new functionality, the conceptual schema on which the information system is based must be modified.

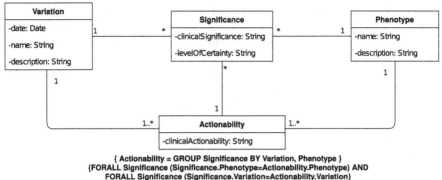

Fig. 2. Conceptual schema to represent the clinical actionability

Figure 2 represents the new Actionability class, associated with the Variation, Phenotype, and Significance classes. The clinicalActionability attribute (Actionability class) represents the practical importance of the variant effect. For each phenotype of a variant (Phenotype class), the clinical actionability is calculated as an aggregate of the different clinical significances (Significance class) provided by experts. Only one clinical actionability is allowed for each Variation-Phenotype pair (represented as a constraint to ensure data integrity).

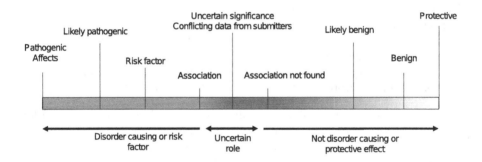

Fig. 3. Distribution of the different clinical significance types according to their likelihood of being the cause of a potentially damaging phenoytpe.

Once the conceptual schema is defined, the next step is to specify how the clinical actionability is calculated. Using the likelihood distribution shown in Fig. 3, we have defined the following terms to describe the different clinical actionability types:

- Disorder causing or risk factor: The variant is the cause of the phenotype, or increases the likelihood of presenting it. This group includes the interpretations whose clinical significance is pathogenic, likely pathogenic, affects, risk factor, or association.
- Not disorder causing or protective effect: The variant is not the cause of the phenotype, or provides a protective effect against it. This group includes the interpretations whose clinical significance is benign, likely benign, association not found, or protective.
- Affects drugs or treatment response: The variant affects the sensitivity or response to the specified drug or treatment. This group includes the interpretations whose clinical significance is drug response or confers sensitivity.
- Uncertain role: The role of the variant in the development of the phenotype is not clear. This group includes the interpretations whose clinical significance is uncertain significance, or when conflicts between interpretations are present.
- Not provided: The variant does not have interpretations and as a consequence the clinical significance is unknown.

Conflicts between interpretations occur when there is less than 75% of agreement in the role of the variant, regarding the development of the associated phenotype. This decision has been taken to avoid situations where an old or not reliable interpretation contradicts the major agreement of the scientific community. Conflicts occur in the following situations:

- Presence of interpretations whose clinical significance belongs to the disorder causing or risk factor group, and to the not disorder causing or protective effect group.
- Presence of interpretations whose clinical significance belongs to the disorder causing or risk factor group, and to the uncertain role group.
- Presence of interpretations whose clinical significance belongs to the not disorder causing or protective effect group, and to the uncertain role group.

Interpretations with no clinical significance provided are not considered for the identification of conflicts. For example, if there are three interpretations for the same phenotype - one of them pathogenic, another one benign, and the third one without the clinical significance specified - only the pathogenic and benign interpretations will be considered, resulting in the presence of conflicts. As a consequence, in this example, the clinical actionability of the variant will belong to the uncertain role group.

Despite the low impact of the changes at the conceptual-model level, the implications for the analytical capabilities of the information system are relevant. The impact of these changes are: i) Abstraction of the different variant effects according to their likelihood of being disease causing or protective, ii) Possibility of evaluating the clinical impact of variants for each associated phenotype, and iii) Decrease of the effort required to add new data sources that use different terms to classify the clinical significance. These changes in the conceptual schema, have been translated into changes in the implementation of the information system that supports the Delfos platform.

3.3   New Delfos Version

The AIS that constitutes the core of the Delfos platform has three main modules:

1. The extraction and transformation module connects to the databases that provide the input data to the system.
2. The identification module is based on an deterministic AI classification algorithm that evaluates the input data, and uses the relationships between the concepts of the CSHG to identify clinically relevant variants.
3. The visualization and exploitation module provides the Graphic User Interface required to query and visualize the knowledge stored in the database that serves as internal data storage.

The main changes affect the AI algorithm, and the way the new knowledge is visualized and accessed by the final user. The rules used to define the different clinical actionability groups, and the criteria required to identify conflicts between interpretations, have been added to the AI algorithm. These changes improve its capability of identifying relevant variants. The internal data storage has been modified to store this new knowledge, according to the specifications of the conceptual schema. Finally, the visualization and exploitation layer has been adapted to provide the required usability.

Thanks to the above mentioned changes, the Delfos platform has been improved to correctly address the problems mentioned in Sect. 2. Using the approach presented in this work, the Delfos platform is able to identify which phenotypes have real conflicts between interpretations, and considers that the effect of the variants could be relevant in other cases. If this information were missing in a genetic analysis, the diagnosis and treatment of patients would be severely affected.

4   Conclusion and Future Work

AIS are key to provide the technological support required to developing correct and accurate genetic diagnosis in the dynamic context of PM. In this work, we have identified two main challenges that led to the need of improving an existing information system (the Delfos platform). The first challenge was the lack of a clear characterization of the variant's clinical significance interpretation at phenotype level; and the second challenge was a generic and sometimes not very precise identification of conflicts between interpretations.

Since Delfos is an AIS supported by a conceptual model and an AI algorithm, we have improved the system by using a MDE approach to: i) consistently represent what a variant interpretation is; ii) allow the efficient management of conflicts between interpretations; iii) ease the integration of interpretations coming from different data sources; and iv) provide a consistent environment aligned with the data analysis requirements in the context of a clinical practice.

Genomics knowledge is under constant evolution. Therefore, the Delfos platform must be frequently updated to adapt to the dynamism of the domain. The main advantage of using and AIS platform is that its extension can be done by reusing what has already been developed, focusing on evolving only the parts that have changed, and reducing the development effort required.

Acknowledgements. This work was supported by the Spanish State Research Agency [grant number TIN2016-80811-P]; and the Generalitat Valenciana [grant number PROMETEO/2018/176] co-financed with European Regional Development Fund (ERDF).

References

1. ClinVar Variant Details (vcv000002777.10). https://www.ncbi.nlm.nih.gov/clinvar/variation/2777/. Accessed 20 Oct 2020
2. Duffy, D.J.: Problems, challenges and promises: perspectives on precision medicine. Briefings Bioinform. **17**(3), 494–504 (2016). https://doi.org/10.1093/bib/bbv060
3. García, S.A., Palacio, A.L., Reyes Román, J.F., Casamayor, J.C., Pastor, O.: Towards the understanding of the human genome: a holistic conceptual modeling approach. IEEE Access **8**, 197111–197123 (2020). https://doi.org/10.1109/ACCESS.2020.3034793
4. Pepin, M.G., Murray, M.L., Bailey, S., Leistritz-Kessler, D., Schwarze, U., Byers, P.H.: The challenge of comprehensive and consistent sequence variant interpretation between clinical laboratories. Genet. Med. **18**(1), 20–24 (2016). https://doi.org/10.1038/gim.2015.31
5. Reyes Román, J.F., Pastor, Ó., Casamayor, J.C., Valverde, F.: Applying conceptual modeling to better understand the human genome. In: Comyn-Wattiau, I., Tanaka, K., Song, I.-Y., Yamamoto, S., Saeki, M. (eds.) ER 2016. LNCS, vol. 9974, pp. 404–412. Springer, Cham (2016). https://doi.org/10.1007/978-3-319-46397-1_31
6. Shah, N., et al.: Identification of misclassified ClinVar variants via disease population prevalence. Am. J. Hum. Genet. **102**(4), 609–619 (2018). https://doi.org/10.1016/j.ajhg.2018.02.019
7. Yang, S., Lincoln, S.E., Kobayashi, Y., Nykamp, K., Nussbaum, R.L., Topper, S.: Sources of discordance among germ-line variant classifications in ClinVar. Genet. Med. **19**(10), 1118–1126 (2017). https://doi.org/10.1038/gim.2017.60

Security Risk Estimation and Management in Autonomous Driving Vehicles

Abasi-amefon O. Affia, Raimundas Matulevičius$^{(\boxtimes)}$, and Rando Tõnisson

Institute of Computer Science, University of Tartu, Tartu, Estonia
{amefon.affia,rma}@ut.ee

Abstract. Autonomous vehicles (AV) are intelligent information systems that perceive, collect, generate and disseminate information to improve knowledge to act autonomously and provide its required services of mobility, safety, and comfort to humans. This paper combines the security risk management (ISSRM) and operationally critical threat, asset, and vulnerability evaluation (OCTAVE *allegro*) methods to define and assess the AV protected assets, security risks, and countermeasures.

Keywords: Autonomous vehicles · Self-driving cars · Security risk management · ISSRM · OCTAVE · Intelligent information systems

1 Introduction

Information systems (IS) involve in the gathering, processing, storing, and distributing information to perform specific tasks and make decisions [14]. Autonomous vehicles (AV), a.k.a., self-driving cars, infer as the intelligent information systems (IIS) because they perceive, collect, generate and disseminate *sensitive* information to improve knowledge to act autonomously and provide its required services of mobility, safety, and comfort to humans. Therefore, it is necessary to secure data and information against malicious use and its resulting security risks. But the current studies focus on the automotive aspect of the AVs and do not consider the AV as an information system. This shortcoming leads stakeholders to miss vital security-related knowledge of the AV information collection, manipulation and actuation activities to make well-informed decisions regarding security investment in AV systems.

In this study, we analyse *how autonomous vehicles as intelligent information systems can be protected against security risks?* Specifically, we focus on vehicles that have achieved autonomy as defined in the SAE J3016 [28] standard – which is level 4 (semi-AVs that autonomously perform all driving functions under certain conditions, e.g. on a specific type of road or at certain times) and level 5 (full AVs that perform all driving functions under all conditions autonomously). We combine the domain model for IS security risk management (ISSRM) [11] with the operationally critical threat, asset and vulnerability evaluation (OCTAVE

© The Author(s) 2021
S. Nurcan and A. Korthaus (Eds.): CAiSE Forum 2021, LNBIP 424, pp. 11–19, 2021.
https://doi.org/10.1007/978-3-030-79108-7_2

allegro) [5] to explore the security risks in AVs through the literature study and case analysis.

2   Research Method

There exist different methods aimed at security risk management, relevant for use in AVs: for example, EVITA [13], ETSI Threat, Vulnerability and implementation Risk Analysis (TVRA) standard [12], HEAVENS security model [21], Security-aware hazard and risk analysis method (SAHARA) [17]. These methods provide guidelines when considering AV security; however, they lack a consistent approach for identifying vulnerabilities, threats/attacks, risk assessment, risk estimation, and risk treatment. Consequently, we did not find a standard or method in the literature that apply to AV security, given its complex capabilities and its overlap across multiple information domains.

In this study, we combine the ISSRM domain model [11] and the OCTAVE [5] method. OCTAVE guides the assessment of information security risks; it contains templates to document risk management activities and guide data collection for probability and security risk impact estimation. But OCTAVE does not support an explicit risk analysis process. The ISSRM domain model guides elicitation of assets, attack methods, vulnerabilities, threats, risks, and solutions to mitigate risks. Initially developed for IS risk management, the ISSRM domain model is also applicable in the AV systems as these systems gather, manipulate, interpret and *disseminate* information for the stakeholders. A combination of OCTAVE and ISSRM strengthens the analysis (*i*) with the ISSRM guidance for the security risk definition and (*ii*) with the OCTAVE templates for security risk estimation.

3   Literature Study

Assets. Following [2], the AV system can be decomposed to perception, network and application layers, as illustrated in Fig. 1. The business assets are defined as data and information that are valuable in the system with its security needs to be estimated using the security criteria (i.e., confidentiality, integrity and availability). The *perception layer* includes the system components responsible for collecting *video, location and travel, surrounding environment and other* data [24,27,28]. The collected data is transmitted to the application layers using the *network layer*. The *application layer* uses the collected data to perform tasks, i.e., calculate routes. An actuation module uses these calculations to perform autonomous functions.

Security Risks. In the literature, we have identified security risks (see Table 1, columns 1–3). Eleven risks (R1–R9, R16) are identified at the perception layer, seven (R10–R11, R19–R23) – at the application layer, and four (R12–R15) at the network layer. R17 can be found at all layers, and R18 is identified at the network and application layers. Details of security risks could also be found in [26]. We do not consider the risks in Table 1 as exhaustive but aim to raise awareness of the AVs' risks.

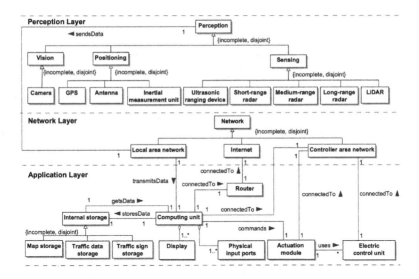

Fig. 1. Literature study: AV system assets (adapted from [26])

Table 1. Literature study: Security risks and countermeasures

Risk ID	Literature	Risk name	Countermeasure	Literature
R1	[19,27,28]	Jamming ultrasonic sensors	Noise detection and rejection; Multiple sensors for redundancy check	[28]
R2	[19,27,28]	Spoofing ultrasound sensors	Noise detection and rejection; Multiple sensors for redundancy check	[28]
R3	[19,23,28]	Acoustic quieting on ultrasound sensors	Multiple sensors for redundancy check	[28]
R4	[19,23,27,28]	Jamming radar	Noise detection and rejection; Multiple sensors for redundancy check	[28]
R5	[19,23,27,28]	Spoofing radar	Noise detection and rejection; Multiple sensors for redundancy check	[28]
R6	[19,24,28]	Blinding cameras	Multiple cameras; Filter to remove harmful light	[24,28]
R7	[24]	Confusing controls using camera inputs	Multiple cameras; Filter to remove harmful light	[24,28]
R8	[19,24]	Relay attack on LiDAR	Multiple LiDAR inputs; Random probing; Shorten pulse period	[24,28]
R9	[19,24,27]	Spoofing LiDAR	Multiple LiDAR inputs; Random probing; Shorten pulse period	[24,28]
R10	[27]	Code modification	Device authentication; Anti-Malware; Isolation	[25,27]
R11	[27]	Code injection	Device authentication; Anti-Malware; Isolation	[25,27]
R12	[25,27]	Packet sniffing	Encryption; Device and user authentication	[25,27]
R13	[19,25,27]	Packet fuzzing	Encryption; Device and user authentication	[25,27]
R14	[23]	Inject CAN messages	Encryption; Device and user authentication	[25,27]
R15	[19,23]	Eavesdropping CAN messages	Encryption; Device and user authentication	[25,27]
R16	[19,22,23]	GPS: Jamming and spoofing	Nullification, Monitoring signals and identification nodes	[20,27]
R17	[23]	EMP attack	Isolation	[25,27]
R18	[23]	Malware injection	Firewall; Anti-Malware; Isolation	[27]
R19	[19,23]	Manipulate map data	User authentication; Device authentication; Isolation	[25,27]
R20	[19]	Extract map data	User authentication; Device authentication; Isolation	[25,27]
R21	[19]	Delete map data	User authentication; Device authentication; Isolation	[25,27]
R22	[19]	Disable actuation module	Isolation; Access control	[25,27]
R23	[19]	Induce bad analysis	Isolation; Access control; Input validation	[25,27]

Countermeasures identified in the literature are presented in Table 1 (see columns 4 and 5). Some key countermeasures at the perception layer are noise detection, rejection, and the use of multiple input sources [24,28]. At the network layer, countermeasures are encryption, special devices and user authentication techniques [25,27]. At the application layer, countermeasures include anti-malware software, firewalls, access control and user authentication.

4   Case Analysis

We have combined the ISSRM and OCTAVE methods to assess the Lexus RX450h AV system in the laboratory environment[1]. The car's architecture is presented in Fig. 2; it is adapted from our literature study (see Fig. 1). The figure also illustrates how risks are associated. Table 2 shows an example of one risk – R6. Here, *an attacker with some expertise and tools sends malicious optical inputs* targeting the AV *cameras*(system assets) because the *cameras are vulnerable to blinding attacks*. If the event happens, it negates the *integrity of video and picture data* leading to unreliable data sensed by the cameras that could

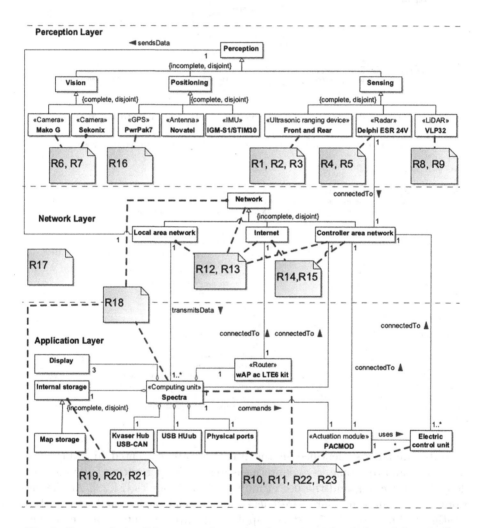

Fig. 2. Case analysis: AV assets and associated security risks (adapted from [26])

provoke wrong decisions when the car is driving/steering. In [26], all considered security risks are explicitly defined using the ISSRM domain model.

Countermeasures are suggested at all three AV layers – perception, network, and application – to mitigate the security risks. We also elicit the relative countermeasure costs. For example, to reduce risk R6, two controls are suggested: (*i*) multiple sensors for redundancy check estimated with a *low* cost and (*ii*) filter to remove harmful light with a *high* cost. The complete risk management documentation of the Lexus RX450h AV system can be accessed in [26].[2,3]

Limitations of Case Analysis. The case study AV is still in the early development phase (i.e., laboratory settings), so we could not consider the system and business assets throughout its life-cycle management; thus, the risk estimations could change. Additionally, we apply security risks found in the literature in our case study. Although we have discovered added risks, our security risk analysis and estimation is limited by those we identified in the literature.

Table 2. Risk estimation using OCTAVE (R6: Blinding cameras)

Business Asset	Video and picture data				
Business Asset's Value	Medium – Car can continue driving but can't recognize signs and traffic lights.				
Area of Concern	An attacker uses their tools to send malicious optical data to the camera causing unwanted blindness, possible hardware damage and loss of integrity of video and picture data.				
Actor Who would exploit the area of concern or threat?	An attacker with some previous experience and tools to send malicious optical inputs (laser etc.).				
Means How would the actor do it? What would they do?	An attacker uses their knowledge and malicious optical emitters to send and blind cameras causing unwanted blindness on the cameras and possibly permanently damage the camera sensors.				
Motive What is the actor's reason for doing it?	Wants to see the car crash and make the company lose reputation.				
Outcome (choose one) What would be the resulting effect be?	Disclosure:	Destruction:	Modification:	Interruption:	x
Security Requirements How would the information asset's security requirements be breached?	Cameras are vulnerable to blinding attacks.				
Likelihood (choose one)	High: x		Medium:	Low:	

Consequences What are the consequences to the organisation as a result of the risk?	**Severity** *3 for highest priority, 2 for medium, 1 for lowest			
	Impact area	**Priority***	**Impact**	**Score**
Blinding attack will cause some blind spots on the image recorded by the cameras.	Confidentiality	1	Low	1
Blind spots can cause not detecting objects and possible accidents because of that. Not having the sensor available without any mitigations will cause the system to not see the outside, possibly other sensors can cover.	Availability	3	High	9
Using lasers to carry out the attack can permanently damage the camera's lens.	Integrity	2	High	6
Relative risk score:				16
Total Risk Score (Rel x likelihood):				48

5   Concluding Remarks

AVs, as IIS, provide a unique perspective on how security risks should be handled while considering the autonomy of data gathering, manipulating, disseminating and actuating functions. In this section, we conclude the paper with the lessons learnt and an overview of the related studies.

---

[2] Full risk management documentation for R6 https://git.io/JkCBf.

[3] Full risk management documentation for other security risks https://git.io/JkCBY.

5.1   Lessons Learnt

Asset-Related Concepts. We have identified the business assets in the perception, network, and application layers. The study results in the systematic examination of the security risks and helps identify countermeasures. For example, the inclusion of multiple sensors could monitor and analyse data from robust and redundant data sources in AVs, which help develop protection strategies that could identify anomalous inputs and behaviour produced by cyber attacks. However, stakeholders must ensure the presence and trust boundary of the sensors as data sources.

Risk-Related Concepts. The assets, alongside attack methods and threat agents, are dynamic. Thus, our estimated scores in the case analysis would change over periods. The dynamic nature of assets, threat likelihood due to evolving attack tools/ methods, and an evolving environment indicate that security risk management must be an *iterative* activity involving dynamic and real-time risk impact estimations as proposed in [16].

We discovered other attacks on the AV not discussed in the literature. One example is carrying out the blinding attack using mirrors to reflect sunlight which could make the likelihood of **R7** (see Footnote 3), *high*. Another is spoofing the *LiDAR* – **R9** (see Footnote 3) with smoke, which increases the likelihood of a spoofing event as it is a low effort attack. Lastly, capability to tamper with the AV code functions used by the *ECU* in the code repository. Efforts must be made to continually improve sensors (i.e. auto-exposure settings for **R7**), algorithms (i.e., improving obstacle detection algorithms for **R9**) and integrity checks for all code used by the *ECU*.

Risk Treatment-Related Concepts. Outlining risk estimations enables treatment prioritisation and return on security on investment analysis in AVs. Using OCTAVE, we can deduce the risk scores based on the relative scores of the impact on the affected assets and threat likelihood while providing a documented risk overview.

Thus, the combination of the ISSRM and OCTAVE methods has filled in the gaps posed by either method's single-use. The ISSRM method refined the security risk management concepts applied in OCTAVE. At the same time, OCTAVE helped provide formal documentation and risk estimation through risk scores based on the relative scores of the affected assets' impact and threat likelihood. The combination provided a useful output to support the AV stakeholders. In [3], Bailey combines the NIST risk assessment process [1] with a probabilistic method and applies the optimisation techniques to recommend the best solutions. Similarly, we have used the countermeasure cost estimation, but we transform the estimates to the qualitative values. This approach allows us to reduce the amount of collected data, but it still supports countermeasure selection decisions.

5.2   Related Work

Related studies analyse security risks in some parts or the whole AV. However, these studies do not consider AVs as information systems. In Table 3, we present

Table 3. Comparing related work

Related work	Risk management				Autonomous focus	Security focus
	Threat	Risk	Solution	Estimation		
Chattopadhyay *et al.* [6]	✓	LD	✓	✗	✓	✓
Parkinson *et al.* [22]	✓	LD	✓	✓	✓	✓
Malik and Sun [18]	✓	LD	✗	✗	✓	✓
Boudguiga *et al.* [4]	✓	✓	✗	✓	LD	SS
Cui *et al.* [7]	✓	LD	✓	✗	✓	SS
Dibaei *et al.* [9]	✓	LD	✓	✗	✓	✓
De La Torre *et al.* [8]	✓	LD	✓	✗	✓	✓
Dominic *et al.* [10]	✓	✓	✓	LD	LD	✓
Kong *et al.* [15]	✓	✓	✗	✗	✓	✓
This study	✓	✓	✓	✓	✓	✓

✓ - Detailed Discussion of concept; LD - Limited Discussion of concept;
✗ - No Discussion of concept; SS - Discusses security and safety.

a comparison illustrating the focus on AV security risk management. It indicates that Dominic *et al.* [10], and Parkinson *et al.* [22] cover the security risk estimation and management in AVs; however, they provide little details on AV system assessment's impact. Other related studies [6–9, 15, 18] address security risk management, some [4, 7] focus on safety and security engineering in AVs. But these studies do not discuss estimations needed for AV stakeholder security investment decisions. In [4], Boudguiga *et al.* TVRA and EVITA methods are combined, but they did not include the cost of countermeasures to assess the severity of the security risks in supporting business decisions. Our study provides a security-focused risk estimation and management analysis on the AV information system, covering the security assets, threats, resulting risks, proposed countermeasures and risk impact estimations based on the mentioned security metrics. We have documented these concepts within the AV case analysis, providing the rationale for making business decisions on securing AVs.

Acknowledgement. This paper is supported in part by EU Horizon 2020 research and innovation programme under grant agreement No 830892, project SPARTA and European Social Fund via Smart Specialisation project with Bolt.

References

1. National Institute of Standards and Technology. SP 800–30 Rev. 1: Guide for Conducting Risk Assessments. https://csrc.nist.gov/publications/detail/sp/800-30/rev-1/final
2. Affia, A.-A.O., Matulevičius, R., Nolte, A.: Security risk management in cooperative intelligent transportation systems: a systematic literature review. In: Panetto, H., Debruyne, C., Hepp, M., Lewis, D., Ardagna, C.A., Meersman, R. (eds.) OTM 2019. LNCS, vol. 11877, pp. 282–300. Springer, Cham (2019). https://doi.org/10.1007/978-3-030-33246-4_18

3. Bailey, D.: Quantitative cybersecurity risk management for autonomous vehicle systems. Master's thesis, Technisch Universitat Munchen (2018)
4. Boudguiga, A., Boulanger, A., Chiron, P., Klaudel, W., Labiod, H., Seguy, J.C.: Race: risk analysis for cooperative engines. In: 2015 7th International Conference on New Technologies, Mobility and Security (NTMS), pp. 1–5. IEEE (2015)
5. Caralli, R.A., Stevens, J.F., Young, L.R., Wilson, W.R.: Introducing OCTAVE allegro: improving the information security risk assessment process. Techical report, SEI (2007)
6. Chattopadhyay, A., Lam, K.Y., Tavva, Y.: Autonomous vehicle: security by design. IEEE Trans. Intell. Transp. Syst. (2020)
7. Cui, J., Liew, L.S., Sabaliauskaite, G., Zhou, F.: A review on safety failures, security attacks, and available countermeasures for autonomous vehicles. Ad Hoc Netw. **90**, 101823 (2019)
8. De La Torre, G., Rad, P., Choo, K.K.R.: Driverless vehicle security: challenges and future research opportunities. Futur. Gener. Comput. Syst. **108**, 1092–1111 (2020)
9. Dibaei, M., et al.: Attacks and defences on intelligent connected vehicles: a survey. Digit. Commun. Netw. (2020)
10. Dominic, D., Chhawri, S., Eustice, R.M., Ma, D., Weimerskirch, A.: Risk assessment for cooperative automated driving. In: Proceedings of the 2nd ACM Workshop on Cyber-Physical Systems Security and Privacy, pp. 47–58 (2016)
11. Dubois, É., Heymans, P., Mayer, N., Matulevičius, R.: A systematic approach to define the domain of information system security risk management. In: Nurcan, S., Salinesi, C., Souveyet, C., Ralyté, J. (eds.) Intentional Perspectives on Information Systems Engineering, pp. 289–306. Springer, Heidelberg (2010). https://doi.org/10.1007/978-3-642-12544-7_16
12. ETSI TS: 182 027: Telecommunications and internet converged services and protocols for advanced networking (TISPAN). IPTV Architecture (2011)
13. EVITA: E-safety Vehicle Intrusion Protected Applications (2011). http://www.evita-project.org/
14. Gupta, E.: Information system. Bajaj, Ankit 197 Bakry, Mohamed Abd El Latif 28 Bala, Shashi 414 Baporikar, Neeta 118, p. 97 (2000)
15. Kong, H.K., Hong, M.K., Kim, T.S.: Security risk assessment framework for smart car using the attack tree analysis. J. Ambient. Intell. Humaniz. Comput. **9**(3), 531–551 (2018)
16. Leite, F.L., Schneider, D., Adler, R.: Dynamic risk management for cooperative autonomous medical cyber-physical systems. In: Gallina, B., Skavhaug, A., Schoitsch, E., Bitsch, F. (eds.) SAFECOMP 2018. LNCS, vol. 11094, pp. 126–138. Springer, Cham (2018). https://doi.org/10.1007/978-3-319-99229-7_12
17. Macher, G., Sporer, H., Berlach, R., Armengaud, E., Kreiner, C.: Sahara: a security-aware hazard and risk analysis method. In: 2015 Design, Automation and Test in Europe Conference & Exhibition (DATE), pp. 621–624. IEEE (2015)
18. Malik, S., Sun, W.: Analysis and simulation of cyber attacks against connected and autonomous vehicles. In: 2020 International Conference on Connected and Autonomous Driving (MetroCAD), pp. 62–70. IEEE (2020)
19. Maple, C., Bradbury, M., Le, A.T., Ghirardello, K.: A connected and autonomous vehicle reference architecture for attack surface analysis. Appl. Sci. **9**(23) (2019)
20. O'Hanlon, B.W., Psiaki, M.L., Bhatti, J.A., Shepard, D.P., Humphreys, T.E.: Real-time GPS spoofing detection via correlation of encrypted signals. Navigation **60**(4), 267–278 (2013)

21. Olovsson, T.: HEAling Vulnerabilities to ENhance Software Security and Safety (HEAVENS) 2015, besucht am 20, pp. 33–89 (2018). https://research.chalmers.se/en/project/5809
22. Parkinson, S., Ward, P., Wilson, K., Miller, J.: Cyber threats facing autonomous and connected vehicles: future challenges. IEEE Trans. Intell. Transp. Syst. **18**(11), 2898–2915 (2017)
23. Petit, J., Shladover, S.E.: Potential cyberattacks on automated vehicles. IEEE Trans. Intell. Transp. Syst. **16**(2), 546–556 (2014)
24. Petit, J., Stottelaar, B., Feiri, M., Kargl, F.: Remote attacks on automated vehicles sensors: experiments on camera and lidar. In: Black Hat Europe (2015)
25. Scalas, M., Giacinto, G.: Automotive cybersecurity: foundations for next-generation vehicles. In: 2nd International Conference on new Trends in Computing Sciences (ICTCS), pp. 1–6 (2019)
26. Tõnisson, R.: Security Risk Management in Autonomous Driving Vehicles: Architecture Perspective. University of Tartu (2020)
27. Thing, V.L., Wu, J.: Autonomous vehicle security: a taxonomy of attacks and defences. In: IEEE International Conference on Internet of Things (iThings) and IEEE Green Computing and Communications (GreenCom) and IEEE Cyber, Physical and Social Computing (CPSCom) and IEEE Smart Data (SmartData), pp. 164–170 (2016)
28. Yan, C., Xu, W., Liu, J.: Can you trust autonomous vehicles: contactless attacks against sensors of self-driving vehicle. In: DEFCON (2016)

BPMN Extensions for Modeling Continuous Processes

Diana Viktoria Strutzenberger[1,2(✉)], Juergen Mangler[3],
and Stefanie Rinderle-Ma[3]

[1] Austrian Center for Digital Production, Vienna, Austria
diana.strutzenberger@acdp.at
[2] Faculty of Computer Science, University of Vienna, Vienna, Austria
[3] Department for Informatics, Technical University of Munich, Munich, Germany
{juergen.mangler,stefanie.rinderle-ma}@tum.de

Abstract. Business process management has focused on discrete processes so far, i.e., processes with identifiable distinct outcomes (e.g., in manufacturing). By contrast, processes known from process and control engineering, e.g., chemical synthesis, have not been fully considered yet. Such processes can be discrete or continuous, i.e., require real-time control systems with constant inlet and outlet flows as well as temporally stable conditions. This paper models continuous processes with existing and standardized means, i.e., BPMN, and provides an exact definition of the parameters and loop conditions. The capabilities of BPMN for modeling continuous processes are analyzed and necessary extensions are provided. The concepts are applied to several real-world use cases from process and control engineering.

Keywords: Process and control engineering · Continuous processes · Process modeling and execution · BPMN extensions

1 Introduction

In process engineering, the design of control systems focuses on the formal description of processes that deal with measuring and controlling complex systems, such as chemical reactors [4] or heat exchangers [5], which are typically applied in mining, production, electricity, gas and water supply as well as waste management. While closed-loop systems take a measured value into consideration for the next control operation (e.g. thermostat), open-loop systems ignore the effect of their output on the system (e.g. temperature control knob on a radiator) [12].

Open-loop systems can be represented as **discrete processes**, closed-loop systems as **continuous processes**. Brewing beer, for example, can be operated as a discrete process, in which a reactor is filled with the ingredients, then started, and at some point in time the next batch of beer is ready. For the continuous operation of the reactor ingredients are continuously added on one side, while

© Springer Nature Switzerland AG 2021
S. Nurcan and A. Korthaus (Eds.): CAiSE Forum 2021, LNBIP 424, pp. 20–28, 2021.
https://doi.org/10.1007/978-3-030-79108-7_3

beer continuously comes out on the other side. The reactor can run forever, its inside is in certain defined states, but it is not possible to track the contents of a glass of water that is added on one side, while it becomes beer.

With ongoing efforts to introduce semantically rich modeling notations such as BPMN[1] into domains like manufacturing [8], it becomes apparent that for reducing the complexity of a system, it is beneficial to model all of its behavior in a single notation, instead of having a collection of modeling and planning artefacts. BPMN is a widely applied standard for modeling business processes and therefore proves to be the right medium to communicate complex processes across industries. Manufacturing processes have already been modeled and orchestrated using BPMN in the Cloud Process Execution Engine (CPEE)[2] [8], enabling dynamic models of complex processes and respective flow description. By contrast, continuous processes still lack such a digital representation despite its advantages for interoperability and for creating digital twins in process engineering; the latter constitutes a research topic which has strongly gained interest in the last years [2,9]. Based on a set of requirements derived from real-world scenarios, the following artefacts are elaborated and evaluated based on real-world use cases: 1) A BPMN extension to simplify the modeling of continuous processes, while increasing their understandability through custom gateways and events. 2) A set of examples that cover the commonly used control engineering patterns, in order to exemplify the expressiveness of our approach. The remainder is structured as follows. Section 2 introduces a set of examples as an evaluation baseline. In Sect. 3 requirements for modeling continuous processes are described. Section 4 introduces BPMN extensions to realize the requirements. In Sect. 5 the solution is evaluated. The paper closes related work in Sect. 6, and conclusion in Sect. 7.

2   Scenario Analysis

To provide a clear understanding of the approach, it is important to analyse how the terms discrete and continuous are used in the fields that specialize on continuous processes, i.e., process and control engineering.

Discrete and Continuous Processes in Process Engineering: In terms of process engineering, processes are divided into two groups, i.e., batch and continuous processes. According to [4], continuous processes are characterized by constant inlet and outlet flows as well as temporally stable conditions. This steady state approach implies a constant progression of the process variables, which can only be achieved after the start-up phase. In contrast, batch or discrete processes present themselves as a one-time input of the materials to be processed. The process steps to be performed mostly run sequentially or are least limited in time by a certain condition or state.

---

[1] BPMN: Business Process Modeling and Notation, www.bpmn-standard.org.
[2] cpee.org.

Discrete and Continuous Processes in Control Engineering: According to [12] continuous systems are characterized by parameters which may take any value in a defined boundary. Further [12] conclude that the frequency in which data access and control tasks are performed determines a discontinuous behavior which needs to be counteracted by finding a fitting control strategy. Due to hardware performance constraints truly continuous behavior may not be realized as physical sensors can only provide data in short time intervals. Among others, control engineering mainly deals with the following three frequently used patterns explained using sample processes.

Feedback and Feedforward Control - Heat Exchanger: As described in [5] there are different options for the implementation of the control system for a heat exchanger. A simple feedback controller such as a PID controller measures the system output, compares the value to the set point and reacts accordingly. Feedforward control is another option for controlling a heat exchanger and reacts to disturbances before they influence the system. A coupled feedback controller compensates the remaining errors [5]. The process model in BPMN is shown in Fig. 1.

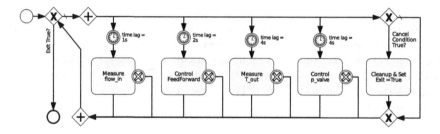

Fig. 1. BPMN model of a feedforward control system for a heat exchanger [5].

Cascade Control - Position Control in Machine Tool: For the position control of drives in machine tools, the cascade control method is usually used. The control model consists of control loops that are nested within each other [11]. The output variable of one control loop is the input variable of the following control loop. Therefore, a direct time dependency between the individual control loops is evident and must be displayed in the workflow. The BPMN workflow model of the control procedure is shown in Fig. 2.

3 Modeling Requirements

Modeling languages and implementation environments must support the realistic representation of continuous processes. Based on the application scenarios presented in Sect. 2, the following modeling requirements for continuous processes are derived that serve as basis for assessing existing modeling languages:

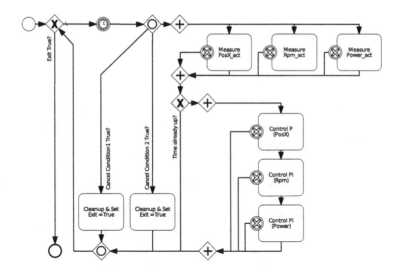

Fig. 2. BPMN model of a cascade control system for position control [11].

Req.1 - Continuity. Continuity needs to be presented in form of a loop. The process model shall imply a continuous flow without having to set a limited number of repetitions or a time limit from the beginning. BPMN supports loop characteristics for tasks and sub-processes [1]. However, this modeling option is confined to individual tasks and sub-processes and thus may lead to complex, multi-level process flows.

Req.2 - Break Conditions. Break conditions can be applied to tasks and sub-processes with loop characteristics [1]. For defining the termination handling of a continuous process and allowing the option to define clean up sequences, Cancel Events can be used. However, for Intermediate Cancelling Events only Boundary Interrupting Events are defined.

Req.3 - Real-Time Process. Due to the critical impact of time regarding continuous processes the role of time needs to be clearly defined. According to [12], a real-time system reacts to simultaneously occurring process signals in time with a corresponding output. BPMN supports Timer Events which need to be applied correctly and comprehensibly in order to understand the implied constraints and display them correctly.

Req.4 - Parallelism. Parallel processing of tasks and task sequences needs to be supported by the chosen modeling environment. Parallelism can be modeled in a way similar to loops in form of attributes for tasks and sub-processes [1]. The orientation of the attribute marker indicates whether the multiple sequences are processed in parallel or sequentially. Again, increasing complexity of the process leads to an incomprehensible model.

Req.5 - Exception Handling. Mechanisms for exception handling have to be available as assurance for real-time processing and determinism. For exception handling BPMN already implies the usage of Intermediate Events [1]. Timer events can be applied to deal with time restrictions which are fundamental for continuous processes.

Req.6 - Limited Complexity. If all necessary details of a continuous process are included in the model, the level of complexity must not exceed to a point at which users no longer understand the process behind the model. To prevent this drawback, modeling conventions need to compensate complex relations, but still lead to a detailed and comprehensible process models.

4   BPMN Extensions for Modeling Continuous Processes

The newly defined symbols are based on common BPMN symbols which have been used to depict similar process models as introduced in Sect. 2. Achieving a completely consistent representation of real control logic for continuous processes is difficult to depict at a reasonable level of complexity. In addition, the requirements set out in Sect. 3 have to be met. Using the standard modeling capabilities in BPMN might result in a complex sequence behind a single control task as demonstrated by the example in Fig. 2.

Closed-Loop Sub-System Gateway: The Closed-Loop Sub-System is a combined version of an Inclusive and an Event-Based Gateway. A Closed-Loop Sub-System combines the advantages of the described gateways and the attributes of loop and multiple-instance characteristics defined in [1]. The symbol and basic definitions of a Closed-Loop Sub-System is introduced in Table 1. Event-based Gateways do not allow Cancel triggers for Intermediate events used in branches after the gateways. Closed-Loop Sub-Systems let tokens traverse each branch which allows processing multiple parallel branches simultaneously (Req. 4). Each branch starts with newly introduced Intermediate Event markers – Measuring, Control and Cancel. Measuring and Control are Intermediate Timer Events indicating an execution interval for each branch as well as individual sections of a sequence to illustrate gradually changing intervals and also dependencies (Req. 3). Cancel is an Intermediate Catching Event which includes conditions for ending the loop (Req. 2). Similar to features of Inclusive and Event-Based Gateways, the Closed-Loop Sub-System is passed through in cycles, which is indicated by an arrow leading back from the converging marker after the branches have been traversed to the first diverging marker (Req. 1). A return to the first marker is only allowed as long as no Cancel Catching Intermediate Event is triggered (Req. 5). The Gateway Direction of a Closed-Loop Sub-System is diverging. It MUST have at least two outgoing Sequence Flows, one starting with a Measuring Intermediate Catching Event and one starting with a Cancel Intermediate Catching Event. It MAY further have multiple outgoing Sequence Flows but MUST have no more than one incoming Sequence Flow. The Closed-Loop Sub-System allows to model continuous processes in a simple structure with necessary attributes, but clearly arranged at one level (Req. 6). Further modeling conventions are described in Table 1.

Table 1. Closed-Loop Sub-System Attributes and Model Associations

Attribute Name	Description/Usage
Interval duration overrun: wait cancel 	When *wait*, the following iteration starts when all branches are finished and the defined interval duration is reached. When *cancel*, the interval duration defines exactly the time each branch takes to finish. If the tasks in a branch are finished early, the branch waits. If not all tasks are finished yet, they are terminated.
Measure-control cycle execution: parallel sequential 	When *parallel*, tasks after Measuring and Control Intermediate Catching Events are performed in parallel. When *sequential*, the tasks after Control Intermediate Catching Events are performed only after all tasks after Measuring Intermediate Catching Events are finished.

Marker	Description
Closed-Loop Sub-System Gateway: 	**Closed-Loop Sub-System Gateway:** contains branches which are triggered for the measuring and control phases of the cycle, as well as branches executed when cancellation events are received.
Intermediate Catching Events: Measuring Control Cancel 	**Measuring:** Receiving events to perform measuring cycles **Control:** Receiving events to perform control cycles **Cancel:** Receiving events to abort closed-loop systems

Intermediate Catching Event Types: To indicate which tasks are executed in one of the parallel branches under the Closed-Loop Sub-System Gateway, three new symbols based on Intermediate Catching Events are proposed in this work. The symbols are shown and described in Table 1.

5 Application

In addition to standard functionalities for modeling with BPMN and support for common workflow patterns the suggested extensions to BPMN are implemented in the CPEE. In order to show the advantages of the proposed extensions in modeling and understanding processes, the process examples identified by the literature study from Sect. 2 were implemented. In the following, some examples are presented. The model of a heat exchanger with a combination of feedback and feedforward control in CPEE is shown in Fig. 3 on the left. The Closed-Loop Sub-System is implemented with the *cancel* attribute set. The control system cancels the execution of every branch in which the tasks are not finished in the given time interval. A position control system with cascade controller is shown in Fig. 3 on the right. The model is implemented in CPEE with the *cancel* attribute set in order to guarantee real-time behavior. Multiple control tasks with different execution frequencies are modeled sequentially to show the order for the execution of the controller elements. Regarding Fig. 2 the effort involved in changing the model can lead to errors in the model and thus the intended semantics of the real process. The modeling convention depicted in Fig. 3 allows the user to modify the model much easier (insert into one branch vs. insert into a combination of loop and parallel as well as inserting additional events and connections).

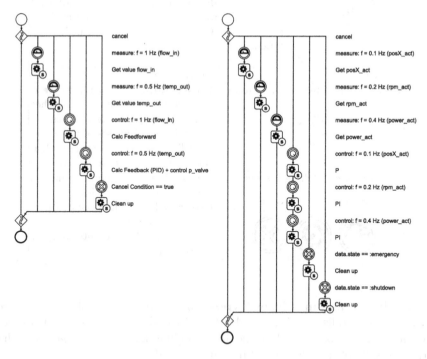

Fig. 3. Feedforward (left) and cascade control (right) - process model with extensions in CPEE.

6   Related Work

Tools for process and control engineering include Aspen Plus [7] and Matlab/Simulink [13]. In general, a common practice is the separation of modeling and execution environment. The linkage between both environments is realized via a code generating solution as presented in [3]. Process patterns provide (partly complex) constructs for describing process flows such as time [6] and resource patterns [10]. Based on the features described in Sect. 3 the usability of the patterns has been assessed. Overall, the most limited support is provided for Req.3 on modeling real-time processes and Req.6 on limited complexity.

7   Conclusion

Process and control engineering constitutes a major industry including mining, gas and water supply, but the continuous processes in this field have not been considered from a business process management perspective yet. This work explains and distinguishes the characteristics of discrete and continuous processes. BPMN is analyzed for representing continuous processes based on set of requirements derived from real-world scenarios. The challenge is to express continuity with break conditions, real-time processing, parallelism, and exception handling in balance with taming the complexity of the resulting models. BPMN extensions in terms of symbols are proposed. The executability in CPEE allows the use of the models also as non-proprietary digital twins.

Acknowledgements. This work has been partially supported and funded by the Austrian Research Promotion Agency (FFG) via the Austrian Competence Center for Digital Production (CDP) under the contract number 854187.

References

1. Business Process Model and Notation (BPMN), Version 2.0, p. 538
2. Bamberg, A., Urbas, L., Bröcker, S., Kockmann, N., Bortz, M.: What makes the digital twin an ingenious companion? Chemie Ing. Technik **92**(3), 192–198 (2020)
3. Chindris, G., Muresan, M.: Deploying simulink models into system-on-chip structures. In: Electronics Technology, pp. 313–317. IEEE (2006)
4. Hertwig, K., Martens, L.: Chemische Verfahrenstechnik: Berechnung. Auslegung und Betrieb chemischer Reaktoren, Oldenbourg (2007)
5. Khare, Y.B., Singh, Y.: PID control of heat exchanger system. Int. J. Comput. Appl. **8**(6), 0975–8887 (2010)
6. Lanz, A., Reichert, M., Weber, B.: Process time patterns: a formal foundation. Inf. Syst. **57**, 38–68 (2016)
7. Luyben, W.L.: Distillation Design and Control Using Aspen Simulation. Wiley, Hoboken (2013)
8. Mangler, J., Pauker, F., Rinderle-Ma, S., Ehrendorfer, M.: centurio. work - industry 4.0 integration assessment and evolution. In: BPM Ind. Forum, pp. 106–117 (2019)
9. Pfeiffer, B.M., Oppelt, M., Leingang, C.: Evolution of a digital twin for a steam cracker. In: Emerging Technologies and Factory Automation, pp. 467–474 (2019)

10. Russell, N., Hofstede, ter, A., Aalst, van der, W., Mulyar, N.: Workflow control-flow patterns : a revised view. BPM reports, BPMcenter.org (2006)
11. Schmid, D., Kaufmann, H., Pflug, A., Strobel, P., Baur, J.: Automatisierungstechnik - Grundlagen, Komponenten, Systeme. Europa Lehrmittel, Nourney, Vollmer GmbH & Co. KG (2015)
12. Tröster, F.: Steuerungs- und Regelungstechnik für Ingenieure. Oldenbourg Lehrbücher für Ingenieure, Oldenbourg
13. Yang, C.H., Vyatkin, V.: Transformation of Simulink models to IEC 61499 function blocks for verification of distributed control systems. Control Eng. Pract. **20**(12), 1259–1269 (2012)

Sensor Data Stream Selection and Aggregation for the Ex Post Discovery of Impact Factors on Process Outcomes

Matthias Ehrendorfer[1]([✉]), Juergen Mangler[2], and Stefanie Rinderle-Ma[2]

[1] Faculty of Computer Science, University of Vienna, Vienna, Austria
`matthias.ehrendorfer@univie.ac.at`
[2] Department of Informatics, Technical University of Munich, Garching, Germany
`{juergen.mangler,stefanie.rinderle-ma}@tum.de`

Abstract. One target of process analysis, monitoring, and prediction is the process outcome, e.g., the quality of a produced part. The process outcome is affected by process execution data, including (external) sensor data streams, e.g., indicating an overheating machine. Challenges are to select the "right" sensors –possibly a multitude of sensors is available– and to specify how the sensor data streams are aggregated and used to calculate the impact on the outcome. This paper introduces process task annotations to specify the selected sensors, their aggregation, and initial impact functions. The initial impact functions are then refined, e.g., threshold values and the impact of sensor data streams are determined. The approach is prototypically implemented. Its applicability is demonstrated based on a real-world manufacturing scenario.

Keywords: Sensor data streams · Process outcome · Process impact analysis

1 Introduction

Companies want to execute processes efficiently by exploiting all available possibilities to avoid undesired outcomes. However, data from sensors and machines being used in the process is often not taken into account, for example, when it does not directly contribute to the control flow of a process. Nonetheless, such data might determine the outcome of tasks or the process itself. This leads to a situation where experienced process operators can anticipate the progression and (final or intermediate) results of a process because they know (1) what they should pay attention to and (2) which behaviour signalises which outcomes.

This work has been partly funded by the Austrian Research Promotion Agency (FFG) via the "Austrian Competence Center for Digital Production" (CDP) under the contract number 881843. This work has been supported by the Pilot Factory Industry 4.0, Seestadtstrasse 27, Vienna, Austria.

© Springer Nature Switzerland AG 2021
S. Nurcan and A. Korthaus (Eds.): CAiSE Forum 2021, LNBIP 424, pp. 29–37, 2021.
https://doi.org/10.1007/978-3-030-79108-7_4

To formalise the knowledge of experienced process operators and make it available at run-time for outcome prediction, we introduce the concept of *Impact Factors*. Impact factors can be derived from process data and external data, e.g., sensor data. The latter is implicitly connected to process tasks and can hold the key to predict the process outcome (see Fig. 1). In most cases, sensor data occurs in the form of a series of data points because machines and sensors measure continuously [7].

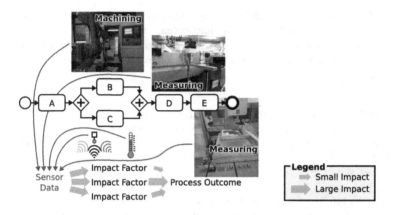

Fig. 1. Deduction of impact factors from sensor data

Determining impact factors based on sensor data raises several challenges. At first, in realistic settings, one has to possibly choose relevant sensors from a multitude of sensors. Secondly, the accessibility of the information, especially at the presence of many sensor streams is crucial. Third, the first and second point require to compare the impact of single sensors vs. the impact of a combination of sensors. Fourth, run-time deviations in sensor information might occur.

These challenges lead to the following research questions. (*RQ1*) How to annotate process models with data sources that are relevant in the context of process task execution? (*RQ2*) How to aggregate and contextualise sensor data for arbitrary process tasks at run-time? (*RQ3*) How to deduce impact factor predictions from the aggregated sensor data?

To tackle *RQ1–RQ3*, this paper provides a method for the structured collection, classification, and correlation of sensor-based impact factors to compare process instances and track their progression. The proposed method works along the following steps: (1) Annotating process tasks to define the extraction of series of data points from data streams (e.g., from sensors) that occur during the execution of those tasks. (2) Annotating process tasks to enable aggregation of the extracted data series. (3) The semi-automatic extraction of impact factors from the collected data. Steps (1)–(3) are implemented in a manufacturing scenario and evaluated based on the corresponding data set. The manufacturing process includes a comprehensible quality assurance as last step, thus allowing for the assessment of the quality of the approach presented in this paper.

The structure is as follows: Section 2 annotates sensors to process tasks and identifies impact factors. Section 3 evaluates the approach. Section 4 discusses the results and Sect. 5 related work. The paper is concluded in Sect. 6.

2   Approach

Manufacturing Scenario: The case presented in this paper is a manufacturing process carried out in the "Pilot Factory Industry 4.0" (http://pilotfabrik. tuwien.ac.at/en/). The steps of the manufacturing process are enacted by a number of machines, humans, and software systems. The orchestration of the steps is defined in a BPMN process model which is executed by a workflow engine. In addition to process data, (sensor-)data is collected. Considering both allows for a deeper analysis of the process along with the possibility for improvements. The manufacturing process used for this paper consists of the following steps on a high abstraction level: (1) Manufacturing with a turning machine. (2) Automated optical quality control measurement directly after part production - fast ($\sim$20 s) but imprecise measurement. (3) Automated final quality control measurement - precise but slow ($\sim$480 s) measurement.

The **Solution Design** aims at annotating process tasks with sensor data.

Sensors define what is extracted from associated data streams and how. As machine and sensor data is often not represented in processes, it must be collected inside the tasks themselves. Therefore, defining how to handle these data streams is necessary, e.g., split data from one machine (like temperature and noise level) or merge data from different sensors (like partial temperature readings).

Aggregators describe how to aggregate the extracted data for analysis. This is necessary because it has to be taken into account that sensors measure differently and therefore different characteristics of a measurement need to be used. For example, measuring a part might result in a massive point-cloud, describing a set of different properties that a part has. An aggregator might (a) throw some data away, and (b) group data so that it becomes accessible for later analysis.

Impact Functions operate on aggregated data, and define how to calculate the deviation between current data and expected data. Expected data leads to the desired outcome, current data might not. An impact function consists of two parts: (1) an expected target value or data pattern, and (2) a function that describes how much a deviation affects the overall process. For example for measurements there may be a certain tolerance until which a part is accepted but when the tolerance is exceeded, the part is considered faulty.

These three types of annotations can be used to derive an **impact value (IV)** by using an **aggregation (A)** for a particular **sensor (S)**. Based on one or more *impact values* together with an **impact function (IFU)** it can be defined how the *impact value(s)* are combined to retrieve an **impact factor (IF)**:

$$IV = (S, A) \text{ and } IF = (IV+, IFU)$$

One or more *impact factors* can then be used to build **impact profiles**, either for individual tasks **(TIP)** or for the whole process **(PIP)**. The combination of the *impact factors* into *impact profiles* is facilitated by an **impact profile function (IPF)**, which works similar to the *IFU* introduced above.

$$TIP = (IF+, IPF) \text{ and } PIP = ((IF, A)+, IPF)$$

While *impact profiles of tasks (TIP)* only use *IFs* of one task, *impact profiles of a process (PIP)* use *IFs* from multiple tasks. *PIPs* therefore need to handle the *aggregation* of *impact factors* differently, because an *impact factor* can be encountered more than once (e.g., in a loop).

When trying to find relevant impact factors for specific outcomes, several pieces of information need to be provided by a human. Firstly, the sensors and data handling have to be specified. E.g., as multiple sensors might be contained in one stream, it has to be split into different data series. This holds for the real-world data set used in this paper, as the turning machine delivers a total of 27 sensors in one data stream. Secondly, one or more aggregation methods that define how the extracted data is interpreted (e.g., is only a specific segment of the measurement important, is only the average of all values important, ...) need to be specified. Lastly, the general impact function (telling how the aggregation of sensor data behaves compared to one where a desired result is achieved) needs to be defined by the user. However, the first interaction of an impact function is seldom the optimum. Thus the impact function is typically refined after enough instances of a process are executed. Furthermore, the actual influence of an impact factor on an outcome is not given, as it is also unknown at design time. The presented approach tries to determine these two missing values based on executed process traces.

Process Outcome: Impact factors have to be refined by determining the optimal impact function parameters as well as the influence of a specific impact factor on the outcome. This refinement requires the following steps: (1) Describe the characteristics of different sensors, i.e., how to aggregate individual values and initial impact functions. (2) Based on executed process traces calculate for each sensor for a specific outcome (a) the ROC curve and AUC value and (b) the impact function parameters to achieve the maximum accuracy. (3) Calculate the influence of individual impact factors on an outcome by using (a) the AUC value or (b) the accuracy achieved with the optimal impact function parameters. (4) Based on the refined impact factors, traces can now be assigned a value showing the severity of dissatisfied impact factors. This value makes it possible to distinguish between different results of the analysed outcome.

The impact of individual factors on the outcome can be determined by higher AUC or accuracy values. Using the share of the majority class for the accuracy or a diagonal ROC curve for the AUC value as a baseline (i.e., minimum expectation for the influence of an impact factor) rewards influential factors and penalises bad ones, thus compensating classes with a high share compared to other classes.

3   Evaluation

The log traces of two batches, referred to as batch 14[1] (38 parts) and 15[2] (41 parts), are used for the evaluation. Both batches contain a valve lifter for a gas turbine (Fig. 2a), produced in a real-world factory setting. The part is produced in a turning machine and taken out by a robot (Fig. 2b). Then the diameter of the part's silhouette is measured by a Keyence measuring machine[3]. Based on semantic knowledge, different segments of the measurement time-series can be identified (Fig. 2c). Finally, a slow but more precise measurement is performed.

■ Keyence Measurement

(a) Part Without Chip   (b) Part Held by Robot   (c) Measurement Segments

Fig. 2. Relationship between physical parts and optical measurement

We use data from a measuring machine yielding the diameter of the part's silhouette and a measuring machine yielding multiple time-series: the workload of the drive (aaLoad) in percent and the axis speed (aaVactB) in millimeters per minute for X, Y, and Z axis alongside the actual speed of the spindle (actSpeed) in turns per minute and the workload of the spindle (driveLoad) in percent. Five aggregation methods are used: min, max, avg, wgtdAvg and wgtdAvgSeg4. To handle different measurement intervals, weighted average (wgtdAvg) assumes that a value is valid until a new one is measured. "Segment 4" (wgtdAvgSeg4, see Fig. 2c) uses only values occurring 5200 to 9600 ms after the first data point. All five aggregation methods are used for analysing the optical measurement and the weighted average is used for the eight sensors observed during machining. A threshold which defines a boundary between different outcome classes is used as method for detecting violations of aggregated sensor data.

The evaluation examines (1) the occurrence of chips (only batch 15) and (2) the result of the "Zylinder Ø4,5-B – Durchmesser" quality control test.

Chip Prediction. Using minimum, average, weighted average, and weighted average of "Segment 4" of the faster but less precise "Keyence" measurement leads to results with a high sensitivity and specificity while the maximum has less impact (Fig. 3a). It can be seen that using the weighted average of machining data (Fig. 3b) does not show if there is a chip.

---

[1] http://cpee.org/~demo/DaSH/batch14.zip [Online; accessed 02-April-2021].

[2] http://cpee.org/~demo/DaSH/batch15.zip [Online; accessed 02-April-2021].

[3] https://www.keyence.com/products/measure/micrometer/ls-9000/ [Online; accessed 02-April-2021].

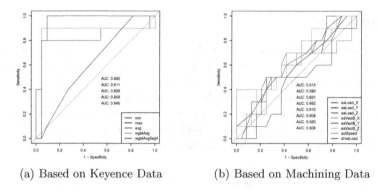

(a) Based on Keyence Data   (b) Based on Machining Data

Fig. 3. ROC curves for predicting chip occurrence for batch 15

Quality Control Test Prediction. When ignoring parts with chips, the weighted average of "Segment 4" has the highest impact (see Fig. 4a). For machining data (see Fig. 4b), actSpeed is the most promising impact factor. Using batch 14 leads to the results shown in Fig. 4c again highlighting actSpeed. "Keyence" measurements are not used because there is no possibility to exclude parts with chips which leads to bad optical measurements.

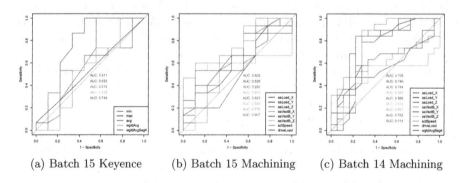

(a) Batch 15 Keyence   (b) Batch 15 Machining   (c) Batch 14 Machining

Fig. 4. ROC curves for predicting quality control test

Using Impact Factors for Outcome Anticipation. The result of calculating the overall impact with the available sensor data is shown in Figs. 5a and 5b for batch 14 and 15. Furthermore, Fig. 5c shows batch 14 results using a training set (75%/27 parts) and test set (25%/9 parts). Due to the low number of parts, data is only split to validate the results achieved and not for all analysis steps.

The results show the overall dissatisfied impact factors (DIF) using different methods (see Sect. 2). The weighted average in segment 4 of the "Keyence" measurement and the weighted average of the machining data are used as impact factors. Although not perfectly separated, higher overall sums of dissatisfied impact factors are calculated for parts being not ok (regarding the quality control test). The effect of using a baseline can be seen in Fig. 5. It has a stronger effect on batch 15 (nearly two-thirds of the part belong to one class) than on batch 14 (classes are evenly distributed). Identifying and combining impact factors as discussed above, is the basis for creating impact profile functions as defined in Sect. 2. The source-code used for the evaluation is available at gitlab[4].

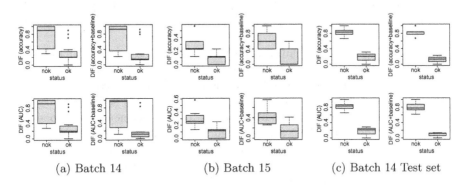

(a) Batch 14   (b) Batch 15   (c) Batch 14 Test set

Fig. 5. Dissatisfied Impact Factors (DIF) for quality control test

4   Discussion

Overall, the presented approach uses sensor data collected during process execution to identify impact factors influencing certain process outcomes. Only the impact of individual sensors on outcomes is examined, a next step would be to consider interdependent impact factors. Also the combination of impact factors to anticipate the outcome should be further examined as only one method (assigning weights representing the influence on the outcome) is exemplary used.

This paper focuses on manufacturing processes. However, transferring the approach to other domains would be interesting. The goal of the approach is to predict the outcome of a process by using sensor data collected throughout the process. A similar use case is the medical domain: the results of examinations or the dosing of administered medication can be collected as data while the health condition of the patient or the costs of the overall therapy process represent outcomes. Another application domain is logistics where sensors measuring temperature, speed, or concussion e.g., in vehicles can be used to find out how long the delivery of a product will take and in which condition it will arrive.

---

[4] https://gitlab.com/me33551/impact-factor-determination [Online; accessed 02-April-2021].

5   Related Work

Process mining mainly focuses on the control-flow perspective [1]. Some approaches examine further perspectives, also referred to as multi-perspective process mining [4], for example, process data [6]. The analysis of time sequence data for explaining concept drifts during run-time is tackled in [6,7]. By contrast, the presented approach aims at including data stream information into the process model to make it usable. [8] compares different outcome-oriented predictive process monitoring techniques. However, the real-life event logs used in [8] do not contain detailed sensor data meaning there is no need to annotate process tasks.

The presented approach can also be positioned in the context of IoT and BPM based on the challenges provided in [3]. The annotation of process tasks with sensor data contributes to C3 (Connection of analytical processes with IoT). Furthermore, C1 (Placing sensors in a process-aware way) is addressed because only explicitly represented sensors allow sensor-aware placement of new ones.

Building on the ideas of [5], this paper focuses on data collection in the context of the enacted process. Earlier work in this field includes [2] which analyses the log files of manufacturing processes containing contextualised data. This paper goes beyond this by explicitly representing data streams in the process model and analysing them with respect to different outcomes of the overall process.

6   Conclusion

This paper presents a way to annotate process tasks for contextualised data collection using (1) "Sensors" defining which data is collected and how this is done, (2) "Aggregators" describing how to aggregate it, and (3) "Impact Functions" allowing to detect the violation from expected sensor behaviour. This provides a basis for finding impact factors. Furthermore, different aggregation methods are evaluated and the conclusion that generic methods like minimum, maximum, or average can already reveal some characteristics is reached. However, advanced aggregations adjusted to the domain and specific case can yield in-depth analysis results. Finally, different methods to determine the impact of aggregated sensor data utilising accuracy and AUC value are presented. After classifying the aggregated data based on a threshold, the overall number of dissatisfied impact factors can then be obtained by combining them based on their influence on the outcome. The evaluation, based on a real-world data set, shows that deducing impact factors allows the prediction of quality variations. Supporting users in defining impact factors depends on domain knowledge, further automating this to improve prediction quality will be the subject of future work.

References

1. van der Aalst, W.M.P.: Process Mining - Data Science in Action, 2nd edn. Springer, Heidelberg (2016). https://doi.org/10.1007/978-3-662-49851-4
2. Ehrendorfer, M., Fassmann, J., Mangler, J., Rinderle-Ma, S.: Conformance checking and classification of manufacturing log data. In: 2019 IEEE 21st Conference on Business Informatics (CBI), vol. 01, pp. 569–577 (2019)
3. Janiesch, C., et al.: The internet of things meets business process management: a manifesto. IEEE Syst. Man Cybern. Mag. **6**(4), 34–44 (2020). https://doi.org/10.1109/MSMC.2020.3003135
4. Mannhardt, F.: Multi-perspective Process Mining. Ph.D. thesis, Technische Universiteit Eindhoven, Eindhoven, February 2018
5. Pauker, F., Mangler, J., Rinderle-Ma, S., Pollak, C.: centurio.work - modular secure manufacturing orchestration. In: BPM Industry Track, pp. 164–171, September 2018
6. Stertz, F., Rinderle-Ma, S.: Detecting and identifying data drifts in process event streams based on process histories. In: CAiSE Forum, pp. 240–252 (2019)
7. Stertz, F., Rinderle-Ma, S., Mangler, J.: Analyzing process concept drifts based on sensor event streams during runtime. In: Fahland, D., Ghidini, C., Becker, J., Dumas, M. (eds.) BPM 2020. LNCS, vol. 12168, pp. 202–219. Springer, Cham (2020). https://doi.org/10.1007/978-3-030-58666-9_12
8. Teinemaa, I., Dumas, M., Rosa, M.L., Maggi, F.M.: Outcome-oriented predictive process monitoring: review and benchmark. ACM Trans. Knowl. Discov. Data **13**(2), 1–57 (2019)

Requirements Elicitation for Applications Running on a Blockchain: Preliminary Results

Sarah Bouraga[1,2](✉) ⓘ, Corentin Burnay[1,2] ⓘ, Ivan Jureta[1,2] ⓘ,
and Stéphane Faulkner[1,2]

[1] Department of Business Administration, University of Namur, Namur, Belgium
{sarah.bouraga,corentin.burnay,ivan.jureta,stephane.faulkner}@unamur.be
[2] PReCISE Research Center, University of Namur, Namur, Belgium

Abstract. Blockchain has been one of Gartner's Top 10 Strategic Technology Trends for several consecutive years. The technology has evolved from a platform allowing transactions of cryptocurrency between peers (e.g. Bitcoin) to a platform allowing the design of Decentralized Applications (DApps). Despite their growing popularity, little attention has been paid to the Software Engineering aspect of DApps. In this work, we aim to start bridging this gap by addressing the Requirements Engineering of DApps. We collect, analyze and integrate DApp user reviews in order to propose a first list of user requirements for DApps. The results can have practical implications for both practitioners and researchers. The former can use the results to guide them in the design of DApps, while the latter can see this paper as a first result to build upon to advance the software engineering field of blockchain-based applications.

Keywords: Blockchain · Requirements engineering · Requirements elicitation · Opinion mining · DApps

1 Introduction

Blockchain can be defined as [31]: *"A blockchain is a distributed ledger that is structured into a linked list of blocks. Each block contains an ordered set of transactions. Typical solutions use cryptographic hashes to secure the link from a block to its predecessor."* Ethereum [3] was launched in 2015, and it has become the world's leading programmable blockchain. Drawing on Bitcoin, Ethereum has offered a platform for anyone to write Smart Contracts and Decentralized Applications (DApps). A Dapp is *"At a minimum, it is a smart contract and a web user interface. A DApp is a web application that is built on top of open, decentralized, peer-to-peer infrastructure services"*[1]. This concept has appealed to early adopters and has since been gaining popularity[2].

---

[1] https://ethereum.org/en/glossary/.
[2] There are more than 3000 DApps on Ethereum (www.stateofthedapps.com) and the number of transactions a day has been around the 1 million mark since August 2020 (www.etherchain.org).

© Springer Nature Switzerland AG 2021
S. Nurcan and A. Korthaus (Eds.): CAiSE Forum 2021, LNBIP 424, pp. 38–46, 2021.
https://doi.org/10.1007/978-3-030-79108-7_5

Despite this growing popularity, little attention has been paid to the Software Engineering (SE) aspect of DApps. Therefore, the goal and corresponding contribution of this work is to propose a preliminary list of Ethereum DApp Requirements. We aim to:

1. **G.1.** Elicit recurring user requirements of applications running on blockchain platforms.
2. **G.2.** Propose an early classification of these requirements.

To address these questions, we first extract various types of data from DApps running on Ethereum (we chose Ethereum because it is one of the leading programmable blockchain platforms). The types of data we extract are: (i) the category of DApp, and (ii) the user reviews for the DApp (App reviews and opinion mining have been recognized as useful in Requirements Engineering (RE) tasks, since they can support Requirements Elicitation and Requirements Prioritization [6]). Next, we analyze each review, identifying the positive and negative feedback communicated by the user. Finally, we organize this feedback into *Functional Requirements*, *Non-Functional Requirements* (NFR), and *Properties*.

The rest of the paper is structured as follows. Section 2 presents a background on blockchain, DApps as well as the related work on RE for the blockchain area. Section 3 introduces the data collection method and describes the sample, while Sect. 4 presents our requirements. Finally Sects. 5 and 6 discusses the results and concludes this paper respectively.

2 Related Work

2.1 Background

In 2008, Satoshi Nakamoto proposed Bitcoin, a decentralized cryptocurrency. Using the Bitcoin network, peers can transfer any amount of Bitcoins (BTC) in a transaction without the need for a trusted or central authority. Blockchain, the underlying technology of Bitcoin, is the "decentralized transparent (public) ledger with the transaction records" [29]. A blockchain offers multiple benefits, namely decentralization, transparency, immutability, security and privacy [23].

Building on the Bitcoin innovation, Ethereum [3] offers a platform which anyone can use to write Smart Contracts and DApps. Smart Contracts can be defined as "programs deployed and run on a blockchain system. Smart contracts can express triggers, conditions, and business logic to enable complex programmable transactions." DApps are a collection of Smart Contracts. Users have access to the code of the DApps - they are typically open-source - expressing the fact that users do not have to trust any single party. Instead, they can simply examine the code made available to them [31].

2.2 RE for DApps

Firstly, software engineering specific to blockchain has been recognized as a potential research field. Its (potential) importance has been emphasized by [7,8,21,25]. For instance, Destefanis et al. [7] advocate the need for a Blockchain-Oriented Software Engineering (BOSE) discipline. The work points to three areas that need to be addressed by BOSE: (i) best practices and development methodology, (ii) design patterns, (iii) testing. Secondly, when dealing with BOSE, most existing works focus on the technical aspects of DApps development. The early requirements are not analyzed in depth [20,21,30]. Other examples are [1,26] which cover many aspects of DApps but does not really address the problem of the early requirements. Thirdly, several works address the development of a blockchain platform for a specific domain [2,9,11,13,16,17,19,24,32], while in this paper, we are interested in the development of blockchain-enabled applications. Moreover, none of these works explicitly address the RE part of such a system. Indeed, they either briefly list the requirements using a very generic RE methodology or jump to the architecture and implementation of the system, the requirements staying implicit.

To conclude, we can claim that the investigation of RE for DApps is a valid field of research. It has been recognized by the literature as a challenge in the blockchain domain. We can also claim that there is a gap that we aim to fill, namely the issue of the early requirements for blockchain-enabled applications.

3   Data Collection

3.1   Data Collection Methodology and Data Summary

Collecting and analyzing requirements from a large group of users or future users has been a topic of interest in the literature [14,15,18,22,27,28]. One way to conduct requirements elicitation from the crowd is to use the app reviews. Indeed, they are a source of user opinions and opinion mining can be valuable in at least 3 scenarios: (i) Validation by users, (ii) Requirements elicitation, and (iii) Requirements prioritization [6].

For this work, we extracted the Top 501 Ethereum DApps[3]. We did not extract more DApps, because after the top 500, barely any reviews were available. Nevertheless, we believe that with 501 DApps, we can still have an accurate view of the DApps market on Ethereum. As indicated on the website, the rank is based on multiple criteria including the number of active users, the volume of transactions on the DApp, the activity of the development team and user recommendation.

For each DApp, we recorded: (i) the name of the DApp, (ii) the category of the DApp, and (iii) the reviews - if any - of the DApp. Table 1 summarizes our sample. From the Table, we can see that many DApps belong to the Finance, Games and Exchanges categories; and that most reviews were written for DApps belonging to these categories as well. Also, we should notice that many DApps (440) were not reviewed at all; which means that the 127 reviews are linked to 61 DApps.

---

[3] We used www.stateofthedapps.com, which offers rankings of DApps running on various platforms.

Table 1. Data distribution.

Category	DApps	Reviews	Category	DApps	Reviews	Category	DApps	Reviews
Development	43	1	Health	4	0	Property	13	6
Energy	3	0	High risk	2	0	Security	6	0
Exchanges	62	17	Identity	8	2	Social	40	13
Finance	113	28	Insurance	1	0	Storage	6	0
Gambling	4	0	Marketplaces	42	15	Wallet	26	2
Games	83	33	Media	27	6			
Governance	17	3	Music	1	1			

3.2   Data Annotation

The manual annotation method was based on feature extraction and sentiment analysis. Specifically, given the reviews collected in the previous step, we labeled each review with features and their associated sentiments. For instance, we recorded terms (e.g. *"Easy set-up"*) or statements (e.g. *"Not many cryptocurrencies. I'd like such a system to work for other cryptocurrencies too and not just ETH"*). Afterwards, we grouped these terms and statements into more traditional requirements and properties. Then, we classified these requirements into functional requirements, non-functional requirements, as well as DApp properties. Finally, for each requirement, we designated whether it was bound to a particular category of DApps or if it was category-agnostic.

4   Results

Tables 2, 3 and 4 summarize the results. For each type of requirements, we provide three elements: (i) the requirements we identified, (ii) (iii) the applicability of the requirements, i.e. is it specific to a category of DApp or is it general to all DApps, and (iii) examples of feedback we used to derive the requirements. Some examples of feedback were negative, and allowed us to elicit the corresponding positive requirement important for users. For instance, "Lack of novelty" was identified as a drawback for a given DApp, therefore, we derived the requirement "Concept of the DApp" as important for the user.

Table 2 displays the NFR. Many definitions for NFR have been proposed in the literature, but there is not necessarily a consensus on a single definition [12]. Nevertheless, it is commonly accepted that NFR describe *how* the future system should do something while functional requirements refer to *what* the system should do [10]. NFR are often referred to as "-ilities" or "-ities" - alluding to the end of the words - yet there are many NFR that do not fit this pattern [5]. In Table 2, when possible, we used the terms proposed by [4] to describe and group the NFR.

Table 2. Non-functional requirements.

Requirements	Category	Examples of feedback
Communication	General	*"No public information on upcoming plans"*
Community	General	*"Slack Community"*
Cost	General	*"Fee too high"*
Documented	General	*"No links to documentation or github or social media"*
Enjoyable	General	*"Fun"*
Global presence	General	*"Globally accessible"*
Inter-operability	General	*"Compatible with my Ether Wallet"*
Interface	General	*"Clear design"*
Mobile app	General	*"Should make the mobile platform more responsive"*
Response time	General	*"Slow transactions"*
Scalability	General	*"Scalable"*
Security	General	*"Smart contracts that are secure"*
Stability	General	*"Stability"*
Support	General	*"Chat support in discord id very good"*
User experience	General	*"Excellent experience for both roles (buyers and sellers)"*
User-friendliness	General	*"Easy-to-use"*

Table 3. Some functional requirements.

Requirements	Category	Examples of feedback
Chat feature	General	*"Private message feature"*
Incentive mechanism	General	*"Creativity is rewarded"*
Multiple payment methods	General	*"Supports an impressive selection of payment methods in fiat currencies"*
No third-party	General	*"No middle man"*
Use of standards	General	*"Use of ERC-20"*
Switch between roles	General	*"Easy way to switch back and forth from Recruiter to Candidate modes"*
Control over the feed	Media	*"Can't control the kinds of articles I want to see in my feed"*
Tag articles	Media	*"Every article carries tags, which will make it easy to locate"*
Visible number of followers	Media	*"Number of followers not clear"*
Active game play	Games	*"Idle game that requires very little active game play"*
Battle replay	Games	*"Battle replay is unique"*
Complex combat system	Games	*"More complex combat system than other blockchain games"*
No minimal order limit	Finance	*"Minimal order limit may restrict micro trader to use the IDEX exchange"*

Table 4. DApp Properties.

Properties	Category	Examples of feedback
Concept of the DApp	General	*"Great idea", "Lack of novelty"*
Transparent	General	*"Publicly available smart contracts"*

5   Discussion

The results show that the NFR are similar to the ones relevant for centralized applications. We can note that DApp users seem to prioritize NFR such as **User-friendliness, Documented**, and **User experience**. Also, the functional requirements are distributed into requirements specific to the blockchain realm (e.g. "support various cryptocurrencies"), while others can be found in centralized applications as well (e.g. "tag articles"). Finally, we identified two DApp properties, namely the DApp should: (i) embody an interesting idea/concept, and (ii) be transparent. The former is relevant for all types of applications. The latter is a property of the blockchain technology.

The practical implications are twofold. Firstly, the results can guide DApp designers in identifying the relevant requirements: the NFR can be used as a checklist, and the functional requirements can serve as examples and guide the designers, particularly to help them prioritize the elicited requirements. Secondly, this requirements structure can be a stepping stone to advances in BOSE.

This work suffers from three main limitations. Firstly, we focused on requirements elicitation based on the user opinions. This results in requirements from a **user perspective**. However, in order to provide a more comprehensive requirements framework, other sources of data are of interest, including: social media and the DApp whitepapers. The former would enable us to enhance and validate the preliminary results here; while the latter would provide us with a better view on features such as dependability and security, which are of the utmost importance with blockchain projects. Thus, while we purposefully focused on users' review, we are aware that other sources for requirements elicitation should be considered. Incidentally, this will be addressed in future work. Secondly, despite considering 501 DApps, we were able to extract only a small amount of reviews. This leads to results that are less robust than we would have liked. It might be due to the fact that DApps are still relatively new compared to more "regular" apps[4]. Finally, we deliberately restricted our analysis to Ethereum. While we believe that the results will not change dramatically when expanding the analysis to other platforms, it would be interesting to examine if our intuition is validated or not.

---

[4] According to Statista (https://www.statista.com), in 2020, there were +3 millions and +2 millions apps on Google Play and on the Apple app store respectively.

6   Conclusion

Given the immutability property of the blockchain - and by extension of DApps - the process of SE needs to be carried out carefully. Consequently, this work aims to be one of the first steps in that direction by addressing the Requirements Elicitation of DApps. We elicited recurring user requirements using user reviews (**G.1.**) and we organized them into: (i) NFR (Table 2), (ii) Functional requirements (Table 3) and (iii) DApp properties (Table 4) (**G.2.**). Future work will consist in addressing the limitations mentioned in Sect. 5.

References

1. Antonopoulos, A.M., Wood, G.: Mastering Ethereum: Building Smart Contracts and Dapps. O'Reilly Media (2018)
2. Axon, L., Goldsmith, M., Creese, S.: Privacy requirements in cybersecurity applications of blockchain. In: Advances in Computers, vol. 111, pp. 229–278. Elsevier (2018)
3. Buterin, V., et al.: A next-generation smart contract and decentralized application platform. White Paper **3**, 37 (2014)
4. Chung, L., Nixon, B.A., Yu, E., Mylopoulos, J.: Non-functional requirements in software engineering, vol. 5. Springer (2012)
5. Chung, L., do Prado Leite, J.C.S.: On non-functional requirements in software engineering. In: Borgida, A.T., Chaudhri, V.K., Giorgini, P., Yu, E.S. (eds.) Conceptual Modeling: Foundations and Applications. LNCS, vol. 5600, pp. 363–379. Springer, Heidelberg (2009). https://doi.org/10.1007/978-3-642-02463-4_19
6. Dabrowski, J., Letier, E., Perini, A., Susi, A.: Mining user opinions to support requirement engineering: an empirical study. In: Dustdar, S., Yu, E., Salinesi, C., Rieu, D., Pant, V. (eds.) CAiSE 2020. LNCS, vol. 12127, pp. 401–416. Springer, Cham (2020). https://doi.org/10.1007/978-3-030-49435-3_25
7. Destefanis, G., Marchesi, M., Ortu, M., Tonelli, R., Bracciali, A., Hierons, R.: Smart contracts vulnerabilities: a call for blockchain software engineering? In: 2018 International Workshop on Blockchain Oriented Software Engineering (IWBOSE), pp. 19–25. IEEE (2018)
8. Drljevic, N., Aranda, D.A., Stantchev, V.: Perspectives on risks and standards that affect the requirements engineering of blockchain technology. Comput. Standards Interfaces **69**, 103409 (2019)
9. D'Oriano, L., et al.: Decentralized blockchain flexibility system for smart grids: requirements engineering and use cases. In: 2018 International IEEE Conference and Workshop in Óbuda on Electrical and Power Engineering (CANDO-EPE), pp. 39–44. IEEE (2018)
10. Eckhardt, J., Vogelsang, A., Fernández, D.M.: Are "non-functional" requirements really non-functional? an investigation of non-functional requirements in practice. In: Proceedings of the 38th International Conference on Software Engineering, pp. 832–842 (2016)
11. Fan, K., Sun, S., Yan, Z., Pan, Q., Li, H., Yang, Y.: A blockchain-based clock synchronization scheme in IoT. Fut. Gener. Comput. Syst. **101**, 524–533 (2019)
12. Glinz, M.: On non-functional requirements. In: 15th IEEE International Requirements Engineering Conference (RE 2007), pp. 21–26. IEEE (2007)

13. Hastig, G., Sodhi, M.S.: Blockchain for supply chain traceability: business requirements and critical success factors. Prod. Oper. Manage. **29**(4), 935–954 (2019)
14. Hosseini, M., Groen, E.C., Shahri, A., Ali, R.: Craft: a crowd-annotated feedback technique. In: 2017 IEEE 25th International Requirements Engineering Conference Workshops (REW), pp. 170–175. IEEE (2017)
15. Jha, N., Mahmoud, A.: Mining non-functional requirements from app store reviews. Empirical Softw. Eng. **24**(6), 3659–3695 (2019)
16. Kassab, M., DeFranco, J., Malas, T., Destefanis, G., Neto, V.V.G.: Investigating quality requirements for blockchain-based healthcare systems. In: 2019 IEEE/ACM 2nd International Workshop on Emerging Trends in Software Engineering for Blockchain (WETSEB), pp. 52–55. IEEE (2019)
17. Khalifa, D., Madjid, N.A., Svetinovic, D.: Trust requirements in blockchain systems: a preliminary study. In: 2019 Sixth International Conference on Software Defined Systems (SDS), pp. 310–313. IEEE (2019)
18. Khan, J.A., Liu, L., Wen, L., Ali, R.: Crowd intelligence in requirements engineering: current status and future directions. In: Knauss, E., Goedicke, M. (eds.) REFSQ 2019. LNCS, vol. 11412, pp. 245–261. Springer, Cham (2019). https://doi.org/10.1007/978-3-030-15538-4_18
19. Kumar, T., Ramani, V., Ahmad, I., Braeken, A., Harjula, E., Ylianttila, M.: Blockchain utilization in healthcare: key requirements and challenges. In: 2018 IEEE 20th International Conference on e-Health Networking, Applications and Services (Healthcom), pp. 1–7. IEEE (2018)
20. Leiding, B., Norta, A.: Mapping requirements specifications into a formalized blockchain-enabled authentication protocol for secured personal identity assurance. In: Dang, T.K., Wagner, R., Küng, J., Thoai, N., Takizawa, M., Neuhold, E.J. (eds.) FDSE 2017. LNCS, vol. 10646, pp. 181–196. Springer, Cham (2017). https://doi.org/10.1007/978-3-319-70004-5_13
21. Marchesi, M., Marchesi, L., Tonelli, R.: An agile software engineering method to design blockchain applications. In: Proceedings of the 14th Central and Eastern European Software Engineering Conference Russia, p. 3. ACM (2018)
22. Munante, D., Siena, A., Kifetew, F.M., Susi, A., Stade, M., Seyff, N.: Gathering requirements for software configuration from the crowd. In: 2017 IEEE 25th International Requirements Engineering Conference Workshops (REW), pp. 176–181. IEEE (2017)
23. Nguyen, C.T., Hoang, D.T., Nguyen, D.N., Niyato, D., Nguyen, H.T., Dutkiewicz, E.: Proof-of-stake consensus mechanisms for future blockchain networks: fundamentals, applications and opportunities. IEEE Access **7**, 85727–85745 (2019)
24. Pop, C., et al.: Blockchain-based scalable and tamper-evident solution for registering energy data. Sensors **19**(14), 3033 (2019)
25. Porru, S., Pinna, A., Marchesi, M., Tonelli, R.: Blockchain-oriented software engineering: challenges and new directions. In: 2017 IEEE/ACM 39th International Conference on Software Engineering Companion (ICSE-C), pp. 169–171. IEEE (2017)
26. Raval, S.: Decentralized Applications: Harnessing Bitcoin's Blockchain Technology. O'Reilly Media, Inc. (2016)
27. Sherief, N., Abdelmoez, W., Phalp, K., Ali, R.: Modelling users feedback in crowd-based requirements engineering: an empirical study. In: Ralyté, J., España, S., Pastor, Ó. (eds.) PoEM 2015. LNBIP, vol. 235, pp. 174–190. Springer, Cham (2015). https://doi.org/10.1007/978-3-319-25897-3_12

28. Snijders, R., Dalpiaz, F., Hosseini, M., Shahri, A., Ali, R.: Crowd-centric require-ments engineering. In: 2014 IEEE/ACM 7th International Conference on Utility and Cloud Computing, pp. 614–615. IEEE (2014)
29. Swan, M.: Blockchain: blueprint for a new economy. O'Reilly Media, Inc. (2015)
30. Wessling, F., Gruhn, V.: Engineering software architectures of blockchain-oriented applications. In: 2018 IEEE International Conference on Software Architecture Companion (ICSA-C), pp. 45–46. IEEE (2018)
31. Xu, X., Weber, I., Staples, M.: Architecture for Blockchain Applications. Springer (2019). https://doi.org/10.1007/978-3-030-03035-3
32. Yang, W., Aghasian, E., Garg, S., Herbert, D., Disiuta, L., Kang, B.: A survey on blockchain-based internet service architecture: requirements, challenges, trends and future. IEEE Access **7**, 75845–75872 (2019)

ISGE: A Conceptual Model-Based Method to Correctly Manage Genome Data

Alberto García S.$^{(\boxtimes)}$ ⓘ, Juan Carlos Casamayor ⓘ, and Oscar Pastor ⓘ

PROS Research Center, Universitat Politècnica de València, Valencia, Spain
{algarsi3,jcarlos,opastor}@pros.upv.es

Abstract. Understanding the Human Genome is one of the most relevant challenges under current investigation. The ongoing genomics revolution promises to change the diagnosis, treatment, and prevention of disease, providing long-term benefits and a transformative impact on personal health. It also has wealth and productivity implications. However, genomics is one of the most complex and data-intensive domains. Fuzzy definitions, data diversity, data heterogeneity, and continuous evolution of knowledge are responsible for an inadequate and inaccurate understanding of the domain, which hinders the unleashing of its full potential. A sound conceptual modeling-practice is essential in achieving the required shared understanding of the domain. This paper presents ISGE, which is a conceptual model-based method to improve genomic data management from two perspectives: first, by performing a sound, new characterization of genomic data; and second, by providing a framework that encourages applying CM techniques and reusing their generated artifacts in order to take advantage of all of the previously accumulated knowledge. Better abstraction capabilities and efficient reuse are intended to facilitate the work of domain experts.

Keywords: Conceptual modeling · Conceptual model-based method · Genomics · ISGE

1 Introduction

Understanding the vast number of processes that drive life as we know it is one of the most challenging goals of the century. Obtaining the needed, well-defined understanding of its associated genomic domain becomes a huge challenge [4]. Genomic data have a high degree of heterogeneity, dispersion, and lack of interconnection. This situation is known as "genomic data chaos" [3]. Besides, there is not an explicit distinction between the problem space and the solution space concepts in genomic data. On the one hand, the problem space concepts are related to purely biological data (e.g., a variation in the genome [5]). On the other hand, solution space concepts refer to non-biological, technologically-related data (e.g., the quality of the identification process of a variation [2]). This context prevent

S. Nurcan and A. Korthaus (Eds.): CAiSE Forum 2021, LNBIP 424, pp. 47–54, 2021.
https://doi.org/10.1007/978-3-030-79108-7_6

domain users from having the required set of precise definitions of genome concepts needed to extract knowledge efficiently.

In this context, conceptual modeling (CM) techniques should play a crucial role in providing a strong, shared understanding of the domain; but they are little used. Existing attempts to apply CM techniques have succeeded in determining relevant information more precisely, but without differentiating between the problem space and the solution space concepts. Two strategies have been identified to better manage genomic data. The first one is to define a new characterization of genomic data by explicitly separating problem space concepts from solution space concepts, which improves understanding of the domain. The second one is to increase the level of reuse of the artifacts generated when applying CM techniques.

This paper presents a conceptual model-based method called **ISGE**, which refers to the phases that make it up (**I**dentify, **S**elect, and **GE**nerate). ISGE implements the two strategies mentioned above, providing a means to enhance the management of genomic data. When ISGE is applied, conceptual schemes that are specific to solution space concepts are generated. These schemes can be assembled, like puzzle pieces, to generate use-case specific conceptual schemes. Domain experts will benefit from this by having an increased level of abstraction and means for managing data.

To achieve these objectives, the paper is organized as follows: Sect. 2 studies and classifies the issues that arise when genomic data is poorly managed. Section 3 details ISGE, which is the main contribution of this work. Our final remarks are presented in Sect. 5.

2   Genome Data Issue Identification

The genomic domain is particularly vast and complex. The consequences of this complexity must be identified to provide valid and valuable solutions. This section determines the impact and consequences of poorly managing genomic data. These consequences have been grouped into three categories, namely, "ontological", "operational", and "knowledge extraction" issues.

First, ontological issues are related to an insufficient understanding of core concepts or a lack of clarity of domain definitions. The available domain knowledge is ever-changing, core concepts are not entirely understood, and their definitions often include plenty of implicit information. Too frequently, these concepts have diverse context-dependent interpretations, and domain experts must infer which one to use or how to interpret crucial aspects of a definition: domain understanding is insufficient and too imprecise. Obtaining a shared understanding of the domain is then a problem that needs to be solved better. The consequences of ontological issues include the existence of fuzzy definitions with implicit information, inadequate and inaccurate communication, or an ontological commitment that is difficult to obtain.

Second, operational issues arise when dealing with a large variety of heterogeneous information from multiple sources, and without any ontological commitment regarding their content or structure. Batini et al. [1] define three levels of heterogeneity: technological, schema, and instance. In most cases, they are a consequence of relying too much on solution space-generated data, ignoring those definitions that belong to the problem space. Technological heterogeneity arises from the large number of existing data sources, file formats, and tools. Schema heterogeneity is a consequence of technological heterogeneity. The existence of different representation models requires an intermediate step to transform the data into a common schema before integrating it. Instance heterogeneity is triggered by schema heterogeneity and other reasons like obsolete data sources or technical failures when generating data. It is not rare to detect redundant or duplicated data as a consequence of the instance heterogeneity. Data quality is a key aspect to avoid inaccurate, unnecessary, or redundant data. The consequences of operational issues include the existence of low-quality data, including inaccurate, unnecessary, or redundant data and integration processes that are too complex and error-prone. The main consequence of knowledge extraction issues is that extracting knowledge is time-consuming and intricate.

Third, Knowledge extraction issues have a direct impact on the quality of the research processes and on the amount of invested time that is needed to perform them. These issues are a direct consequence of ontological and operational issues. Extracting knowledge is a hard task when there is not a solid, ontological background and genomic data has low quality.

The reported issues justify the need to implement the two characteristics defined above. On the one hand, having an explicit separation between the data from the problem space and the data from the solution space can facilitate the understanding of the domain. Solution space data does provide domain experts with contextual and data-quality information, but not having a real separation between them distorts how problem space concepts are studied, discussed, and represented. It is a cross-cutting problem that reduces domain clarity by polluting the problem space (ontological issues), complicates any attempt of data integration by increasing domain heterogeneity (operational issues), and slows knowledge extraction (knowledge extraction). On the other hand, increasing the level of reuse can help to obtain a clearly defined single point of truth to reduce ontological issues and reduce schema heterogeneity, helping to solve many operational and knowledge extraction issues.

3   Method Definition

The correct and efficient management of genomic data that we want to achieve is strongly dependent on the specification of a clear, single point of truth. The use of CM techniques can serve as a basis for a sound integration layer. The aim of our work is to provide a solution to this problem. We have identified two strategies to address this situation: i) to explicitly separate problem space concepts from solution space concepts, and ii) to increase the level of reuse of the artifacts generated when applying CM techniques. The method that we present faces the challenge of effectively implementing these strategies.

The first strategy is achieved with the definition of the two elements that support ISGE. The first one is a CS, called the Conceptual Schema of the Genome

(CSG), which conceptualizes biological concepts (i.e., the problem space). Specific conceptual views (with a subset of CSG concepts) can be instantiated to adapt to the particularities of the use cases of the working domain.

The second strategy is a catalog of solution space-specific conceptual schemes. These conceptual schemes include, but are not limited to, technologies, software, file formats, or defined standards. These elements provides a means to have an explicit separation between the problem space and the solution space.

ISGE is divided into three phases. Phase 1 identifies the essential components of the use case. Phase 2 selects the set of conceptual schemes of the catalog. Phase 3 generates the final CS. The generation is divided into two activities.

Method Elements

ISGE is supported by two elements. The first element is the CSG, which conceptualize biological concepts (i.e., the problem space concepts). The second element is the catalog of conceptual schemes of technological aspects (i.e., the solution space).

The **CSG** provides a well-grounded ontological basis that describes an extensive set of domain definitions and how they are related. To deal with the great variety of use cases in the genomic domain, ISGE allows the instantiation of conceptual views of the CSG in order to adapt to their particularities.

The **catalog of conceptual schemes of technological aspects** contains a set of conceptual schemes, each of which models a technological aspect. The SAM file-format specification, the Variant Call Format, or the UniProt database are examples of these technological aspects.

Each CS of the catalog includes a set of rules that indicates its relationships with the other conceptual schemes of the method, including the CSG and other conceptual schemes of the catalog. There are two types of rules. The first type is the "chain rule", which indicates that two classes of different conceptual schemes are somehow related and are connected when represented together. The second type is the "equality rule", which indicates that two classes of different conceptual schemes refer to the same concept and are merged when represented together.

The catalog allows additional technological aspects to be conceptualized, thereby enriching the method. By executing ISGE, the most suitable CS for a specific use case is obtained by merging a generated view from the CSG and a set of relevant conceptual schemes of the technological aspects used. The resulting CS takes into account the specific particularities of the use case under study while keeping the holistic perspective of the CSG.

Method Phases

The method is applied through a three-phase workflow that is composed of six activities Phase 1 consists of studying the particularities of the case under study. Phase 2 consists of selecting the elements of the method that are required for the use case. Phase 3 consists of merging the identified conceptual schemes in order to obtain the final CS.

Phase 1 – Identify the Essential Components of the Use Case

Phase 1 consists of obtaining the knowledge that is needed to generate a CS that is specifically adapted to the working use case. The process is carried out in a series of meetings with domain experts, and it is divided into two activities:

1. Identification of Relevant Concepts activity, where the CSG is used to identify the basic building units required to develop an appropriate conceptual view. The CSG is the graphical representation of the ontological framework that provides a common, shared understanding to facilitate the interaction with the domain experts. The CSG is discussed on a per-view basis with domain experts to identify those concepts that play a determinant role in their use case. The result of this activity is the list of classes of the CSG that make up the conceptual view that will be generated in Phase 3.
2. Identification of Technological Aspects Used activity, where the technological aspects (file formats, standards, processes, data sources, etc.) that are used to manage data in the case under study are identified. The result of this activity is the set of technological aspects used. The conceptual schemes of the catalog that model the technological aspects will be selected in Phase 2.

Phase 2 – Select Conceptual Schemes of the Catalog

Phase 2 consists of selecting the relevant conceptual schemes of the catalog that represent the identified technological aspects. These conceptual schemes will be assembled in Phase 3 to generate the final CS. This phase is divided into two activities:

1. Conceptualization of missing technological aspects activity, where those technological aspects that are missing in the catalog are conceptualized and included in it. The conceptualization exercise includes creating the corresponding CS, the chain rules, and the equality rules. The number of solution space elements that ISGE covers is increased each time a new item is included in the catalog.
2. Selection of the Conceptual Schemes of the Catalog activity, where the corresponding conceptual schemes of the technological aspects identified as *used* in Phase 1 are selected.

Phase 3 – Generate the Final CS

Phase 3 consists of generating the final CS. Two activities make up this phase, which are supported by the outputs of Phases 1 and 2.

1. Generation of the Biological View activity, where a biological view is instantiated from the CSG based on the list of classes identified in Phase 1. This view is discussed with the domain experts, who validate it.
2. Merging of the conceptual schemes activity, where the selected conceptual schemes of the catalog are merged to the biological view generated in the previous activity. This process is driven by the chain and equality rules.

4   Application of the Method

In this Section, an example of how IGSE has been applied in a real-world use case is presented. The use case under study pertains to the agri-food field, and its objective is twofold: **i)** to provide more efficient and valuable citrus crops by identifying genotype-phenotype relationships regarding specific traits of interest, like sweetness or drought resistance; and **ii)** to establish phylogenetic relationships between citrus species to determine their origin and closeness. These goals are achieved through comparison exercises involving hundreds of whole-genome sequences of citrus varieties.

In Phase 1, we started by interviewing eight domain experts in a series of ten meetings to perform the first phase of the method, which allowed us to identify the unique particularities of their use case. The CSG was discussed in the *identification of relevant concepts* activity to identify relevant concepts that play a key role in their comparison exercises. 17 concepts out of the 62 defined in the CSG will make up the biological view. Our approach allowed us to narrow down the number of elements to work with and focus on the relevant concepts from a more general, holistic starting point. Consequently, conceptual schemes that are adapted to the unique particularities of the various use cases of the genomic domain are generated without renouncing the much needed holistic perspective. At this point, the *identification of technological aspects used* activity begins, in which four technological aspects have been identified as used:

- **Scaffolding technology:** to store DNA sequences of chromosomes.
- **Gene Ontology data source:** to characterize biological processes and how they relate to genes.
- **Variant Call Format (VCF) file format:** to store identified variations.
- **SnpEff variant annotation software:** to annotate identified variations with additional information regarding the effect they cause at a molecular level.

In Phase 2, we gathered the required conceptual schemes of the catalog that conceptualize those technological aspects that are used. For the sake of brevity, we assume that there are no missing concepts in the catalog. Therefore, the *conceptualization of missing technological concepts* activity was not triggered. The technology identification activity in Phase 1 identified four technological aspects, and the conceptual schemes corresponding to them were selected from the catalog in the *selection of the conceptual schemes of the catalog* activity.

In Phase 3, we generated the final CS. In the *generation of the biological view* activity, we generated the biological view adapted to the particularities of the working use case. Figure 1 shows the classes of the biological view with a white background. Its content focuses on establishing the consequences of genetic variations in every step of the protein-coding process. This includes analyzing changes and their implications at the DNA level in genes, at the RNA level in primary transcripts and mRNA, at the amino acid level in proteins and enzymes, and at the metabolic level in pathways. The view also allows studying citrus lineage by performing evolutionary studies that analyze ortholog groups.

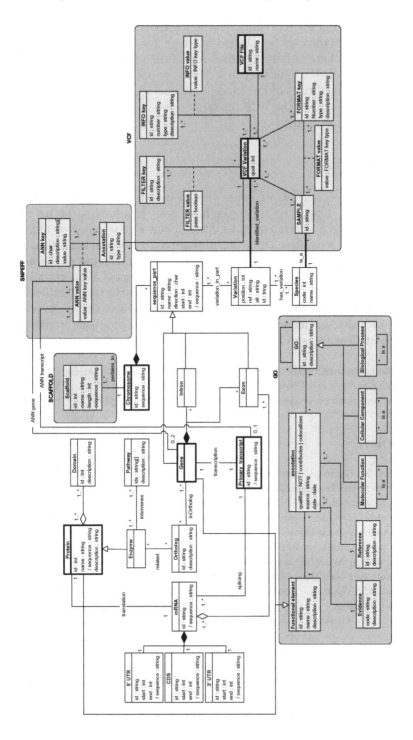

Fig. 1. Generated CS after applying ISGE

In the *merging of the conceptual schemes* activity, we merged the set of conceptual schemes of the catalog selected in Phase 2 with the biological view generated in the previous activity. Figure 1 shows the selected conceptual schemes of the catalog shaded in light gray in a dark gray background. This process was driven by the defined rules of the conceptual schemes. As can be observed, only one technological aspect, the VCF file format, has chain rules, but every aspect has equality rules defined.

5   Conclusions

We have identified a series of issues that demonstrate that genomic data is poorly managed. Thus, two strategies have been proposed to better manage genomic data. The first strategy is to define a new characterization of genomic data by explicitly separating the problem space concepts from the solution space concepts. The second strategy is to increase the level of reuse of the artifacts generated when applying CM techniques. We have presented a conceptual model-based method, called ISGE, that effectively implements the two identified strategies, providing a means to enhance genomic data management. Future work is oriented to providing more efficient data integration processes by developing model-based algorithms to provide automated, on-demand data integration.

Acknowledgements. This work was funded by the Spanish Ministry of Science and Innovation through Project DataME (ref: TIN2016-80811-P) and the Generalitat Valenciana through project GISPRO (PROMETEO/2018/176).

References

1. Cabitza, F., Batini, C.: Information quality in healthcare. In: Batini, C., Scannapieco, M. (eds.) Data and Information Quality. DSA, pp. 403–419. Springer, Cham (2016). https://doi.org/10.1007/978-3-319-24106-7_13
2. Cingolani, P., et al.: A program for annotating and predicting the effects of single nucleotide polymorphisms, SnpEff: SNPs in the genome of drosophila melanogaster strain w1118; iso-2; iso-3. Fly **6**(2), 80–92 (2012)
3. León Palacio, A.: SILE: a method for the efficient management of smart genomic information. Ph.D. thesis (2019)
4. Pearson, H.: What is a gene? Nature **441**(7092), 398–401 (2006). https://doi.org/10.1038/441398a
5. Pierce, B.A.: Genetics: A Conceptual Approach. W. H. Freeman, New York (2010)

Case Level Counterfactual Reasoning in Process Mining

Mahnaz Sadat Qafari$^{(\boxtimes)}$ and Wil M. P. van der Aalst

Rheinisch-Westfälische Technische Hochschule Aachen (RWTH), Aachen, Germany
{m.s.qafari,wvdaalst}@pads.rwth-aachen.de

Abstract. Process mining is widely used to diagnose processes and uncover performance and compliance problems. It is also possible to see relations between different behavioral aspects, e.g., cases that deviate more at the beginning of the process tend to get delayed in the later part of the process. However, correlations do not necessarily reveal causalities. Moreover, standard process mining diagnostics do not indicate how to improve the process. This is the reason we advocate the use of *structural equation models* and *counterfactual reasoning*. We use results from causal inference and adapt these to be able to reason over event logs and process interventions. We have implemented the approach as a ProM plug-in and have evaluated it on several data sets.

Keywords: Process mining · Counterfactual statement · Structural equation model

1   Introduction

Humans tend to learn from the past (their experiences) by analyzing possible alternatives of what happened in the reality and reflecting on their findings aiming for better results in future similar cases (e.g., not doing the same mistakes). Thinking about possible alternatives to what happened in the past is called *counterfactual thinking*.

The information systems of companies save data about the process instances (cases) in their event logs. Process mining extracts knowledge from the event logs for discovering the process model, monitoring process KPIs, and improving processes. Process improvement requires a deep comprehension of the process behavior and its cases. In this paper, we tailor the concept of *counterfactual thinking* to process mining and explain why a specific situation has a special outcome. Given an instance with an undesirable outcome, we aim at providing a set of counterfactual statements (we call them *explanations*) to explain such an outcome.

Companies can boost customer satisfaction and build trust by providing explanations for their specific cases without putting other people's rights and privacy in danger [7]. Case level explanation can be used to explain why a customer has received a particular result, was it fair, or how to approach to get a better result. Moreover, the process manager can benefit from this method as it can be used to explain why something happens in a specific case and how to act differently to get different results in the future.

© Springer Nature Switzerland AG 2021
S. Nurcan and A. Korthaus (Eds.): CAiSE Forum 2021, LNBIP 424, pp. 55–63, 2021.
https://doi.org/10.1007/978-3-030-79108-7_7

Two important aspects of an explanation are accuracy and applicability. Both of them can be amended by distinguishing between correlation and causation among the process features, which prevents misleading explanations that recommend altering features with non-causal relationships with the result. For this matter, we propose using the *structural equation model (SEM)* of the features in the procedure of generating explanations.

Case level explanations are case dependent, which means, an explanation that is useful for a customer may not be favored by another customer with the same undesirable outcome. To overcome this issue, in the proposed method, we present a set of diverse explanations (i.e. explanations that differ from the given instance in different features) to the user such that the user can decide which one to apply. Moreover, as the explanations are meant to be used by the human, the readability and understandability of the explanations are important. Therefore those explanations with a smaller number of features with different values from the given instance, are preferred [10].

The rest of the paper is organized as follows. In Sect. 2, a brief overview of the related work is presented. In Sect. 3, the method is presented. The experimental results are presented in Sect. 4. Finally, in Sect. 5 the conclusion is presented.

2   Related Work

There are already several approaches in the domain of process mining that deal with root cause analysis using the findings of a classification techniques [2,9]. The drawback of these methods is that the classification techniques are based on correlation and not causal relationships. Also, there are several works considering causal relationships among different process features at the process level [3,4,6]. Moreover, in [1] a method for generating case-level recommendations of treatments that maximize the probability of a given outcome is proposed. In this method a subset of candidate treatments that are most correlated with the outcome is extracted by applying an association rule mining technique. Then the subgroups with causal relation between treatment and outcome are identified using uplift tree. Finally, the subgroups are sorted by the ratio of the score associated to them by the uplift trees and their cost.

It is worth noting that counterfactual reasoning for explainability has been studied extensively in the field of data mining and machine learning (e.g., [8,10]).

3   Method

The general overview of the proposed method is presented in Fig. 1. First, we enrich the event log. Then, several random counterfactual instances similar to the current instance are generated. Among them, those that have a desirable outcome regarding a given threshold are selected and optimization techniques are used to make them as close as possible to the current instance. The resulting desirable counterfactual instances are ordered according to their distance with the current instance, and finally, converted into a set of explanations and presented to the people involved.

In the following, we first explain how we extract the data from the event log and then we describe the explanation generation method.

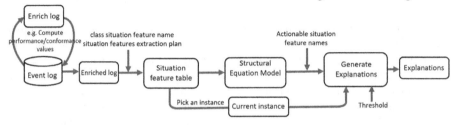

Fig. 1. The general overview of the proposed method.

3.1 Situation Feature Table Extraction

Here, we mention how to extract features from the event logs of processes. An event log is a collection of traces where each trace is a collection of events. Each event indicates that specific activity has happened at a specific time for a specific case. A trace is a sequence of chronologically ordered events that belong to a specific case. Both traces and events may have several attributes. Here we assume the uniqueness of the events in the event log. We define an event log as follows:

Definition 1 (Event Log). *An event log is a set of traces where each trace is composed of a chronologically ordered sequence of events and trace attributes (if applies). Moreover, each event refers to a case, an activity, a timestamp, and event attributes (if applicable).*

Fig. 2. The process of the repair company.

Through this paper, we consider a company that repairs a specific product as the running example. The Petri-net model of this repair company is shown in Fig. 2. Each trace in the event log is corresponding to the process of repairing one product. In the "inspection" activity, several tests are done to determine the defects of a product. Then it is repaired, and afterward "final check" is done. We know that the newer products are more complicated and harder to deal with. In this example, "model" is a trace level attribute where newer products have higher model numbers. "team size" is another trace-level attribute that indicates the number of resources involved in repairing the product. "num test" is an event-level attribute indicating the number of tests that have been done in the "inspection" activity. A snapshot of an event log is shown in Table 1. The manager of the repair company believes that in the trace with "case id" = $c1$ the "repair" activity (event $e2$) was too long and should have taken at most 500 h. He/She needs to know if it was the case, and if so, how they could had prevented it.

When we are interested in features not existing in the event log, we need to enrich the event log by adding new derived features from the event log or possibly other sources to its traces and events. For example, we can enrich the repair company event log by adding an attribute named "duration" to its events indicating the duration of that event in hours. In the repair company example, the value of the "duration" attribute can be computed by subtracting the timestamp of two consecutive events in each trace.

With respect to the time precedence of the cause and effect, we consider just the features that have been extracted from that part of a trace that has been recorded before a specific feature as possible causes of it. For example, in the repair company, extracting the data from the "final check" activity is meaningless when we want to find the features that causally influence the "duration" of the "repair" activity. So we need to extract the data from a proper prefix of a trace, which we call a *situation*. Also, we define the *situation set* of an event log as the set of all situations generated using its traces. Some of the subsets of the situation set of a given event log are more meaningful. For example the set of all the situations that end with an event with a specific activity name or the set of all traces. In the repair company example, we can have a subset of situations that end with an event whose activity name is "repair". In this case, the situation subset would include all the prefixes of traces which include the events with the activity name "inspection" and "repair". The situation extracted from the first trace would include the two events with "event id" $e1$ and $e2$. Let's call this situation s_1.

An event log may have both event and trace level attributes. Moreover, it is possible to have the same attribute name in both levels. To concretely determine the attributes that we are interested in their values, we use *situation feature* notion. A situation feature refers to an attribute and an activity name (or possibly "trace"). For example in the repair company, $sf_{teamsize}$ and sf_{model} are two situation features indicating "team size" and "model" attributes in the trace level. While, $sf_{inspDuration}$ and $sf_{inspNumTest}$ are the situation features referring to the "duration" and "num test" in the "inspection" activity. Also, $sf_{repairDuration}$ refers to the "duration" of the "repair" activity. The situation feature value extraction mechanism from a given situation is as follows:

- If the situation feature refers to an attribute name and "trace", then the value of that attribute in the trace-level is assigned to the situation feature.
- If the situation feature refers to an attribute name and an activity name, then the value of that attribute from an event with the given activity name, with the maximum timestamp is assigned to the situation feature.

For example, for the situation s_1, the value assigned to $sf_{inspDuration}$ is 71 (computed using timestamps) and the value assigned to sf_{model} is 7.

To generate explanations, we need to know the situation feature that identifies the problem (we call it *target situation feature*) and a set of descriptive situation features that are those features that may have causal effect on the problem. We call the set including the descriptive situation features and the target situation feature a *situation feature extraction plan* and denote it by $\boldsymbol{SF}$. We can look at the $\boldsymbol{SF}$ as the schema in a tabular data. For example in the repair company, as the manager believes that the duration of "repair" activity for some cases should have been shorter, the target situation feature is $sf_{repairDuration}$. Also he has considered sf_{model}, $sf_{teamsize}$, $sf_{inspNumTest}$, and $sf_{inspDuration}$ as descriptive situation features. So, in this example we have $\boldsymbol{SF}_{repair} = \{sf_{model}, sf_{teamsize}, sf_{inspNumTest}, sf_{inspDuration}, sf_{repairDuration}\}$.

Table 1. A snapshot of the event log of the repair company.

Event id	Case id	Activity name	Timestamp	Team size	Num test	Model
e1	c1	Inspection	01-04-2020T08:00:00	2	42	7
e2	c1	Repair	04-04-2020T07:00:00	2	42	7
e3	c1	Final test	28-04-2020T08:00:00	2	42	7
e4	c2	Inspection	01-05-2020T08:00:00	3	26	5
e5	c2	Repair	03-05-2020T11:00:00	3	26	5
e6	c2	Final test	19-05-2020T20:00:00	3	26	5
$\vdots$	$\vdots$	$\vdots$	$\vdots$	$\vdots$	$\vdots$	$\vdots$

Given a situation feature extraction plan, SF we can map each situation to a data point by simply extracting the values of situation features in SF using the proper mechanism. We call such a data point an *instance*. Moreover, we can define a target-dependent tabular data, called *situation feature table*, extracted from a given situation subset, as the bag of the instances extracted from the situations in a given situation subset. As an example, using SF_{repair} instance $i_{repair} = \{(sf_{model}, 7), (sf_{teamsize}, 2), (sf_{inspNumTest}, 42), (sf_{inspDuration}, 71), (sf_{repairDuration}, 577)\}$ is generated from s_1.

3.2 Explanation Generation Method

Consider an instance i in the situation feature table with an undesirable target situation feature value regarding a threshold t. For example, in the repair company the threshold is 500. W.l.o.g., in this paper, we always assume that the values lower than the given threshold are desirable. Explanations are diverse instances which are close to i and have a desirable target situation feature value. As it is vain to investigate the effect of intervention on those situation features that their value can not be altered by the user, we study the effect of changing the value of those situation features that are modifiable by the user. We call the set of modifiable situation features *actionable situation features* and denote it with ASF. We define a set of counterfactual explanations for a given instances as follows.

Definition 2 (A Set of Counterfactual Explanation). *Let i be an instance for which the target situation feature value is undesirable. A set of explanations for i is a set of diverse instances that are close to i and yet differ from i in a subset of ASF and have a desirable result for the target situation feature.*

To generate the set of counterfactual explanations, we take the following three steps:

1. Generating candidates. We generate several candidates for the values that could had been assigned to the actionable situation features. Each candidate is a value assignment to a subset of situation features in ASF. We generate candidates such that for half of them the situation feature values are selected from their distribution in the situation feature table and for the other half, they are selected randomly from their domain.

2. Predicting the value of the target situation feature. In the second step, we compute the effect of replacing the values of the situation features in the given instance with those in the generated candidates on the value of target situation feature using the SEM of the situation features. The SEM of the situation features of a situation feature table can be provided by a customer who possesses the process domain knowledge or can be inferred in a data-driven manner using several methods that already exist in the literature (e.g., [4,6]). Loosely speaking, a SEM is a set of equations that determine how to generate the observational and interventional distributions. More formally:

Definition 3 (Structural Equation Model (SEM)). *Let SF be a situation feature extraction plan, the SEM of SF is defined as $\mathcal{E}Q \in SF \rightarrow Expr(SF)$ where for each $sf \in SF$, $Expr(SF)$ is an expression over the situation features in SF and possibly some noise N_{sf}. Moreover, the noise distributions of N_{sf} for all $sf \in SF$ have to be mutually independent.*

We assume that SF includes all relevant situation features and there is no common hidden confounder for the situation features in SF. Also, we assume that the SEM does not include any loop. In Table 2, a possible SEM for the repair company is presented.

Table 2. A possible SEM for the repair company.

$sf_{model} = N_{sf_{model}}$	$N_{sf_{model}} \sim Uniform(1, 10)$
$sf_{teamsize} = N_{sf_{teamsize}}$	$N_{sf_{teamsize}} \sim Uniform(1, 3)$
$sf_{repairDuration} = 10sf_{model} + N_{sf_{repairDuration}}$	$N_{sf_{repairDuration}} \sim Uniform(-2, 4)$
$sf_{inspNumTest} = 5sf_{model} + 3sf_{teamsize} + N_{sf_{inspNumTest}}$	$N_{sf_{inspNumTest}} \sim Uniform(-1, 2)$
$sf_{repairDuration} = 50sf_{model} + 5sf_{inspNumTest} + N_{sf_{repairDuration}}$	$N_{sf_{repairDuration}} \sim Uniform(10, 20)$

Using SEM $\mathcal{E}Q$, prediction of the class situation feature value for each candidate involves three steps *abduction*, *action*, and *prediction* [5]. We explain these steps using the repair company example.

- **Abduction.** First we need to incorporate the observed data, instance i, into the model, $\mathcal{E}Q$, and generate a *counterfactual SEM* that explains the conditions and the behavior of the system and the environment when i was happening. A *counterfactual SEM*, $\mathcal{E}Q'$, is obtained by replacing the distribution of noise terms in $\mathcal{E}Q$ with the corresponding noise distributions condition on $SF = i$. Considering the SEM in Table 2 and i_{repair}, the equations of the counterfactual SEM $\mathcal{E}Q'_{repair}$ are: $sf_{model} = 7$, $sf_{inspNumTest} = 2$, $sf_{inspDuration} = 10sf_{model} + 1$, $sf_{inspNumTest} = 5sf_{model} + 3sf_{teamSize} + 1$, and $sf_{repairDuration} = 50sf_{model} + 5sf_{inspNumTest} + 17$.
- **Action.** The second step is taking action toward enforcing changes in the counterfactual SEM $\mathcal{E}Q'$, regarding candidate c. The result is a SEM $\mathcal{E}Q''$ where $sf = c_{sf}$

where c_{sf} is the value assigned to sf by c if $sf \in dom(c)$ and $sf = \mathcal{E}Q'(sf)$ where sf is not in the domain of c. As an example, suppose that we are interested in predicting the value of $sf_{repairDuration}$ for the candidate $\{(sf_{teamSize}, 3)\}$. Intervention on the counterfactual SEM $\mathcal{E}Q'_{repair}$, results in replacing $sf_{teamSize} = 2$ with $sf_{teamSize} = 3$.

– **Prediction.** The third step involves using the modified SEM to predict the counterfactual value of the target situation feature by simply computing the value of targer situation feature (or its distribution) in the counterfactual SEM under the intervention. In this step, we remove those situation features from the domain of c that do not affect the target situation feature value. In the above example, computing the values of the situation features we have: $\{((sf_{model}, \perp), 7), (sf_{teamSize}, 3), (sf_{inspNumTest}, 45), (sf_{inspDuration}, 71), (sf_{repairDuration}, 592)\}$. We call such an instance a *counterfactual instance*.

3. Selecting a subset of candidates. We want explanations to be a set of diverse candidates with a small domain and a desirable predicted target situation feature value. Also we want them to be close to the given instance. To compute the distance between instances, we use L_1 metric on the normalized situation features. As mentioned in [10], using L_1 metric, more sparse explanations would be generated. For the diversity, we partition candidates with desirable predicted outcome based on their domain and then sort them in each partition according to their distance from the given instance. A set of these candidates are selected one by one from different partitions, with the priority of those partitions that have a smaller domain.

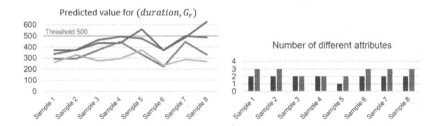

Fig. 3. The result of applying the implemented method on the synthetic event logs. (Color figure online)

4   Experimental Results

The implemented plugin is available in ProM nightly build under the name *counterfactual explanation*. In the implemented plugin, we can apply several classifiers (including Regression Tree (RT), Locally Weighted Learning (LWL), Multi-layer perceptron (NN)), as well as SEM, to predict the target situation feature value of candidates.

We applied the implemented plugin on a synthetic event log to see how different might be the explanations generated by the SEM and by a machine learning technique with the highest accuracy in terms of predicted target situation feature values and the number of situation features with different values in the given instance and the explanations. So, we did not use optimization on the selected desirable counterfactual instances.

For the synthetic event log, we have used the repair company example and i_{repair} as the instance with the undesirable target situation feature. Also, the values lower than the given threshold 500 were desirable. We considered all the descriptive situation features as actionable. We have generated 1000 traces such that the SEM of its situation feature values is the one in Table 2. Then, we generate a set of 8 explanations by generating several candidates and using the SEM in Tabble 2 to evaluate them.

We have used the classifier with the highest accuracy for predicting the value of $sf_{rapairDuration}$ on the selected candidates in the previous step. The accuracy of RT, LWL, and NN on the data were 0.818, 0.990, and 0.984, respectively. But their accuracy reduced on the counterfactual instances to 0.74, 0.77, and 0.76, respectively.

The results of applying the proposed method using SEM and three mentioned machine learning techniques are presented in Fig. 3. In left part of Fig. 3, the predicted $sf_{rapairDuration}$ of the selected desirable candidates using SEM (red line), RT (blue line), LWL (green line), and NN (light green line) are presented. In the right side of Fig. 3, the size of the domain of the selected candidates is demonstrated.

Discussion. As demonstrated in Fig. 3, there is a gap between the values predicted by the machine learning techniques and by SEM. Also, the accuracy of the classifiers predicting the value of the counterfactual instances drops dramatically. This phenomenon can be explained by the difference in their mechanism of predicting counterfactual values. Using a machine learning technique, neither the behavior of the environment nor the effect of an intervention is considered; but, the generated instance is regarded as a new instance, which may result in wrong predictions.

The difference in the number of effective situation features with different values between the given and explanations comes from the fact that machine learning techniques do not distinguish among the situation features with causal and mere correlation relationship with the target situation feature. On the other hand, using SEM the changes in the values of the situation features that have no causal relationships with the target situation feature in the counterfactual instances are simply ignored.

5 Conclusion

We have presented a method that can be used by companies to explain to their customers why they have received a specific outcome in a case-specific manner and help them to prevent the same outcome in the future. As a result, the interpretability and accountability of the companies would be boosted.

The results of the evaluations have shown that ignoring the causal relationships among the situation features may end up in explanations that suggest changing situation features with no causal effect on the class situation feature. Moreover, using a machine learning technique, regardless of its accuracy, for predicting the value of the target situation feature may result in wrong explanations or missing some of the good explanations.

References

1. Bozorgi, Z.D., Teinemaa, I., Dumas, M., Rosa, M.L., Polyvyanyy, A.: Process mining meets causal machine learning: discovering causal rules from event logs. In: ICPM (2020)
2. Ferreira, D.R., Vasilyev, E.: Using logical decision trees to discover the cause of process delays from event logs. Comput. Ind. **70**, 194–207 (2015)
3. Hompes, B.F.A., Maaradji, A., La Rosa, M., Dumas, M., Buijs, J.C.A.M., van der Aalst, W.M.P.: Discovering causal factors explaining business process performance variation. In: Dubois, E., Pohl, K. (eds.) CAiSE 2017. LNCS, vol. 10253, pp. 177–192. Springer, Cham (2017). https://doi.org/10.1007/978-3-319-59536-8_12
4. Narendra, T., Agarwal, P., Gupta, M., Dechu, S.: Counterfactual reasoning for process optimization using structural causal models. In: Hildebrandt, T., van Dongen, B.F., Röglinger, M., Mendling, J. (eds.) BPM 2019. LNBIP, vol. 360, pp. 91–106. Springer, Cham (2019). https://doi.org/10.1007/978-3-030-26643-1_6
5. Pearl, J., et al.: Models, Reasoning and Inference. Cambridge University Press, Cambridge (2000)
6. Qafari, M.S., van der Aalst, W.: Root cause analysis in process mining using structural equation models. In: Del Río Ortega, A., Leopold, H., Santoro, F.M. (eds.) BPM 2020. LNBIP, vol. 397, pp. 155–167. Springer, Cham (2020). https://doi.org/10.1007/978-3-030-66498-5_12
7. Reddix-Smalls, B.: Credit scoring and trade secrecy: an algorithmic quagmire or how the lack of transparency in complex financial models scuttled the finance market. UC Davis Bus. LJ **12**, 87 (2011)
8. Russell, C.: Efficient search for diverse coherent explanations. In: Proceedings of the Conference on Fairness, Accountability, and Transparency, pp. 20–28 (2019)
9. Suriadi, S., Ouyang, C., van der Aalst, W.M.P., ter Hofstede, A.H.M.: Root cause analysis with enriched process logs. In: La Rosa, M., Soffer, P. (eds.) BPM 2012. LNBIP, vol. 132, pp. 174–186. Springer, Heidelberg (2013). https://doi.org/10.1007/978-3-642-36285-9_18
10. Wachter, S., Mittelstadt, B., Russell, C.: Counterfactual explanations without opening the black box: automated decisions and the GDPR. Harv. JL Tech. **31**, 841 (2017)

Evaluating Fidelity of Explainable Methods for Predictive Process Analytics

Mythreyi Velmurugan[(✉)] [ID], Chun Ouyang [ID], Catarina Moreira [ID],
and Renuka Sindhgatta [ID]

Queensland University of Technology, Brisbane, Australia
{m.velmurugan,c.ouyang,catarina.pintomoreira,renuka.sr}@qut.edu.au

Abstract. Predictive process analytics focuses on predicting the future states of running instances of a business process. While advanced machine learning techniques have been used to increase the accuracy of predictions, the resulting predictive models lack transparency. Explainable machine learning methods can be used to interpret black-box models. However, it is unclear how fit for purpose these methods are in explaining process predictive models. In this paper, we aim to investigate the capabilities of two explainable methods, LIME and SHAP, in reproducing the decision-making processes of black-box process predictive models. We focus on *fidelity* metrics and propose a method to evaluate the faithfulness of LIME and SHAP when explaining process predictive models built on a Gradient Boosting Machine classifier. We conduct the evaluation using three real-life event logs and analyze the fidelity evaluation results to derive insights. The research contributes to evaluating the trustworthiness of explainable methods for predictive process analytics as a fundamental and key step towards human user-oriented evaluation.

Keywords: Predictive process analytics · Explainable AI · Evaluation metrics · Explanation fidelity

1 Introduction

Predictive process analytics focuses on applying predictive analytics to forecast future states of business process executions [10]. While advanced machine learning techniques have been used to increase accuracy of process predictions, the resulting predictive models become 'black-box' models. Methods and techniques have been proposed in machine learning to explain black-box models, forming a new research theme known as explainable AI (XAI) [3]. Several recent studies in predictive process analytics (e.g., [2,9]) have attempted to apply existing XAI methods to interpret black-box process predictive models. However, there have been few studies on evaluating how well available XAI techniques interpret process predictions. One key measure of explanation fitness is *fidelity*, which aims to determine how faithful the explanation is to the black-box predictive model, i.e., how well the explanation method can mimic the black-box model [3].

ⓒ Springer Nature Switzerland AG 2021
S. Nurcan and A. Korthaus (Eds.): CAiSE Forum 2021, LNBIP 424, pp. 64–72, 2021.
https://doi.org/10.1007/978-3-030-79108-7_8

In this paper, we identify and draw on fidelity evaluation studies in XAI, and propose a method for evaluating explanation fidelity for process predictions. We apply the proposed method to evaluate the performance of LIME and SHAP in interpreting process predictive models built on XGBoost, which has been shown to be most accurate in process outcome predictions [10], and analyse the evaluation results to derive insights. The research contributes to evaluating the trustworthiness of explainable methods for predictive process analytics as a fundamental and key step towards human user-oriented evaluation.

2   Background and Related Work

2.1   Explainable AI

While more complex algorithms often produce more accurate results, it is harder for a human to understand their internal workings, thus becoming a 'black box' and requiring interpretation [3]. Post-hoc interpretation refers to the interpretation of a predictive model, a data neighbourhood or a prediction created after the model has been generated, typically by an interpretation mechanism external to the predictive model [3]. Two popular black-box-model-agnostic, local explanation methods in literature are LIME and SHAP. LIME determines the importance of all features in an input by perturbing the dataset to create a surrogate linear model that captures the black-box model's behaviour at a specific neighbourhood [8]. SHAP uses a game theoretic approach to assign a value, known as SHAP value, to each feature at the instance level, describing its contribution to the final output—the prediction [5].

2.2   Fidelity of Explanations

While post-hoc explanation methods can be used to interpret complex models, because the explanation method is distinct from the prediction method, it is possible that the explanation generated is not always faithful to the decision-making of the original black box. Hence, it is important to understand the fidelity of the explanation method. Two ways of measuring fidelity are defined in [6]: external and internal fidelity. *External fidelity* measures the similarity of decisions made by a surrogate model or interpretation of a black box and the black box itself, but this does not measure the similarity of their decision-making processes – defined as *internal fidelity* [6]. A common method of evaluating the fidelity of post-hoc approaches is to remove or change features identified by the interpreter and comparing the changes in prediction probability of the black box [1,4], though this is typically applied to image or text data.

2.3   Problem Statement

Explainable predictive process analytics has emerged as a new research topic, and current studies have attempted to use existing explainable methods in XAI [2,9].

However, it is as yet unclear how fit for purpose these methods are for explaining process predictions, given the relatively complex multidimensional structure of event log data. As such, it is important to understand how well explainable methods can mimic the decision-making of process prediction black boxes. However, methods of assessing internal explanation fidelity for tabular data like event logs remain unexplored. In literature, internal fidelity evaluation methods often apply ablation, in which the most influential features are removed from the input [1]. However, this is typically applied to text or image data, where the "removal" of features is relatively simple, and would not be appropriate for tabular data. This has motivated us to draw on existing work to *build a method to assess the fidelity of post-hoc methods used in explainable predictive process analytics.*

3   Fidelity Evaluation Method

We evaluate the *internal fidelity* of explanations as we are interested in the fidelity of the interpreter's decision-making processes, not the decision (i.e., prediction) itself. An ablation approach to measuring internal fidelity will not hold for tabular data like event logs, particularly when using XGBoost which automatically imputes missing data. As such, a *perturbation strategy* was judged to be more effective. For the prediction of each instance, ten explanations were generated—to mitigate the effects of explanation instability—and the top 10% of features that were most common in the explanations were identified. For each feature, LIME presents the feature value or feature value distribution which affected the black box's prediction. For example, an explanation including "1 < Activity_A < 3" indicates that the occurrence of "Activity_A" more than once, but fewer than three times was influential. As SHAP presents only the feature's influence on the end result, feature value distributions were generated based on the SHAP value for a specific feature, for a specific instance (i.e., what feature values would produce similar SHAP values in the entire test dataset). For example, if "Activity_A" has a SHAP value between 0.5 and 0.6 only when the feature value is between 1 and 3, this would be the distribution attributed to a SHAP value of 0.54. Using these distributions, for each instance:

1. A prediction using input vector x was generated, along with the prediction probability for the predicted class $Y(x)$
2. For each feature to be perturbed, a new, uniform distribution outside of the existing distribution was created to draw new feature values from
3. For each feature to be perturbed, a new value was randomly sampled from the new distribution to replace the original value for that feature, creating the perturbed feature vector x'
4. The prediction probability for the originally predicted class was determined for input x' resulting $Y(x')$, and the difference between $Y(x)$ and $Y(x')$ was computed

Each instance was perturbed ten times, and the differences in prediction probability were used to calculate the mean absolute percentage error (MAPE) of the differences as the fidelity score for each instance (see Eq. 1). We chose to perturb the feature vectors, instead of the event logs used to derive the feature vectors, as the input for both the black box and the explanation methods were the derived features, and not the original event log.

It is important to note that the definition of the measure in Eq. 1 focuses on the (local) explanations at the process instance level. The overall evaluation of such a measure over the entire event log can be calculated as the average of the scores for all instances in the event log. Error functions have previously been applied to quantify internal fidelity, averaged out over the size of a dataset [1]. As such, MAPE is used to measure the fidelity of explanations, and we calculate the fidelity ($\mathcal{F}$) of an explanation for a single process instance in an event log as follows:

$$\mathcal{F} = \frac{\sum_1^{|X'|} \frac{|Y(x)-Y(x')|}{Y(x)}}{|X'|} \tag{1}$$

where:
- x = original feature vector for the process instance
- X' = Set of perturbations for x and $x' \in X'$
- $Y(x)$ = Prediction probability given input x
- $Y(x')$ = Prediction probability given input x'

Note that this measure is naturally bounded by the fact that prediction probabilities fall between 0 and 1.

4 Evaluation and Analysis

4.1 Design of Experiments

The prediction target is process instance outcomes, as outcome classification is one of the most common process prediction problems. Since XGBoost is generally the most accurate algorithm for outcome prediction [10], it was used to create the underlying black-box models. The XGBoost classifiers were trained on different data encoding and bucketing methods. The following combinations of bucketing and encoding methods were used:

- Aggregate encoding for dynamic attributes with prefix-length bucketing
- Index-based encoding for dynamic attributes with prefix-length bucketing
- Aggregate encoding for dynamic attributes with no bucketing

In the "no bucketing" method, all data is compiled as one bucket and a single classifier is trained on this bucket. When prefix-length bucketing is used, data is grouped (bucketed) based on shared prefix length (the number of activities that have already been completed in a process instance), and a classifier is trained for each bucket. For example, in a dataset with process traces ranging from prefix length of 1 to 40, forty classifiers will be trained. Aggregate encoding, as the name implies, aggregates the details of the entire case into a summary, while index-based encoding attempts to preserve the temporal details of the case as much as possible. As such, combining aggregate encoding with single bucketing preserves the characteristics within the original event log the least, while combining index-based encoding with prefix-length bucketing preserves the most.

SHAP and LIME, two popular post-hoc interpretation methods, were chosen for evaluation due to their prevalence in explainable predictive analytics [2, 9].

4.2 Datasets

We use three open-source, real-life event logs, all varying in the amount of cases recorded, types of attributes present and context (see Table 1). We follow the preprocessing, bucketing and encoding methods used in [10].

Table 1. A summary of statistics of three event log datasets

Event log		Production[a]	Sepsis cases[b]	BPIC2012[c]
Description		A manufacturing process	Hospital event log showing sepsis cases	Loan application process
No. of cases (before encoding)		220	782	4,685
Proportion of positive cases		55.0%	16.0%	53.4%
Maximum prefix length		23	29	40
Prefix lengths used		1–20	1–25	1–25
Feature vector shape	Single bucket & aggregate encoding	162	274	134
	Prefix-length buckets & aggregate encoding	Min: 137 Max: 156	Min: 153 Max: 218	Min: 43 Max: 134
	Prefix-length buckets & index-based encoding	Min: 100 Max: 844	Min: 147 Max: 535	Min: 11 Max: 1654

[a] https://doi.org/10.4121/uuid:68726926-5ac5-4fab-b873-ee76ea412399
[b] https://doi.org/10.4121/uuid:915d2bfb-7e84-49ad-a286-dc35f063a460
[c] https://doi.org/10.4121/uuid:3926db30-f712-4394-aebc-75976070e91f

The Production dataset has the fewest cases and a substantial number of static and dynamic attributes (though more dynamic than static), and around 55% of the cases were completed with a positive outcome. The Sepsis Cases dataset is highly unbalanced with only 16% positive cases. It also contains considerably more static than dynamic attributes, which will result in comparatively longer feature vector lengths when using aggregate encoding, but comparatively shorter feature vector lengths at higher prefix lengths when using index-based encoding. The training dataset was balanced through downsampling, but the testing data remains unbalanced. The BPIC2012 event log contains one (numerical) static attribute and a number of dynamic attributes, most of which are categorical, resulting in comparatively smaller feature vectors when using aggregate encoding, but the feature vector size will increase considerably as prefix length increases when using index-based encoding.

4.3   Results and Analysis

The source code implementing the proposed evaluation method in Sect. 3 and the design of experiments in Sect. 4.1 as well as the associated experiment results are available at: https://git.io/JIYtH.

Evaluation Results. Overall, fidelity scores were low-to-moderate for both explainable methods (see Table 2). SHAP is the better performer, though generally by small margins. Both explanation methods were generally least faithful when single bucketing and aggregate encoding are used, whereas the best combination of bucketing and encoding that produced better results varied across datasets.

Table 2. Overall fidelity results for each of the three datasets

		Production	Sepsis cases	BPIC 2012
Single bucket aggregate encoding	LIME	0.26	0.36	0.37
	SHAP	**0.27**	**0.46**	**0.41**
Prefix-length buckets aggregate encoding	LIME	0.47	0.37	0.38
	SHAP	**0.51**	**0.49**	**0.42**
Prefix-length buckets index-based encoding	LIME	0.36	0.51	0.32
	SHAP	**0.51**	**0.56**	**0.4**

LIME and SHAP are almost comparable when evaluating fidelity. In many cases, such as with SHAP for the BPIC2012 dataset (see Fig. 1), the faithfulness of explanations varies across instances in an almost uniform distribution. This suggests that only some explanations are faithful, but there appears to be no pattern or trend of faithfulness with regards to prefix length, encoding method, bucketing method or the initial prediction probability.

There is generally no link between prefix length and fidelity, except with BPIC2012 (most noticeable in LIME), where a higher prefix length generally results in a more faithful explanation. The large size of the BPIC2012 dataset (at least in comparison to the other two) has resulted in more reasonable black-box accuracy at the higher prefix lengths (see Fig. 2), which in turn appears to have ensured that LIME's surrogate models better fit the data.

Analysis and Findings. At first glance, these low scores seem to suggest that LIME and SHAP cannot accurately mimic process prediction black boxes. However, a further analysis indicates that the reasons for poor fidelity results may lie in the following aspects.

Firstly, event logs are inherently complex due to their multidimensional nature and variety of event attributes, and it is possible that the processing of the event log to a simpler, algorithm-readable feature vector could have led

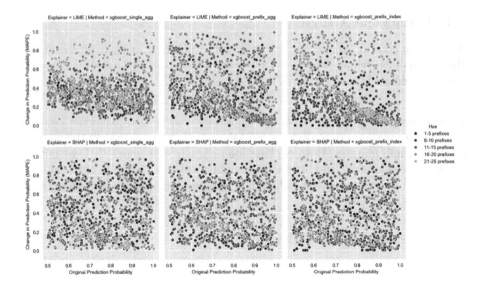

Fig. 1. Fidelity results over original prediction probability and prefix length of LIME and SHAP for the BPIC2012 dataset.

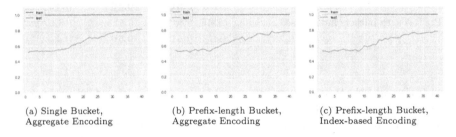

(a) Single Bucket, Aggregate Encoding

(b) Prefix-length Bucket, Aggregate Encoding

(c) Prefix-length Bucket, Index-based Encoding

Fig. 2. Accuracy of predictive models at each prefix length for the BPIC2012 dataset

to the poor fidelity results. As noted, perturbation of the input was conducted using the feature vector, not the underlying event log, and potential dependencies between the features (such as events and their attributes) could also have contributed to these poor results. If this is true, it is possible that the combination of single bucketing with aggregate encoding produced the least faithful explanations as it preserves the complexity of event logs the least.

Secondly, the poor fidelity results may also be due to some internal mechanisms of the explanation methods. In particular, sampling methods used by LIME to produce surrogate models are known to often produce poor results [7]. It is possible that the underlying mechanisms of LIME and SHAP cannot appropriately recreate the complex dependencies between the features that can be derived from event logs.

Thirdly, it is likely that the characteristics of the underlying black box also affected the fidelity results. This is most noticeable in the BPIC2012 dataset, when fidelity increased as the accuracy of the black-box model increased at higher prefix lengths. This phenomenon of increased accuracy closer to the completion of a running instance is expected in predictive process monitoring [10]. It is possible that the poor performance of the black-box models at smaller prefix lengths led to overall low fidelity and a poorly-fit surrogate model. Also, in predictive process analytics, an accurate prediction as early as possible during the process is valuable. Accordingly, any corresponding explanations will also perform better if they are faithful at an earlier stage during process prediction.

Insights for Future Work. Based on the above findings, we propose that a number of considerations should be made when assessing the fidelity of process prediction explanations. Firstly, a closer investigation needs to be made of the perturbation method used, with consideration of whether perturbation of the event log would be more appropriate than perturbation of the features extracted from it. Secondly, it would also be useful to consider the assumptions made when developing the proposed evaluation method, including the assumption that the boundaries derived from the explanation are absolute. Thirdly, to better understand whether the poor results stem from the use of event logs as datasets, the proposed method should be applied with more standard, less complex tabular datasets. Furthermore, evaluations should also be conducted with other types of black-box models, to understand how the underlying black box, including accuracy, contribute to the faithfulness of explanations.

5   Conclusion

As black-box models are often applied in predictive process analytics, explainability becomes necessary to help understand why certain predictions are made by the underlying predictive models. To determine the quality of explanations, we have proposed a method to assess explanations of process predictive models. The application of this proposed method to three event log datasets using a variety of bucketing and encoding techniques has provided observations regarding the faithfulness of process prediction explanations. Insights derived from the observations can be used to guide future refinement of the proposed method and evaluations as well as understanding of process prediction explainability.

References

1. Du, M., Liu, N., Yang, F., Ji, S., Hu, X.: On attribution of recurrent neural network predictions via additive decomposition. In: The World Wide Web Conference, WWW 2019, pp. 383–393. ACM (2019)
2. Galanti, R., Coma-Puig, B., de Leoni, M., Carmona, J., Navarin, N.: Explainable predictive process monitoring. In: 2nd International Conference on Process Mining, pp. 1–8. IEEE (2020)
3. Guidotti, R., Monreale, A., Ruggieri, S., Turini, F., Giannotti, F., Pedreschi, D.: A survey of methods for explaining black box models. ACM Comput. Surv. **51**(5), 93:1-93:42 (2019)

4. Kindermans, P.-J., et al.: The (un)reliability of saliency methods. In: Samek, W., Montavon, G., Vedaldi, A., Hansen, L.K., Müller, K.-R. (eds.) Explainable AI: Interpreting, Explaining and Visualizing Deep Learning. LNCS (LNAI), vol. 11700, pp. 267–280. Springer, Cham (2019). https://doi.org/10.1007/978-3-030-28954-6_14

5. Lundberg, S.M., Lee, S.: A unified approach to interpreting model predictions. In: Annual Conference on Neural Information Processing Systems, pp. 4765–4774 (2017)

6. Messalas, A., Kanellopoulos, Y., Makris, C.: Model-agnostic interpretability with shapley values. In: 10th International Conference on Information, Intelligence, Systems and Applications, IISA 2019, pp. 1–7. IEEE (2019)

7. Rahnama, A.H.A., Boström, H.: A study of data and label shift in the lime framework (2019). arXiv: 1910.14421

8. Ribeiro, M.T., Singh, S., Guestrin, C.: "why should I trust you?": explaining the predictions of any classifier. In: Proceedings of the 22nd ACM SIGKDD International Conference on Knowledge Discovery and Data Mining, pp. 1135–1144 (2016)

9. Sindhgatta, R., Ouyang, C., Moreira, C.: Exploring interpretability for predictive process analytics. In: Kafeza, E., Benatallah, B., Martinelli, F., Hacid, H., Bouguettaya, A., Motahari, H. (eds.) ICSOC 2020. LNCS, vol. 12571, pp. 439–447. Springer, Cham (2020). https://doi.org/10.1007/978-3-030-65310-1_31

10. Teinemaa, I., Dumas, M., Rosa, M.L., Maggi, F.M.: Outcome-oriented predictive process monitoring: Review and benchmark. ACM Trans. Knowl. Discov. Data 13(2), 17:1-17:57 (2019)

Data-Driven Process Performance Measurement and Prediction: A Process-Tree-Based Approach

Sebastiaan J. van Zelst[1,2]([✉]), Luis F.R. Santos[2], and Wil M. P. van der Aalst[1,2]

[1] Fraunhofer Institute for Applied Information Technology (FIT),
Sankt Augustin, Germany
sebastiaan.van.zelst@fit.fraunhofer.de
[2] RWTH Aachen University, Aachen, Germany

Abstract. To achieve operational excellence, a clear understanding of the core processes of a company is vital. Process mining enables companies to achieve this by distilling historical process knowledge based on recorded historical event data. Few techniques focus on the prediction of process performance after process redesign. This paper proposes a foundational framework for a data-driven business process redesign approach, allowing the user to investigate the impact of changes in the process, w.r.t. the overall process performance. The framework supports the prediction of future performance based on anticipated activity-level performance changes and control-flow changes. We have applied our approach to several real event logs, confirming our approach's applicability.

Keywords: Process mining · Process improvement · Process redesign

1 Introduction

Information systems, e.g., Enterprise Resource Planning (ERP), support the execution of a company's core processes. These systems capture at what point in time an activity was performed for an instance of the process. *Process mining* techniques turn such *event data* into actionable knowledge [1]. For example, various *process discovery techniques* exist that transform the event data into a *process model* describing the process behavior as captured in the data [2]. Similarly, *conformance checking techniques* quantify whether the process behaves as recorded in the event data w.r.t. a given reference model [3].

The overarching aim of process mining techniques is to *improve the process*, e.g., decreasing the process duration while maintaining the same quality level. Yet, a relatively small amount of work focuses on data-driven techniques to support decision-makers in effectively improving the process. For example, in [4], the authors propose to discover *simulation models* on the basis of recorded event data, which can be used to simulate the process under different "What if" scenarios. In [5], a similar approach is proposed, explicitly focusing on macro-level

© Springer Nature Switzerland AG 2021
S. Nurcan and A. Korthaus (Eds.): CAiSE Forum 2021, LNBIP 424, pp. 73–81, 2021.
https://doi.org/10.1007/978-3-030-79108-7_9

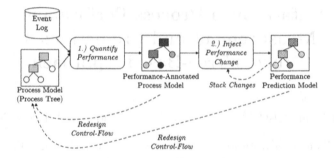

Fig. 1. Overview of our proposed framework. The current process performance is quantified in the context of a (given) process model. Anticipated performance changes are injected to compute possible future performance.

aspects of the process, e.g., average case duration. The work presented in this paper acts in the middle of the two spectra covered by the work mentioned. Similar to [4], we measure performance on the *activity-level*. However, we do not learn a complete simulation model. Instead, we explain the historical behavior captured in the event log in the context of a model specifying the process behavior. We use the annotated model for the prediction of future behavior.

In Fig. 1, we depict the proposed framework. An event log and a process model act as the input artifacts. We compute *timed partial order alignments*, which we use to quantify the process's historical performance in the context of the given model. Our framework supports the assessment of changes in the time-performance of activities (either waiting or service time), and it supports stacking multiple anticipated improvements of the process. Since our framework takes an arbitrary process tree as an input, it is possible to extend it to calculate the effect of control-flow changes. We have evaluated a prototypical implementation of our framework using several collections of real event logs. Our experiments confirm that our framework allows us to identify the main bottlenecks of the process. Furthermore, we observe that, in some cases, the process model used as an input influences the measured performance of the bottlenecks identified.

The remainder of this paper is organized as follows. Section 2 discusses related work. In Sect. 3, we present background notions. In Sect. 4, we present our framework, which we evaluate in Sect. 5. Section 6 concludes this paper.

2   Related Work

We refer to [1] for an overview of process mining. Most papers on prediction, focus on *intra-case prediction*, e.g., see [6]. Early work, e.g., [7], learns and uses annotated transition systems to predict possible future states of running processes. In [8], LSTM neural networks for predicting the next activity/remaining time for a process instance are studied. Data-driven global performance measurement and prediction are studied less intensively. In [9], the authors structure the field and identify the lack of relevant work in this space. Arguably the first work in this domain, i.e., [10], proposes to learn simulation models. In [11], a generic framework describing the integration of data-driven simulation models in process improvement/redesign is presented. More recently, the application of *system dynamics modeling* in the context of process mining has been studied [5].

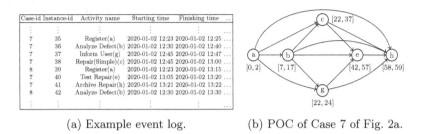

Case-id	Instance-id	Activity name	Starting time	Finishing time	...
⋮	⋮	⋮	⋮	⋮	...
7	35	Register(a)	2020-01-02 12:23	2020-01-02 12:25	...
7	36	Analyze Defect(b)	2020-01-02 12:30	2020-01-02 12:40	...
7	37	Inform User(g)	2020-01-02 12:45	2020-01-02 12:47	...
7	38	Repair(Simple)(c)	2020-01-02 12:45	2020-01-02 13:00	...
8	39	Register(a)	2020-01-02 12:23	2020-01-02 13:15	...
7	40	Test Repair(e)	2020-01-02 13:05	2020-01-02 13:20	...
7	41	Archive Repair(h)	2020-01-02 13:21	2020-01-02 13:22	...
8	42	Analyze Defect(b)	2020-01-02 12:30	2020-01-02 13:30	...
⋮	⋮	⋮	⋮	⋮	...

(a) Example event log.   (b) POC of Case 7 of Fig. 2a.

Fig. 2. Example event log (Fig. 2a) and Partially-Ordered Case (POC) (Fig. 2b).

3 Background

Event Data. Information systems store the historical execution of processes in *event logs*. In Fig. 2a, we depict an example event log. Each row refers to an *activity instance* describing an executed activity. Activity instances describe several data attributes, e.g., the activity name, timestamps, resource, etc. The first row of Fig. 2a describes an instance with id 35, describing activity *Register*, executed on January 2nd 2020, from 12:23 until 12:25, in the context of a *process instance* with identifier 7. Activity instances referring to the same process instance compose a *case*, e.g., in the context of case-id 7: *Register(a), Analyze Defect(b), Inform User(g), Repair(Simple)(c), Test Repair(e), Archive Repair(h)*. Hence, a *case describes a collection of activity instances*. Since activity instances record a start and an end time, they may overlap in time, e.g., consider instance 37 (Inform User) and instance 38 (Repair (Simple)). We assume a *strict partial ordering* (an irreflexive, anti-symmetric and transitive relation) of the activity instances that belong to a case. In Fig. 2b, we depict a *Partially Ordered Case* (POC) representation for Case 7. An *event log* is a collection of cases.

Process Trees. We use *process trees* as a process modeling formalism, i.e., rooted trees in which the internal vertices represent control-flow constructs and the leaves represent activities. In Fig. 3a, we depict an example process tree. The *sequence* operator ($\rightarrow$) specifies sequential behavior, i.e., first its left-most child is executed, then its second left-most child, etc. The *exclusive choice* operator ($\times$) specifies an exclusive choice between its children. Parallel behavior is represented by the *parallel operator* ($\wedge$), i.e., all children are executed simultaneously/in any order. Repetition is represented by the *loop operator* ($\circlearrowright$). The $\rightarrow$, $\times$, and $\wedge$-operator can have an arbitrary number of children. The $\circlearrowright$-operator has exactly two children. Its left child is always executed, i.e., at least once. When executing

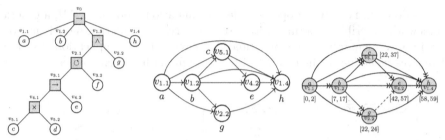

(a) Example process tree Q_1. Leaf vertices describe activity labels, internal vertices describe control-flow operators.

(b) Labeled Partial Order (LPO) that is in the language of Q_1.

(c) Partially-Ordered Alignment (POA) of the POC in Fig. 2b and the LPO in Fig. 3b.

Fig. 3. Example process tree (Fig. a) and a member of its language (Fig. b).

its right child, we again execute its left-most child to finish the operator. We assume that a process tree describes a set of strict partial orders as its language, e.g., in Fig. 3b we depict one Q_1. Due to the loop operator ($v_{2.1}$), the process tree in Fig. 3a describes an infinite amount of LPO's.

Partially-Ordered Alignments. Alignments [3, Chapters 7–9] quantify the behavior captured in an event log in terms of a reference process model. We consider *Partially-Ordered Alignments* (POAs) [12]. POAs align a POC with a partial order in a process model's language. The elements of alignments are called *moves*. An observed activity for a case that is also described by the process model is referred to as a *synchronous move*, e.g., for the POC in Fig. 2b the first activity instance describes activity a, which is in line with any partial order described by Q_1. We record a *synchronization* as a tuple $(a, v_{1.1})$ aligning the observed activity instance with label a, with the execution of vertex $v_{1.1}$. If an activity occurred that is not described by the model, we write $(a, \gg)$, i.e., referred to as a *log move*. If the model describes behavior that is not observed, written as $(\gg, v)$ (here v is some leaf node), we refer to a *model move*. The ordering among the moves is extracted from both the POC and the model. In Fig. 3c, we depict a POA of the POC in Fig. 2b and the partial order in Fig. 3b, i.e., only describing synchronous moves. The double-headed arrows represent ordering relations that are both described by the process model and the POC. The single-headed dashed arrow represents an order relation that is only present in the POC.

4 POA-Based Performance Measurement and Prediction

Here, we present our framework for data-driven process performance measurement and prediction. We focus on time-based performance, i.e., *waiting*, *service*, *idle* and *cycle time*. These metrics are schematically visualized in Fig. 4.

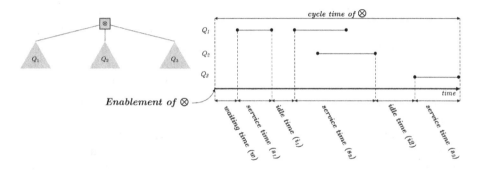

Fig. 4. Overview of the performance metrics considered.

In the remainder, we describe the steps of the approach: *1.) Performance Quantification* and *2.) Performance Change Injection* (cf. Fig. 1).

4.1   Performance Quantification

To measure time performance, i.e., as recorded in an event log and conditional to a given process model, we use the notion of *Timed Partially-Ordered Alignments* (TPOA). In a TPOA, the moves of a POA are associated with timestamps derived from the event log. For synchronous and log moves, the time range is copied from the event log. Model moves are interpreted as *point-intervals*, i.e., having a zero-duration (this design decision is easily changed, e.g., by taking the log-based average duration of the activity described by the model move). To compute a point-interval for a model move, we obtain the maximum interval value x of any of its predecessors in the POA, i.e., according to the model's ordering-relations, which is used as a point-interval of the form $[x, x]$ or $[0, 0]$ if the move has no predecessors.

   In the remainder of this section, we describe and exemplify the computation of the three core metrics considered for an arbitrary subtree of a process tree and a given trace, i.e., based on timed moves.

Service Time. The service time of a (sub)tree comprises all intervals at which it is *active*, i.e., work has been performed. In Fig. 4, the service time of the root operator, i.e., $\otimes$, consists of three time ranges, i.e., s_1, s_2 and s_3. The service time range s_2 consists of the service times observed for Q_2 and Q_3. In the running example (Fig. 3c), the service time of $v_{3.1}$ comprises the service times of moves $(c, v_{5.1})$ and $(e, v_{4.2})$, i.e., ranges $\{[22, 37], [42, 57]\}$. The service time of $v_{1.3}$ is the same, i.e., $(g, v_{2.2})$ is executed concurrently with $(c, v_{5.1})$.

Waiting Time. The waiting time of a (sub)tree, i.e., w in Fig. 4, is the time between the tree's enabling until the first activity observed in any of its children. Given a subtree Q' of a process tree Q, its waiting time is computed by subtracting the *minimum* starting time of any of the model/synchronous move related to Q', from the *maximum* finishing time of any synchronous/model move preceding any move related to Q'. Consider move $(e, v_{4.2})$ in Fig. 3c. The move starts at time 42. The maximum finishing time of any move preceding the move is 37 recorded by $(c, v_{5.1})$. Hence, the waiting time of the move is captured by the range $[37, 42]$. We ignore the finishing time of move $(g, v_{2.2})$, since $v_{2.2}$ does not precede $v_{4.2}$, i.e., their common ancestor is $v_{1.3}$ (parallel operator).

Idle Time. Idle time comprises all time ranges in which we observe no activity, yet the process tree has been active before and has not finished yet. For example, the waiting time of $(e, v_{4.2})$, i.e., $[37, 42]$ represents the idle time of the subtree formed by $v_{3.1}$. We obtain the idle time of an arbitrary subtree by taking the union of all active times of the moves that are part of it, i.e., according to the POA's timed moves. Subsequently, we intersect the *complement* of the aforementioned set of ranges with the range formed by the first start-time and maximum end-time of any of the subtree's moves.

Cycle Time. Each observed instance of a subtree Q' of some process tree Q, generates a singleton waiting time interval as well as a set of service and idle times respectively. Hence, the *cycle times* of a subtree are calculated by computing the union of the related sets of waiting, service and idle time.

4.2   Performance Change Injection

We assume that the process owner calculates the effect of changing the process's time-performance at the *activity level*, e.g., assessing the impact of a *waiting time reduction of* 20% of an activity of the process. Given an expected change (either positive or negative), we assume that all other events behave the same. Adopting such a scenario for performance prediction translates to *shifting* the time range of the timed moves, according to the desired improvement. Consider improving the performance of activity c in the running example (Fig. 2b and Fig. 3c) by 20%. This results in a new service time range of $[22, 34]$ $(0.8 \cdot (37 - 22) = 12)$. We shift the range of moves $(e, v_{4.2})$ and $(h, v_{1.4})$ by 3, i.e., to $[39, 54]$ and $[55, 56]$

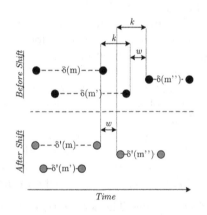

Fig. 5. Computation of the new start point of a move (m''). Before shifting, move m' directly precedes m'', after shifting, it precedes m''.

respectively. Hence, the reduction on activity c, yields a $\sim$5% reduction in the overall flow-time $(\frac{3}{59})$.

We use a *move shift function*, describing how to shift a timed move based on a proposed change. The core idea is to maintain a shift value on both the *start* and *end time* of a move of a TPOA. The shift function allows us to derive the (new) interval boundaries described by the timed move. Given some move m with time interval $[a, b]$ and a corresponding shift function value x for the

Table 1. Experimental results. Measured performance is in hours (rounded). The impact of the bottleneck reductions is relative to the original cycle time.

Event Log	Discovery Threshold	Detected Bottleneck	Avg. Bottleneck Sojourn Time	Abg. Overall Cycle Time	Rel. Cycle Time Red. (1% Bott. Red.)	Rel. Cycle Time Red. (2.5% Bott. Red.)
BPI 2017 [14]	10%	O_Cancelled	479	397.6	0.57355%	1.43387%
	60%	O_Cancelled	479	397.6	0.57355%	1.43387%
BPI 2020 Domestic Declarations [15]	10%	Declaration APP...	107	304.8	0.27794%	0.69486%
	30%	Declaration APP..	107	304.8	0.27794%	0.69486%
BPI 2020 International Declarations [15]	10%	Start trip	500.7	1244.8	0.40223%	1.00558%
	20%	Start trip	500.7	1244.8	0.39700%	0.99251%
BPI 2020 Request Payment [15]	10%	Payment Handled	102.3	315.7	0.32398%	0.80995%
	20%	Payment Handled	102.3	315.7	0.32398%	0.80995%
BPI 2020 Travel Permit [15]	10%	Send Reminder	1249.4	1331	0.19091%	0.47728%
	20%	Send Reminder	1349	1331	0.16858%	0.42145%
Road Traffic [16]	10%	Send for Credit...	11704.8	6976.8	0.66604%	1.66510%
	20%	Send for Credit...	11704.8	6976.8	0.66604%	1.66510%
Hospital Billing [17]	10%	FIN	560.2	556.7	0.65105%	1.62763%
	20%	FIN	560.2	556.7	0.65105%	1.62763%

start and y for the end time of m. The new time interval for m, is equal to the interval $[a + x, b + y]$ (shift forward in time: $x<0$ and $y<0$). Moves that have no predecessors in the TPOA are not shifted or shifted on their start/end time according to the performance change, e.g., a 5% reduction of service time on $(a, v_{1.1})$ in Fig. 3c, yields a shift on its end time of $2 - 0.95 \cdot 2 = 0.1$. For a move m that does have predecessor moves, first, a new time range for all its predecessors is computed, i.e., by applying (accumulated) shifting on top of the initially recorded time annotation of the TPOA. The initial shift values of move m are the difference between the maximum end point of its predecessors excluding any shift (i.e., based on the original time ranges of the predecessors) and the maximum ending point of its predecessors including any shift (i.e., based on the new time ranges of the predecessors). If a move relates to an activity with an anticipated performance change, the change is computed on top of the initially computed shift values. Figure 5 shows an exemplification of the computation.

5 Evaluation

In this section we evaluate our approach. We conducted our experiments using a publicly available implementation of our framework (https://github.com/luisfsts/KPIAlgebras). We use seven publicly available event logs. For each log, we discover two process trees by using different noise threshold values in the discovery algorithm [13] (starting with threshold 10% and increasing with steps of 10% until we discover a different process tree). To reduce time consumption, we sampled 1000 cases per event log.

The results of the experiment are presented in Table 1. In all cases, as expected, we observe that using a 2.5% reduction on the bottleneck yields a better improvement on the overall cycle time of the process, i.e., roughly 2.5 times the 1% reduction. Only in the BPI 2020 Travel Permit data [15], the model impacts the measured cycle time of the identified major bottleneck in the process. Upon inspection, this is the case because the 10%-model incorporates more synchronizations of the bottleneck activity, and hence, more performance measurements, leading to a slightly lower measured activity sojourn time. Furthermore, the aforementioned event log and the BPI 2020 International Declarations [15] event log are the only two event logs in which the process model has an influence on the global performance reduction.

6   Conclusion

In this paper, we presented a foundational framework that allows us to measure the time-based performance of a process, based on historically logged event data. The framework exploits partially ordered alignments (POAs), which are annotated with time-based performance information derived from the data. The use of POAs supports the use of data that records both start and end times of events. The effect of anticipated changes of activity-level performance can be injected into the framework. In our evaluation, we highlight the applicability of our tool using real event data.

References

1. van der Aalst, W.M.P.: Process Mining - Data Science in Action, 2nd edn. Springer, Heidelberg (2016). https://doi.org/10.1007/978-3-662-49851-4
2. Augusto, A., et al.: Automated discovery of process models from event logs: review and benchmark. IEEE Trans. Knowl. Data Eng. **31**(4), 686–705 (2019)
3. Carmona, J., van Dongen, B.F., Solti, A., Weidlich, M.: Conformance Checking - Relating Processes and Models. Springer, Heidelberg (2018). https://doi.org/10.1007/978-3-319-99414-7
4. Rozinat, A., Mans, R.S., Song, M., van der Aalst, W.M.P.: Discovering simulation models. Inf. Syst. **34**(3), 305–327 (2009)
5. Pourbafrani, M., van Zelst, S.J., van der Aalst, W.M.P.: Scenario-based prediction of business processes using system dynamics. In: Panetto, H., Debruyne, C., Hepp, M., Lewis, D., Ardagna, C.A., Meersman, R., (eds.) OTM 2019 Conferences - CoopIS, ODBASE, C&TC 2019, Rhodes, Greece, October 21–25, 2019, Proceedings. LNCS, vol. 11877, pp. 422–439. Springer, Heidelberg (2019). https://doi.org/10.1007/978-3-030-33246-4_27
6. Márquez-Chamorro, A.E., Resinas, M., Ruiz-Cortés, A.: Predictive monitoring of business processes: a survey. IEEE Trans. Serv. Comput. **11**(6), 962–977 (2018)
7. van der Aalst, W.M.P., Schonenberg, M.H., Song, M.: Time prediction based on process mining. Inf. Syst. **36**(2), 450–475 (2011)
8. Tax, N., Verenich, I., La Rosa, M., Dumas, M.: Predictive business process monitoring with LSTM neural networks. In: Dubois, E., Pohl, K. (eds.) CAiSE 2017. LNCS, vol. 10253, pp. 477–492. Springer, Cham (2017). https://doi.org/10.1007/978-3-319-59536-8_30
9. Martin, N., Depaire, B., Caris, A.: The use of process mining in business process simulation model construction - structuring the field. Bus. Inf. Syst. Eng. **58**(1), 73–87 (2016)
10. Rozinat, A., Mans, R.S., Song, M., van der Aalst, W.M.P.: Discovering colored Petri nets from event logs. Int. J. Softw. Tools Technol. Transf. **10**(1), 57–74 (2008)

11. Maruster, L., van Beest, N.R.T.P.: Redesigning business processes: a methodology based on simulation and process mining techniques. Knowl. Inf. Syst. **21**(3), 267–297 (2009)
12. Lu, X., Fahland, D., van der Aalst, W.M.P.: Conformance checking based on partially ordered event data. In: Fournier, F., Mendling, J. (eds.) BPM 2014. LNBIP, vol. 202, pp. 75–88. Springer, Cham (2015). https://doi.org/10.1007/978-3-319-15895-2_7
13. Leemans, S.J.J., Fahland, D., van der Aalst, W.M.P.: Discovering block-structured process models from event logs containing infrequent behaviour. In: Lohmann, N., Song, M., Wohed, P. (eds.) BPM 2013. LNBIP, vol. 171, pp. 66–78. Springer, Cham (2014). https://doi.org/10.1007/978-3-319-06257-0_6
14. van Dongen, B.F.: BPI Challenge 2017, February 2017. https://doi.org/10.4121/uuid:5f3067df-f10b-45da-b98b-86ae4c7a310b
15. van Dongen, B.F.: BPI Challenge 2020, March 2020. https://doi.org/10.4121/uuid:52fb97d4-4588-43c9-9d04-3604d4613b51
16. de Leoni, M.M., Mannhardt, F.: Road traffic fine management process, February 2015. https://doi.org/10.4121/uuid:270fd440-1057-4fb9-89a9-b699b47990f5
17. Mannhardt, F.: Hospital billing - event log, August 2017. https://doi.org/10.4121/uuid:76c46b83-c930-4798-a1c9-4be94dfeb741

Detecting Privacy, Data and Control-Flow Deviations in Business Processes

Azadeh S. Mozafari Mehr$^{(\boxtimes)}$(ID), Renata M. de Carvalho(ID),
and Boudewijn van Dongen(ID)

Department of Mathematics and Computer Science,
Eindhoven University of Technology, Eindhoven, The Netherlands
{a.s.mozafari.mehr,r.carvalho,b.f.v.dongen}@tue.nl

Abstract. Existing access control mechanisms are not sufficient for data protection. They are only preventive and cannot guarantee that data is accessed for the intended purpose. This paper proposes a novel approach for multi-perspective conformance checking which considers the control-flow, data and privacy perspectives of a business process simultaneously to find the context in which data is processed. In addition to detecting deviations in each perspective, the approach is able to detect hidden deviations where non-conformity relates to either a combination of two or all three aspects of a business process. The approach has been implemented in the open source ProM framework and was evaluated through controlled experiments using synthetic logs of a simulated real-life process.

Keywords: Process mining · Multi-layer alignment · Data privacy · Conformance checking · Multi-perspective analysis

1 Introduction

In recent years, data privacy issues are of increasing concern to organisations and governments. Organisations often define sets of rules as privacy policies for protecting sensitive data of their processes. However, regulations like GDPR (https://gdpr-info.eu) impose more strict privacy requirements. New privacy rules which denotes "who can access data for which purpose" relate to multiple perspectives of a business process, as they are closely related to the tasks being executed (control-flow perspective), the flow and processing of information (data perspective) and legitimate role allocation (resource or privacy perspective). Employees should follow these policies while performing activities within business processes. However, it is well documented in the literature that real process behavior often deviates from the expected process which often opens the way to the fraudulent behaviour or performance issues [5,13]. Unfortunately, standard preventative access control, which regulates who may carry out which data operations in a system is not sufficient for data protection as access is independent of context since it is not checked for which purpose data are processed

© Springer Nature Switzerland AG 2021
S. Nurcan and A. Korthaus (Eds.): CAiSE Forum 2021, LNBIP 424, pp. 82–91, 2021.
https://doi.org/10.1007/978-3-030-79108-7_10

Table 1. Data model of treatment process. R: Read, C: Create

Activity	Data operations
Identify patient (ip)	R(ID)
Admission (ad)	R(ID,PatientID,Name)
	C(AdmissionID)
Visit (vi)	R(AdmissionID,PatientID,MedicalHistoryID)
	C(VisitID,PrescriptionID)
Lab appointment (la)	R(AdmissionID,PatientID
	C(LabAppointment)
Basic lab test (bt)	R(AdmissionID,PatientID,PrescriptionID)
	C(BLabPID)
Advanced tests (at)	R(AdmissionID,PatientID,PrescriptionID)
	C(ALabPID)
Evaluate (ev)	R(AdmissionID,PrescriptionID,
	BLabPID,ALabPID)
	C(TestResultID)
Consult request (co)	R(AdmissionID,PatientID)
	C(ConsAppointment)
Inter-colleague	R(AdmissionID,PatientID,VisitID,
consultation (in)	PrescriptionID,TestResultID,MedicalHistoryID)
	C(VisitID,CPrescriptionID)
Treatment	R(AdmissionID,VisitID,MedicalHistoryID)
prescription (tr)	C(TreatmentPlan)
Discharge (di)	R(AdmissionID,PatientID)
	C(Confirmation)
Billing (bi)	R(AdmissionID,PatientID,PaymentID)
	C(PaymentReceipt)

after access to data has been granted [10]. In this paper, we address this issue by proposing a novel approach for multi-perspective conformance checking. By considering all control-flow, data, and privacy perspectives of a business process simultaneously, our approach brings two main contributions: a) we detect spurious data access and identify privacy infringements where data have been processed for unclear or secondary purposes by an authorised role; and b) we detect important deviations in each perspective such as unexpected activities, missing data operations or illegitimate role allocations. As a proof of concept, we implemented and tested our approach over synthetic logs generated from simulation of a real-life process.

This paper is organized as follows. Section 2 introduces a running example along with some scenarios as the motivation of this work. Section 3 illustrates

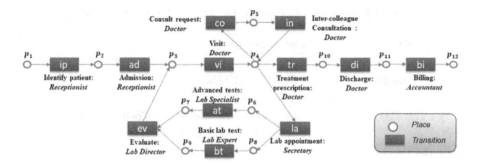

Fig. 1. An example of healthcare treatment process in Petri net notation (adapted from [3])

our approach. Section 4 presents experimental results. Section 5 discusses related work. Section 6 concludes the paper and provides directions for future works.

2   Motivating Example

As a running example, consider a healthcare treatment process derived from Alizadeh *et al.* [3]. Figure 1 shows the process as a Petri net. The process starts with the patient identification and admission by the receptionist. Next, the patient is visited by a doctor. The doctor might request a basic lab test and advanced tests such as MRI scans, for which the secretary makes an appointment. After a lab expert and a lab specialist perform the tests, a lab director evaluates the results. Based on the evaluation, the doctor may request inter-colleague consultation ((co) followed by (in)), request more lab tests, or prescribe a treatment plan. Finally, the patient is discharged and a bill is sent to the patient's insurance company by an accountant. In this process, certain data operations on specific data fields are required to be performed during each activity. Table 1, presents these data operations.

An example of an execution of this process is depicted in Fig. 2. This figure shows observed behavior from three perspectives which can be extracted from the recorded behavior in the process and data logs. For each activity, a start event and a complete event are expected. Whenever they both occur and are performed by the same resource, they are linked as a yellow rectangle as shown in Fig. 2(a). The sequence of yellow triangles in Fig. 2(b) shows a data trace consisting of twenty data events. The events in the process trace and data trace record information regarding the process instance or case, the corresponding activity and data operation, the time of the execution, and the actor who executed the activity or data operation, separately. Each hexagon presents the role of the actor under whose name the event is registered in the system.

Below, we present some scenarios to motivate the need for investigating the data, privacy and control-flow conformance to detect the hidden deviations:

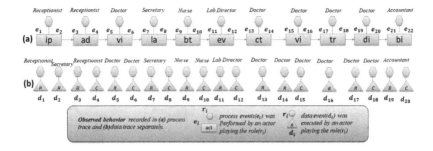

Fig. 2. An executed process instance of the healthcare process depicted in Fig. 1.

Scenario 1: According to the presented process and data models, several roles like doctors and lab experts are allowed to access sensitive data of patients. A curious actor may exploit this privilege to access patient information for personal or financial gain. For instance, a doctor who has access to patient information for providing medical treatment, can use this information to conduct a clinical trial (ct) which does not contribute to the fulfilment of the treatment process.

Scenario 2: A nurse, instead of a lab expert, takes a blood sample from the patient. Based on both data and control-flow perspectives, the occurrence of this activity and related data operations are allowed but from the privacy perspective they are not. This is a case where all three layers of process, data and privacy should be considered together to detect the hidden deviation.

Scenario 3 [3]**:** During each visit, doctors are expected to add a prescription or treatment plan to the patient's medical history. A doctor may negligently forget to update it. This missing data operation may cause other doctors to prescribe an incompatible drug to the patient. In this case, from a control-flow perspective there is no violation while from the data perspective there is a missing data operation.

3 Proposed Multi-layer Alignment Approach

In this section, we propose our approach for multi-perspective conformance checking. The main goal of this approach is to align process, data and privacy policy layers to find hidden deviations between these three perspectives of a business process in addition to detecting the deviations in each layer.

Figure 3 shows an overview of our approach together with its inputs and outputs. A Process log (❶) records process executions and a data log (❷) contains data operations showing which user accessed which data. These two inputs indicate observed behaviors.

To represent the modeled behaviors the approach considers a process model (❹), a data model (❺) and an organisational model (❸). A process model describes the activities to be performed in a specific order to reach a certain business goal. The data model relates the process logic to the data layer by

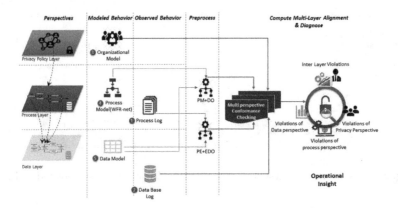

Fig. 3. An overview of the proposed approach

indicating which data operations must be executed in order to complete a given activity. The organisational model links users to their roles. The role of actors in the process log and data log can be retrieved from this model. As discussed before, using only an organisational model for access control is not sufficient to check data privacy. Therefore, in order to find the context of data access, first we integrate the activities with their corresponding roles in the process model to unify the two perspectives of process and privacy into a single model. Second, using the data model, we enrich the aforementioned process model with expected data operations in a pre-processing step, shown as "PM+DO" in Fig. 3. In another pre-processing step, we enrich the events of the process log with the expected data operations using the data model ("PE+EDO" in Fig. 3).

The combination of the process model with role information, the process event log showing the start and complete of activities performed by specific resources and the data log showing who accessed what at which time is translated into a large *synchronous product model*. Such synchronous product is the foundational model for conformance checking and techniques exist [1] to find the optimal execution given a cost function that penalizes specific deviations.

In this synchronous product, totally synchronous moves represent expected behavior. We further distinguish six kinds of deviations:

- A *move on data log* happens when a not-allowed data operation was executed.
- A *move on process log* happens when an unexpected activity was performed.
- A *move on model* happens when there is a missing activity in the process log.
- A *partially synchronous move with correct role* happens when there is a missing data operation in the data log. In this case, the expected activity was performed by a legitimate role.
- A *partially synchronous move with wrong role*, as the previous, but performed by a not-allowed role.
- A *totally synchronous move with wrong role* happens when an expected activity and data operation were done by a not-allowed role.

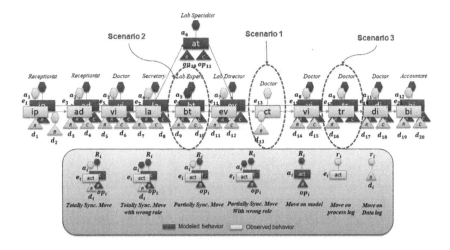

Fig. 4. Multi-perspective alignment between modeled and observed behavior

A cost function in our approach assigns a cost equal to 4 for move on data log, move on process log and move on model. It assigns a cost equal to 2 to partially synchronous moves and cost 0 to totally synchronous moves. Finally, it adds the penalty cost 1 if the actor plays a not-allowed role. This cost function is a parameter of the approach and can be changed per use-case, but it is an essential parameter to compute the optimal alignment.

The optimal alignment we get from the synchronous product model is translated back into a multi-perspective alignment as shown in Fig. 4. Returning to the running example in Sect. 2, by using our technique for multi-perspective alignment we can identify the three scenarios of Sect. 2 as shown in Fig. 4.

4 Evaluation

We implemented the approach illustrated in Fig. 3 as a package named MultiLayerAlignment in the ProM framework (https://www.promtools.org/). The output is a csv file including the alignment results that can be used by other applications for visualization or further analysis. In order to conduct controlled experiments, we simulated the process model depicted in Fig. 1 using CPN tools (http://cpntools.org) to generate process and data logs with real-life complexity(e.g. loops or considerable trace length). Table 2 summarizes the differences of conducted experiments in terms of the type of deviations and the perspectives in which the deviations happened. The numbers in parentheses show the percentage of inserted noise and the filled cells in each row represent the type of deviations that were included in the experiment. For instance, E0 is the fully fitting base line and experiments E1 to E3 are the simulation of the three scenarios described in Sect. 2. We inserted all kinds of deviations at the level of traces in the E7 and at the level of the entire log in E8.

Table 2. The result of experiments

Deviation happened in	All three layers	Process layer	Data layer	Data layer	Data layer & Privacy layer	Privacy layer	_
Legal Move	Move on model	Move on process log	Move on data log	Partially sync. move	Partially sync. move with penalty cost	Totally sync. move with penalty cost	Totally sync. move
	P-R-F1	P- R- F1	P- R- F1	P- R- F1	P- R- F1	P- R- F1	P- R- F1
E0 (0 %)							1.00-1.00-1.00
E1 (5 %)		1.00-1.00-1:00	1:00-1:00-1:00				
E2 (5 %)						1.00-1.00-1.00	
E3 (5 %)				1.00-1:00-1:00			
E4 (5 %)	1.00-1.00-1.00						
E5 (5 %)			1.00-1.00-1.00				
E6 (5 %)					1.00-1.00-1.00		
E7 (5 %)	1.00-1.00-1.00	1.00-1.00-1.00	1.00-1.00-1.00	1.00-1.00-1.00	1.00-1.00-1.00	1.00-1.00-1.00	
E8 (26 %)	1.00-1.00-1.00	1.00-1.00-1.00	1.00-1.00-1.00	1.00-1.00-1.00	1.00-1.00-1.00	1.00-1.00-1.00	

To assess the approach's capability of detecting different kinds of deviations and the accuracy of obtained results, we computed the precision, recall, and F_1-measure [9]. Precision is computed as the fraction of detected deviations that are actual deviations, whereas recall is the fraction of the inserted deviations that are detected. The F_1-measure is the harmonic mean of precision and recall. In each experiment, the ground truth was known since deviations were introduced artificially.

As shown in Table 2, overall, our results show high precision and recall. Considering all experiments, we conclude that the approach is able to detect all deviations that happened in one, two, or all three combinations of process perspectives (control-flow, data and privacy policy).

5   Related Work

Process mining is a set of techniques that aim at analyzing business process execution data recorded in event logs. We limit related work to the research approaches most related to our contribution to the field of conformance checking.

Besides the control-flow, there are also other perspectives like data or resources that are often crucial for conformance analysis. Few approaches have investigated how to include these perspectives in the conformance analysis: De Leoni et al. [4] extend the alignment approach to bring other perspectives' impact in the identification of non-conformity. This approach considers data, resource, and time as data attributes of process events. Thus, control-flow is aligned first, and then data are considered. Mannhardt et al. [6] extend the work in [4] to propose a more balanced approach using data-aware Petri net as the prescribed model and check executed behaviors in the process log with respect to the values of the variables in the guards in addition to control-flow conformance. Both approaches are unable to consider the three perspectives separately since these methods give priority to the control-flow. Accordingly, some important violations such as missing data operations or not allowed data access can be missed in the alignment results.

Alizadeh *et al.* [3] proposed an approach for linking data and process perspectives for conformance analysis. Similarly to [4] and [6] they extend the alignment approach to handle the data perspective in which control-flow is aligned first and then data are considered. In contrast to the proposed approaches in [4] and [6], Alizadeh *et al.* [3] aligned data and process perspectives independently. They applied a CRUD matrix that relates process activities to data operations and defined two criteria functions to link data operations in the data traces and events in the process traces.

We have extended the work in [3] and added privacy perspective in addition to process and data perspectives. To this end, we integrate the activities with corresponding roles in the process model in addition to using organisational model. Therefore, our approach can provide more comprehensive diagnostics than [3]. Similar to [3], we use a data model that relates process activities to data operations. However, we employed the data model in a completely different way to bring data perspective into conformance analysis. In [3], the approach applies a data model along with two criteria functions to link data operations in data traces with events in process traces. They performed this step in post-processing (after alignment computation) locally for each event in the alignment trace to find the deviations related to the data layer. This is the reason why their approach is not able to identify all the deviations correctly. For instance, in the presence of concurrent process events, a data operation can be linked to different process events with the same activity name. We solved this problem globally by allowing the alignment algorithm to find the best match. In contrast to [3], we use the data model in the pre-processing step to enrich the process model with related data operations in order to model prescribed behavior from all three perspectives. By constructing it, our approach is able to link data and process layer in a more robust way.

A large body of literature is related to privacy-preserving process/data mining i.e. [2,7,8,11,12] . They are not compared here since they consider privacy issue at design time to minimise privacy risks while maximising data utility for analysis. However, they do not consider the run-time perspective of business process management.

To the best of our knowledge, the work in this paper is the first work that proposes a novel technique for computing alignment by considering all control-flow, data, and privacy perspectives of a business process at the same time without giving priority to one perspective.

6   Conclusion

In this work, we presented a new method for multi-perspective conformance checking. We discussed that by considering more perspectives, our approach is able to find the context of data accesses in addition to detect hidden deviations between control-flow, data, and privacy perspectives of business processes.

As proof of concept, we implemented the approach in the ProM framework. An evaluation of the proposed approach has been carried out using synthetic logs generated from the simulation of a real-life process. The evaluation shows the applicability of our implementation to real-life complexity. The experiments confirm that our approach is able to provide more accurate diagnostics of deviations than control-flow based conformance checking approaches. The results also implied that the proposed approach allows the user to identify violations that cannot be detected by taking into consideration only one or two aspects.

In future work, we plan to improve the visual representation of the results to guide users towards an in depth identification of problems in the business processes execution. Extending the application of the approach and making it suitable for online process mining would be another direction of future work.

Reproducibility. The source code and inputs required to reproduce the experiments can be found at https://github.com/AzadehMozafariMehr/Multi-Layer-Alignment

Acknowledgement. The author has received funding within the BPR4GDPR project from the European Union's Horizon 2020 research and innovation programme under grant agreement No. 787149.

References

1. Adriansyah, A., van Dongen, B.F., van der Aalst, W.M.P.: Towards robust conformance checking. In: zur Muehlen, M., Su, J. (eds.) BPM 2010. LNBIP, vol. 66, pp. 122–133. Springer, Heidelberg (2011). https://doi.org/10.1007/978-3-642-20511-8_11
2. Aggarwal, C.C.: Data Mining. Springer, Cham (2015). https://doi.org/10.1007/978-3-319-14142-8
3. Alizadeh, M., Lu, X., Fahland, D., Zannone, N., van der Aalst, W.: Linking data and process perspectives for conformance analysis. Comput. Secur. **73**, 172–193 (2018)
4. de Leoni, M., van der Aalst, W.M.P.: Aligning event logs and process models for multi-perspective conformance checking: an approach based on integer linear programming. In: Daniel, F., Wang, J., Weber, B. (eds.) Business Process Management, pp. 113–129. Springer, Berlin Heidelberg, Berlin, Heidelberg (2013)
5. de Leoni, M., van der Aalst, W.M.P., van Dongen, B.F.: Data- and resource-aware conformance checking of business processes. In: Abramowicz, W., Kriksciuniene, D., Sakalauskas, V. (eds.) Business Information Systems, pp. 48–59. Springer, Heidelberg (2012)
6. Mannhardt, F., de Leoni, M., Reijers, H.A., van der Aalst, W.M.P.: Balanced multi-perspective checking of process conformance. Computing **98**(4), 407–437 (2015). https://doi.org/10.1007/s00607-015-0441-1
7. Mannhardt, F., Koschmider, A., Baracaldo, N., Weidlich, M., Michael, J.: Privacy-preserving process mining differential privacy for event logs. Bus. Inf. Syst. Eng. **61**, 1–20 (2019)

8. Michael, J., Koschmider, A., Mannhardt, F., Baracaldo, N., Rumpe, B.: User-centered and privacy-driven process mining system design for IoT. In: Cappiello, C., Ruiz, M. (eds.) Information Systems Engineering in Responsible Information Systems, pp. 194–206. Springer, Cham (2019). https://doi.org/10.1007/978-3-030-21297-1_17

9. Perry, J.W., Kent, A., Berry, M.M.: Machine literature searching x. Machine language; factors underlying its design and development. Am. Docum. **6**(4), 242–254 (1955)

10. Petković, M., Prandi, D., Zannone, N.: Purpose control: did you process the data for the intended purpose? In: Jonker, W., Petković, M. (eds.) SDM 2011. LNCS, vol. 6933, pp. 145–168. Springer, Heidelberg (2011). https://doi.org/10.1007/978-3-642-23556-6_10

11. Pika, A., Wynn, M.T., Udiono, S., Ter Hofstede, A.H.M., van der Aalst, W.M.P., Reijers, H.A.: Privacy-preserving process mining in healthcare. Int. J. Environ. Res. Public Health **17** (2020)

12. Rafiei, M., van der Aalst, W.M.P.: Privacy-preserving data publishing in process mining. CoRR abs/2101.02627 (2021)

13. Zhang, S., Genga, L., Dekker, L., Nie, H., Lu, X., Duan, H., Kaymak, U.: Towards multi-perspective conformance checking with aggregation operations. In: Lesot, M.-J., et al. (eds.) IPMU 2020. CCIS, vol. 1237, pp. 215–229. Springer, Cham (2020). https://doi.org/10.1007/978-3-030-50146-4_17

Dynamic Strategic Modeling
for Alliance-Driven Data Platforms:
The Case of Smart Farming

István Koren[1]($\boxtimes$), Stefan Braun[2], Marc Van Dyck[3],
and Matthias Jarke[2,4]

[1] Process and Data Science, RWTH Aachen University, Aachen, Germany
koren@pads.rwth-aachen.de
[2] Information Systems & Databases, RWTH Aachen University, Aachen, Germany
{braun,jarke}@dbis.rwth-aachen.de
[3] Technology and Innovation Management, RWTH Aachen University,
Aachen, Germany
vandyck@time.rwth-aachen.de
[4] Fraunhofer FIT, Birlinghoven Castle, Sankt Augustin, Germany

Abstract. The increasing availability of data offers opportunities for
advancing business models, e.g., by combining hardware sales with value-
added services. Besides platform companies aiming for a dominant market position, other configurations are relevant especially in contexts of
highly qualified smaller enterprises in the industrial sector, where players
in alliance-driven platforms cooperate to jointly create and capture value.
The challenge is to identify and assess these opportunities early on. In
this paper, we propose the combination of strategic modeling and setting
control points to support organizations in adjusting and evaluating possible business models. Our approach was initiated in an extensive case
study in the agriculture industry, yet we are confident that the results
are transferable to other industrial areas with emerging alliance-driven
data platforms.

Keywords: Data platform · Conceptual modeling · Industry 4.0

1 Introduction

The ongoing digitalization is changing entire value chains for industrial organizations. As one effect, networked devices produce more and more data. This
data has the potential to increase productivity due to faster and more practical insights through features such as predictive maintenance, which enables the
early detection of defective components, based on historical repair data. A challenge for many companies is not only to deal with these enormous amounts of
data but also to create and capture value from them. Towards this goal, organizations increasingly rely on external data and service exchange within business
networks. New data-driven business models provide potential for existing big

© Springer Nature Switzerland AG 2021
S. Nurcan and A. Korthaus (Eds.): CAiSE Forum 2021, LNBIP 424, pp. 92–99, 2021.
https://doi.org/10.1007/978-3-030-79108-7_11

players but also for startups, as there is a low entry barrier without investments in industrial hardware. Examples are service-oriented business models, enabling new interrelations such as multi-angular relationships between companies, as well as value co-creation [28]. However, policies and agreements between stakeholders are required to regulate collaboration between parties for data sharing [1].

Platform ecosystems evolved that connect various stakeholders from established business partners to emerging market entrants like complementors [32]. In industrial settings, physicality and complexity hamper value capture. Technological complexity results from connected physical components such as industrial assets and their association to information systems, business processes, and "smart" services on top [29,30]. Challenges are manifold; first, potential needs to be recognized in time, so that firms can take strategic decisions in advance. Second, data sovereignty of enterprises in terms of self-determination with regard to the use of their data needs to be taken care of. This is particularly valid for emerging alliance-driven platforms [24], where multiple players cooperate to jointly create value. The approach described in this paper combines i*-based strategic conceptual modeling, the setting of so-called control points, and the recognition of control points set by competitors.

Strongly extending an initial set of i* models [6], the paper is organized as follows. First, we discuss related work in the area of platform ecosystems and ecosystem modeling. Then, we discuss the specific needs for a dynamic strategic modeling approach for ecosystems, describe the basics of our approach, which differs by its multi-player approach from the existing alternative modeling approaches to adaptive resp. coopetition systems modeling. We validate these claims by modeling a large-scale evolution case study in the smart farming ecosystem. Finally, we discuss our findings and give a conclusion and point to ongoing and future work.

2   Related Work

An ecosystem is "an interdependent network of self-interested actors jointly creating value" [5]. Platform ecosystems consist of a central platform with multiple peripheral firms connected to it [17]. They are a sub-group of innovation ecosystems, where multiple actors mutually depend on each other to create value. Thereby, platform orchestrators hope to benefit from network effects [1,16], achieving a winner-takes-all (WTA) position [12,13]. Therefore, in common WTA ecosystems, a dominant industry platform has arisen, where the orchestrator is the de-facto leader. In integrated platform ecosystems relying on a modular architecture, openness is relevant [4] as value proposition and the underlying innovations are created jointly by platform owners and third-party contributors [1]. Openness is critical to building momentum at this stage [8].

Software vendors face the challenge of relying on third-party interfaces, libraries, and resellers, leading to numerous dependencies on technical and business levels. A clear view on technical dependencies on integrated libraries, their licenses, and update policies regarding, for instance, security aspects needs to be kept. To this end, visual modeling languages have been proposed. Software supply network (SSN) diagrams include material and monetary flows [18]. Product deployment context (PDC) models, in contrast, focus on the software in the running architecture [22]. Yu & Deng describe software ecosystems by modeling strategic goals of their stakeholders with the i* modeling language [36]. On top of the SSN and PDC approaches, i* modeling helps to highlight the intentional and strategic dimension of relationships. In the remainder of this paper, we profit from the findings of Yu & Deng by showing i*'s capabilities to a) make relationships explicit, b) facilitate exploring strategies and alternatives, as well as c) bring out structure for systematic reasoning.

From an *information systems perspective*, openness is enabled by standardized interfaces and autonomous data exchange, connecting formerly isolated companies [7]. The platform thereby embraces technology standards that support the integration of offerings and manage the interdependencies in the ecosystem [31]. The International Data Spaces (IDS) [25] Association has introduced an architecture, blueprint and standards for data-sharing among member organizations in a reliable, transparent, compliant and accountable manner. The IDS principles are also the basis for the ongoing GAIA-X initiative to enable the exchange of sensitive and valuable data [23]. The main idea behind the IDS is that actors can trustfully, and with full sovereignty over usage of their data, exchange data without knowing each other. Significant effort has been invested in creating a coherent standardized information meta model about all aspects of the IDS reference architecture [2,19]. IDS itself does not offer a conceptual abstraction for the actual valuable data objects to be exchanged. To address this issue, we have proposed the notion of *Digital Shadows* and are exploring it in the context of Aachen's large-scale research initiative Internet of Production [21] which is also the context for the approach and case study reported in this paper.

3   An Integrative Approach to Dynamic Ecosystems Modeling

Like ecosystems in nature, data-related ecosystems are not only highly complex but also need to be adaptive to outside developments and shifts in internal relationships. As illustrated by the IDS initiative and its multi-faceted metamodel [2], this applies to the operational and technical level of data management, service exchange, and IT security mechanisms, but equally to the business aspects of collaborative value creation, and to the strategic level of setting regulations for the ecosystem as well as developing strategies for the individual players. In this paper, we are mostly interested in concepts on the strategic level. While the i* concepts of goal orientation (Strategic Rationale) are the basis for managerial decision making of individual players in the network (considering or changing the dependency context), achieving a balanced network of dependencies is an important prerequisite especially for alliance-driven ecosystems setup [24] and stability. However, it is clear that actions from inside and outside the ecosystem will constantly challenge and not rarely change this structure.

This need for dynamic complements to the i* infrastructure has been recognized at least since the early 2000's. In cooperation between computer science and sociology [14], the dynamic nature of trust in networks was recognized and modeled by linking i* dependencies to workflow or AI planning models through which trust could be built up by kept commitments, and distrust monitored by suitable controls. In a complementary approach, Mylopoulos and colleagues conducted in-depth studies of adaptive IS engineering essentially by exploiting the structure of "alternative" links within Strategic Rationale models (e.g., [20]).

Closest to our approach is Vik Pant's recent study of an i* extension for modeling coopetition, i.e. how the combination of competition and cooperation can be modeled and analyzed [26,27]. In particular, his extension of reciprocality offers an interesting dynamic concept for our current research question. Pant and Yu combine Game Trees with i* dependencies as an operationalization of this dynamics [26]. Pant's case studies focus so far on binary coopetions, possibly facilitated by a third abstract platform actor like the IDS infrastructure and regulations. In alliance-driven settings, the more general case of multi-sided coopetition applies. For companies in such a platform it is of immense strategic importance to anticipate their future role at an early stage and plan appropriate steps along the way. Strategically, this is best done in a top-down way, as actively placed management decisions. In our approach, we therefore augment i* with *Control Points*. Control points, also referred to as bottlenecks [3,15], are technical and strategic decisions representing solutions to issues constraining value creation. In that sense, they can be set to grant access or impose certain behavior [11], analogous to the data usage control policies of IDS.

4   Case Study: Analysis and Dynamic Modeling of a Smart Farming Ecosystem

The farming sector is dominated by a few large manufacturers, with two strong market leaders in Europe and North America respectively. The European leader, under pressure from potential threats by market participants in other parts of the traditional supply pipeline (e.g. seed companies) as well as generic web-based marketing platforms, began in the 2010s with setting up its own platform-based ecosystem as a broad alliance-driven network including players in its supply chain as well as customers (farmers and their supporting contractors), service units, and the like. Recently, even competitors have been joining forces such that coopetition is becoming a strong element of the alliance. Our case study started as a qualitative analysis by the innovation researchers in the author team [33,34], accompanying the emerging ecosystem for a long time, but eventually the need for a conceptual modeling approach resulted from the observed complexity.

We adopted a qualitative case study approach, following the suggestions for rigorous case study research by Yin [35]. First, we conducted 55 interviews with key actors from the agricultural sector, e.g. manufacturers, input firms (seed, crop protection) and other relevant members (customers, suppliers, complementors, competitors, dealers, or new entrants). These platform actors are categorized and described in the next section. We then evaluated over 100 h of interview and workshop material in total. Extensive secondary data like information on connected machines, digital service usage, strategy documents, or annual reports

were additionally analyzed. Based on this large-scale study of a competitive platform provider, cooperatives, as well as their internal strategies, we identified the
interactions between ecosystem members.

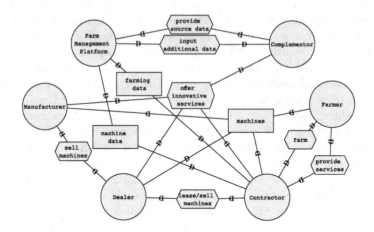

Fig. 1. Strategic dependency view of stakeholder relationships

For a detailed description of our models, created using the recent iStar 2.0
notation of i* [9], we refer the reader to our earlier publication [6]. Here, we
shortly point out the actors. Market participants present in a pipeline ecosystem
as well as a platform ecosystem are **Manufacturers, Dealers, Contractors**,
and **Farmers**. When changing from a pipeline to a platform ecosystems, a **Farm
Management Platform** and **Complementors** are joining. An i* strategic
dependency model shows these actors and their goals, as well as the dependency
relationships between them. Figure 1 depicts such a view of the stakeholder relationships in the smart farming ecosystem.

5   Control Points in Emerging Platform Strategies

Much of the relationships between the actors of the traditional agricultural
value chain are changed with the appearance of the platform and emerging IT-
related market participants. We hereby consider control points as active strategic
decisions, that platform participants can exercise to achieve a certain ecosystem behavior. Organizations can set up control points, by adhering to specific
technical standards. In this sense, this also signals a willingness to cooperate.
Thus, in an emerging setting like industrial platforms, where roles and rules are
yet unclear, control points are even more important [10]. The major strategic
and technical control points concerning platform ecosystems and their relation
concerning value capture and innovation paths are empirically identified and
described in detail by [34]. For instance, the machinery firm could decide to
technically modularize its offering, i.e. separate its hardware from its software-
based services, to enable access for third-party complementors to create the basis

for an innovation ecosystem. From a strategic perspective, a platform provider could try to impose multi-homing costs (costs for affiliating with multiple platforms) in order to increase the likelihood of a market to tip towards a dominant platform.

For the extensive discussion of identified control points, the reader is kindly referred to an earlier publication [34]. For instance, through passing the control point *Modularization*, value can be captured in a pipeline business model. By the control points *Opening* and *Prizing*, a platform model can be reached. In contrast, the traditional ultimate goal is a WTA approach, where one dominant market leader captures the entire value. Turning away from a WTA approach, additional value can be captured by a trust-enabled data sharing approach in an alliance-like platform ecosystem. Specifically, the actor concepts of the IDS model [25] can be mapped to the platform model. For example, The IDS concepts Data Owner and Data Provider are roles of our existing market participant. The interface represents the App Store and Broker for new complementor services. The IDS Clearing House is responsible for checking whether community rules are observed.

6 Discussion and Conclusion

Platform ecosystems in industrial settings are characterized by high complexity in terms of technology layers [29] and relationships [30]. In addition, interdependencies change as the ecosystem evolves. Questions are, for example, whether there will be one dominant platform, or two? How will future technical achievements change this interplay? We introduced two strategic tools to accompany this research: conceptual modeling using the i* language as well as control points.

The main contribution of our paper is the integration of strategic, technical and decisional perspectives, validated by a major real-world case study from industry. They result in decision making instruments that platform participants can use to plan their next step within an alliance-driven platform ecosystem. The strategic framework can also be used to identify, at an early stage or in face of major expected disruptions, which control points other companies are setting in relation to their competitors. This allows companies to react early and adapt their strategy or even enter negotiations for a new alliance or joining existing ones. Therefore, we claim that the right configuration of control points helps by indicating viable transition paths within and for platform ecosystems. In future work, the synthesis of these ideas by combining the comparison of platform variants with code generation may lead to a faster and more holistic analysis of data ecosystem variants. Ultimately, a repository of available graphical representations and code structures may facilitate automated, easier, and faster decision support for stakeholders in new data-driven ecosystems. Besides seeing their current status, this would allow organizations to see missing links, and potentially extend their current portfolio from a model repository.

Acknowledgement. Thanks to Frank Piller for inspiring discussions. Funded by the Deutsche Forschungsgemeinschaft (DFG, German Research Foundation) under Germany's Excellence Strategy - EXC-2023 Internet of Production - 390621612.

References

1. Adner, R.: Ecosystem as structure. J. Manag. **43**(1), 39–58 (2017)
2. Bader, S., Pullmann, J., Mader, C., Tramp, S., et al.: The international data spaces information model - an ontology for sovereign exchange of digital content. In: Pan, J.Z., et al. (eds.) The Semantic Web (ISWC 2020). LNCS, vol. 12507, pp. 176–192. Springer, Cham (2020)
3. Bottlenecks. Apress, Berkeley, CA (2017). https://doi.org/10.1007/978-1-4842-2580-6_23
4. Baldwin, C.Y., Woodard, C.J.: Competition in modular clusters. Harvard Business School Working Paper (08–042) (2007)
5. Bogers, M., Sims, J., West, J.: What is an ecosystem? Incorporating 25 years of ecosystem research. Acad. Manag. Proc. **2019**(1), 11080 (2019)
6. Braun, S., Koren, I., Van Dyck, M., Jarke, M.: An agricultural data platform iStar model. In: Renata, G., Gunter, M. (eds.) Proceedings of the iStar Workshop co-located with RE 2020. CEUR Workshop Proceedings, vol. 2641, pp. 19–24 (2020)
7. Brettel, M., Friederichsen, N., Keller, M., Rosenberg, M.: How virtualization, decentralization and network building change the manufacturing landscape: an industry 4.0 perspective. Int. J. Mech. Ind. Sci. Eng. **8**(1), 37–44 (2014)
8. Cusumano, M.A., Gawer, A.: The elements of platform leadership. MIT Sloan Manag. Rev. **43**(3), 51 (2002)
9. Dalpiaz, F., Franch, X., Horkoff, J.: iStar 2.0 Language Guide (2016)
10. Dattée, B., Alexy, O., Autio, E.: Maneuvering in poor visibility: how firms play the ecosystem game when uncertainty is high. Acad. Manag. J. **61**(2), 466–498 (2018)
11. Eaton, B., Elaluf-Calderwood, S., Sørensen, C., Yoo, Y.: Distributed tuning of boundary resources: The case of apple's ios service system. MIS Q. **39**(1), 217–243 (2015)
12. Eisenmann, T., Parker, G., van Alstyne, M.: Platform envelopment. Strateg. Manag. J. **32**(12), 1270–1285 (2011)
13. Farrell, J., Klemperer, P.: Coordination and lock-in: competition with switching costs and network effects. Handb. Ind. Organ. **3**, 1967–2072 (2007)
14. Gans, G., Jarke, M., Kethers, S., Lakemeyer, G.: Continuous requirements management for organisation networks: a (dis)trust-based approach. Requirements Eng. **8**(1), 4–22 (2003)
15. Hannah, D.P., Eisenhardt, K.M.: How firms navigate cooperation and competition in nascent ecosystems. Strateg. Manag. J. **39**(12), 3163–3192 (2018)
16. Iansiti, M., Levien, R.: Strategy as ecology. Harv. Bus. Rev. **82**(3), 68–78 (2004)
17. Jacobides, M.G., Knudsen, T., Augier, M.: Benefiting from innovation: value creation, value appropriation and the role of industry architectures. Res. Policy **35**(8), 1200–1221 (2006)
18. Jansen, S., Brinkkemper, S., Finkelstein, A.: Providing transparency in the business of software: a modeling technique for software supply networks. In: Camarinha-Matos, L.M., Afsarmanesh, H., Novais, P., Analide, C. (eds.) PRO-VE 2007. ITIFIP, vol. 243, pp. 677–686. Springer, Boston, MA (2007). https://doi.org/10.1007/978-0-387-73798-0_73
19. Jarke, M.: Data sovereignty and the internet of production. In: Dustdar, S., Yu, E., Salinesi, C., Rieu, D., Pant, V. (eds.) CAiSE 2020. LNCS, vol. 12127, pp. 549–558. Springer, Cham (2020). https://doi.org/10.1007/978-3-030-49435-3_34
20. Jureta, I.J., Borgida, A., Ernst, N.A., Mylopoulos, J.: The requirements problem for adaptive systems. ACM Trans. Manag. Inf. Syst. **5**(3), 1–33 (2014)

21. Liebenberg, M., Jarke, M.: Information systems engineering with digital shadows: concept and case studies. In: Dustdar, S., Yu, E., Salinesi, C., Rieu, D., Pant, V. (eds.) CAiSE 2020. LNCS, vol. 12127, pp. 70–84. Springer, Cham (2020). https://doi.org/10.1007/978-3-030-49435-3_5

22. Lucassen, G., Brinkkemper, S., Jansen, S., Handoyo, E.: Comparison of visual business modeling techniques for software companies. In: Cusumano, M.A., Iyer, B., Venkatraman, N. (eds.) ICSOB 2012. LNBIP, vol. 114, pp. 79–93. Springer, Heidelberg (2012). https://doi.org/10.1007/978-3-642-30746-1_7

23. Otto, B.: GAIA-X and IDS (2021). https://internationaldataspaces.org/download/19016/

24. Otto, B., Jarke, M.: Designing a multi-sided data platform: findings from the international data spaces case. Electron. Mark. **29**(4), 561–580 (2019). https://doi.org/10.1007/s12525-019-00362-x

25. Otto, B., et al.: Reference Architecture Model for the Industrial Data Space (2017)

26. Pant, V., Yu, E.: Generating win-win strategies for software businesses under coopetition: a strategic modeling approach. In: Wnuk, K., Brinkkemper, S. (eds.) ICSOB 2018. LNBIP, vol. 336, pp. 90–107. Springer, Cham (2018). https://doi.org/10.1007/978-3-030-04840-2_7

27. Pant, V., Yu, E.: Modeling simultaneous cooperation and competition among enterprises. Bus. Inf. Syst. Eng. **60**(1), 39–54 (2018). https://doi.org/10.1007/s12599-017-0514-0

28. Pfeiffer, A., Krempels, K.H., Jarke, M.: Service-oriented business model framework: a service-dominant logic based approach for business modeling in the digital era. In: Proceedings of the 19th International Conference on Enterprise Information Systems, pp. 361–372. SciTePress (2017)

29. Schermuly, L., Schreieck, M., Wiesche, M., Krcmar, H.: Developing an industrial iot platform - trade-off between horizontal and vertical approaches. In: Ludwig, T., Pipek, V. (eds.) 14. Internationale Tagung Wirtschaftsinformatik (WI 2019), Siegen, Germany. pp. 32–46. University of Siegen/AISeL (2019)

30. Sisinni, E., Saifullah, A., Han, S., Jennehag, U., Gidlund, M.: Industrial internet of things: challenges, opportunities, and directions. IEEE Trans. Ind. Inform. **14**(11), 4724–4734 (2018)

31. Thomas, L.D.W., Autio, E., Gann, D.M.: Architectural leverage: putting platforms in context. Acad. Manag. Perspect. **28**(2), 198–219 (2014)

32. van Alstyne, M.W., Parker, G.G., Choudary, S.P.: Pipelines, platforms, and the new rules of strategy. Harv. Bus. Rev. **94**(4), 54–62 (2016)

33. Van Dyck, M., Lüttgens, D.: Design faktoren und strategien für digitale plattformgeschäftsmodelle im b2b-kontext am beispiel der agrarindustrie. In: Gausemeier, J., Bauer, W., Dumitrescu, R. (eds.) Vorausschau und Technologieplanung, pp. 215–232 (2019)

34. Van Dyck, M., Lüttgens, D., Piller, F., Diener, K., Pollok, P.: Positioning strategies in emerging industrial ecosystems for industry 4.0. In: Proceedings of the 50th Hawaii International Conference on System Sciences. ScholarSpace (2020)

35. Yin, R.K.: Case Study Research and Applications: Design and Methods. Sage Publications, sixth edition edn. (2018)

36. Yu, E., Deng, S.: Understanding Software Ecosystems: A Strategic Modeling Approach. In: IWSECO@ICSOB (2011)

Modelling Cyber-Physical Security in Healthcare Systems

Fatma-Zohra Hannou, Faten Atigui, Nadira Lammari,
and Samira Si-said Cherfi[✉]

CEDRIC, Conservatoire National des Arts et Métiers (CNAM), Paris, France
{fatma-zohra.hannou,faten.atigui,nadira.lammari,samira.cherfi}@lecnam.net

Abstract. Health organizations are critical cyber-physical infrastructures. By relying on last technological advances, healthcare organizations are now able to provide more personalized services through open and controlled platforms. Unfortunately, these new technologies that rely on common communication interfaces and standards, enhance security breaches and exposes hospitals to several threats.

The paper presents an ontology that allows (1) modelling cyber-physical security concepts in healthcare systems and (2) helps designing incidents propagation mechanisms by focusing on cyber-physical interactions among critical assets.

Keywords: Critical health services · Cyber-physical assets · Ontology-based model · Cyber-physical incidents · Security attacks scenario

1 Introduction

Healthcare organizations are complex socio-technical systems with the involvement of humans, business processes and sophisticated cyber-physical systems (CPS). They integrate cyber and physical infrastructure where patients, their health and their security are in the center. In CPS, frontiers between cyber and physical worlds are becoming more and more blurred. Indeed, with the recent advances in cloud computing, the Internet of Things (IoT) and other information technologies, the face of healthcare systems is changing. By adopting the usage of Electronic Patient Records, wearable sensors or in-home remote patients monitoring, healthcare organizations are now able to provide more personalized services. This progress induces sharing information about health services, resources availability (beds and medical personnel) or patients' data through open and controlled platform. It also offers new opportunities for new applications such as disease treatment, medical research, care services, etc. Unfortunately, these developments rely on common communication interfaces and standards and thus enhance security breaches exposing hospitals to several threats.

Besides, as healthcare organizations deal with human being health and lives, damages are mostly more severe. According to the Ponemon IBM data breach

© Springer Nature Switzerland AG 2021
S. Nurcan and A. Korthaus (Eds.): CAiSE Forum 2021, LNBIP 424, pp. 100–108, 2021.
https://doi.org/10.1007/978-3-030-79108-7_12

report [13], healthcare organizations had the highest costs associated with data breaches with $6.45 million. To increase the efficiency of solutions, it is necessary to examine all the problem facets.

2 Problem Statement

To a better understanding, we present an example of a cyber-physical attack scenario. Alike any critical infrastructure, the hospital has a building management system, including a network of connected cyber-physical objects dedicated to building management automation. Connected objects are implemented to control accesses (camera) or measure some indicators (temperature sensors, fire detectors, etc.). In a very simplified way, we assume that the temperature management includes three parts: sensors, PLC (Programmable Logic Controller) receiving measures and processing data, and actuators such as air cooling or heating to act on the hospital's air.

An attacker targets the temperature management system and executes the following sequence:

1. The attacker identifies the maintenance company operating in the hospital and gets the technical maintainer email;
2. He/she sends a spearfishing email;
3. He/she acquires control of the maintainer computer;
4. He/she goes to the hospital and steals the access codes to the technical room;
5. He/she enters the technical room which hosts the building management interfaces;
6. He/she connects to the building management system and identifies the PLC;
7. He/she simulates a fake temperature sensor indicating low temperature in different areas;
8. **Result:** the cooling ventilation system does not start, the temperature rises excessively in the concerned sectors.

The direct serious consequences on the hospital's processes are: the unavailability of surgery rooms, patients suffering from injuries can be super-infected or contaminated by viruses, data-center crashes, leading to the unavailability of the hosted servers services and of course, hospitals reputation and loss of trust. The behavior described in the previous example exploits several information on assets, their vulnerabilities, the protection mechanisms in place, their interconnections as well as the nature of the attack and its ability to propagate.

The purpose of the work presented in this paper is to propose a solution able to:

- identify the critical assets and their properties;
- evaluate the risk to which they are exposed tacking into account the nature of assets, their relationships, and the protections in place;
- provide information to help prevent the propagation of incidents in case of attacks;

The remaining of the paper is organised as follows: Sect. 3 reports on related works. Section 4 presents our solution including both knowledge acquisition and knowledge conceptualisation before concluding.

3   Related Work

Ensuring system's security and facing cyber or physical attacks raised major concerns for both practitioners and academics. As commonly known knowledge bases, we mention the Common Vulnerabilities and Exposures (CVE)[1], the Common Weakness Enumeration (CWE) (See footnote 1), and the Common Vulnerability Scoring System (CVSS)[2]. In [14], the authors present the Unified Cyber security Ontology (UCO) that unifies most commonly used cyber security standards. The NIST institute promotes a more general vulnerabilities ontology [4].

Based on the modeled security breach, we can classify the existing work into two main categories: risk & threat, and attacks & incident modeling approaches. For each category, a particular attention is given to ontology-based and healthcare dedicated contributions.

Risk & Threat Modeling Framework. The European Commission reported a generic classification of threats in which natural hazards are distinguished from non-malicious man-made hazards and malicious man-made hazards [15]. In [5], the author present an ontology-based approach that provides classification, relationships, and reasoning about vulnerabilities and threats.

For physical risk assessments, in [16], the authors present an ontology of hazards and threats that could affect a critical infrastructure. In the healthcare field, the work presented in [7], provide an overview of the cyber threats that jeopardize smart hospitals. In [2], the authors present taxonomies of threats for healthcare infrastructures.

Attack and Incident Modeling Framework. The MITRE provides the CAPEC[3] knowledge base that reports attack patterns in cyber security. In [11], the authors propose a taxonomy for classifying security incident that focuses on the cross domain and impact oriented analysis. The work presented in [10], provide a detection model for events occurring in CPS. In [1], the authors propose a model-driven framework based on EBIOS [6] and on attack trees method, in order to identify the critical parts of the systems.

The study of the state of the art shows that the provided standards, knowledge bases, and research contributions differ according to their main objectives: storing the common vulnerabilities, modeling or assessing risks and threats, or modeling incidents and their cascading impacts. Despite the escalating integration of networked cyber and physical components, physical security and cyber security remain handled separately. A security mechanism should be designed for the entire system rather than addressing only a part of it [3]. It is important

---

[1] https://cve.mitre.org/.
[2] https://www.first.org/cvss/.
[3] https://capec.mitre.org/index.html.

to provide an approach that considers the different aspects of both cyber and physical security and provides a semantic description of the assets, their vulnerabilities, and the kinds of threats that could affect them, as well as the incidents and their cascading effects.

4 An Ontology for Cyber-Physical Security Management

Existing ontology construction approaches [8] present common 3 main phases that we follow to build our ontology, i.e. **knowledge acquisition** (Sect. 4.1), **conceptualization** (Sects. 4.2; 4.3), and **implementation** (Sect. 4.4).

4.1 Knowledge Acquisition

This activity involved security experts, either belonging to the hospital staff (end-users) or other stakeholders by the means of questionnaires and preformatted files, onsite attack scenarios simulations and discussion workshops for validation. Afterward, this knowledge is refined based on literature taxonomies and security standards for better genericity and adequacy with the field practices. During this process we had to manage 2 main issues: (i) **heterogeneity of terminologies**: the interviewed experts came from hospitals belonging to 3 different countries (France, Italy, and Netherlands), so they use different terminologies, and (ii) **difficulties to get engagement**: collecting business experts' knowledge is a heavy and time consuming task.

To successfully conduct this process, we collaborate with our partners to develop 12 security attack scenarios classified into three groups: physical, cyber, or hybrid, based on the attacks and impacts types. These scenarios are confidential, but the example shown in the introduction, is inspired by one of these scenarios. For each scenario, we carried out the following actions:

1. Phase 1: identify the list of involved assets, the related risks, and the protections in place;
2. Phase 2: identify the inter dependencies between assets and the information about the surrounding infrastructures;
3. Phase 3: collect knowledge about the propagation process and how it is related to both the nature of incidents and the type of assets.

4.2 SafecareOnto: Assets Identification

An overview of the obtained ontology is shown in Fig. 1 with a central module said `Core ontology` and two related and additional modules dedicated to `protection` and `impact propagation`.

The Core Ontology captures the static knowledge about critical assets and their structural relationships detailed in Table 1. **An asset** is an entity that someone places value upon. Within healthcare services context, assets could be business assets such as "personal data" or support assets such as "IT devices".

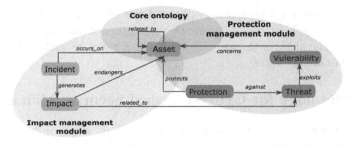

Fig. 1. The conceptual view of SafecareOnto

The Protection Management Module describes protection of assets against attacks. Each asset could have one or several weaknesses said `vulnerabilities` that could be exploited by a `threat` that is a potential of impairment of an asset. A `protection` could be an asset or a policy that protects an asset from `threats`. For example, a <u>camera</u> is protection against a threat that is <u>unauthorized access</u>.

The Impact Management Module defines the concepts that are essential to the computation of impact propagation and provide indicators to help decide about the suitable countermeasures to face attacks. It relies on `Incident` and `Impact` concepts.

An incident is adverse actions performed by a threat agent on an asset. When an `incident` occurs, there is a risk that it propagates to related assets. An `impact` is the result of such propagation. This propagation needs to be precisely qualified and/or quantified to efficiently help decide about the mitigation plans.

4.3   SafecareOnto Conceptualization

During the conceptualisation phase, the concepts and their relationships are refined. For space consideration, only the asset concept is detailed.

. **Asset** concept is a subclass of owl: Thing ($Asset \sqsubseteq \top$) and is further specialised into a set of subclasses that constitute a partition of the concept "Asset" since they have no common instances and that their union completely covers the concept "Asset" as defined for the domain [9].
  - **Support Asset** concept ($SupportAsset \sqsubseteq Asset$) gathers all the assets that help the achievement of the hospitals missions. The specialisation into more precise concepts considers propagation channels.
    * $ITAsset \sqsubseteq SupportAsset$
    * $NetworkedMedicalDevice \sqsubseteq MedicalDevice \sqsubseteq SupportAsset$
    * etc.
  - **Business Asset** ($BusinessAsset \sqsubseteq Asset$) is an asset that is directly related to the hospital mission such as care processes, personnel, etc.
    * $StaffAsset \sqsubseteq BusinessAsset$

  * $BusinessProcess \sqsubseteq BusinessAsset$
  * etc.

Relations Identification. The relationships depict how assets interact in the healthcare context and what are their properties. We have identified two families of relations:

- The first one corresponds to concepts Attributes (data properties in OWL): a staff `hasRole`, a building `hasLevel`, a software `hasVersion`, etc.

Table 1. Structural patterns

Pattern	Description
	The whole-part pattern assumes that if an incident happens on a whole, then it could impact its parts. Inversely, if parts are attacked, the whole could also suffer from the consequences of the attack. This pattern applies to several assets and essentially to assets representing locations. In SafecareOnto, they are referred to as `Building assets`. the propagation through theses structures are essentially "physical incidents" such as "unauthorized access". For example, an intrusion on one floor of a hospital could potentially affect all the rooms on that floor.
	Leads to pattern captures the access and communication possibilities between assets. This access applies for both physical or cyber flows and is materialized through a specific asset referred to as `Access point`. As an example we could mention a door that allows access from a room to another or a port that is a communication end point in a network. An access point could be one way or bidirectional to represent the possible flow directions explicitly.
	Controls pattern allows specifying the conditions and mechanisms for granting or revoking access to assets. The pattern is composed of three elements: the `Controller` applies the access policy, the `Control point` representing the access point and the `Data` representing the policy applied by the controller. For example, a smart card based system is composed of: the access rights stored locally or remotely, door readers to check whether data on the card is consistent with the policy and the door.
 a1 = Asset.content a2= Asset.host (a1.category=device AND a2.category=softwar OR (a1.category=device AND a2.category=data) ..	The hosts-content pattern assumes that if an incident happens on an asset named `host asset` then the content, referred to as `content asset` could be affected by this incident. The structure of the pattern is enriched by rules to enhance the validity of the relationships description. For example, if the host is a device, IT or medical, a content could be software.

– The second family of relations results from our analysis of propagation channels. This analysis revealed that there exist some structural patterns that help reasoning on propagation of incidents according to their nature (cyber or physical). We detail some of these patterns in Table 1.

4.4 SafecareOnto Implementation

To implement the ontology, We have used Protégé [12], which is an ontology and knowledge base editor that enables the construction of domain ontologies,and comes with visualization packages. Figure 2 depicts an extract of the Safecare ontology designed in Protégé. Here, we present concepts that belong mostly, to the core ontology like `Asset` that could be `Staff`, `Device`, `Data`, or `Building`, etc. with their links, as for instance, a `Device hots Data`. Also, we show the concept `Threat`, `Vulnerability`, and `Protection` that belong to the protection management module as well as, `Impact` and `Incident` that belong to the impact management module.

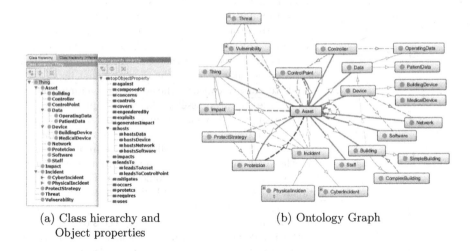

(a) Class hierarchy and Object properties   (b) Ontology Graph

Fig. 2. SafecareOnto implementation in Protégé

5   Conclusion and Future Work

Healthcare systems lack a formal knowledge repository to assist security managers for effective security solutions design. In this paper, we propose an ontology-based model for both cyber and physical security in healthcare systems able to support incident propagation and mitigation reasoning. Our modular ontology is built around a core ontology focusing on assets, and comprises protection and impact propagation modules.

The knowledge acquisition process conducted with experts provided a business domain expert knowledge that we still analyse to construct a decision support system for risks mitigation. The modular structure of the solution proved to be very useful as the acquisition of domain knowledge could not be done on one shot given the variety and geographical spread of stakeholders. The next step is to develop the protection and the impact management modules.

Acknowledgment. This work is part of the SAFECARE project. This project has received funding as part of the "Secure societies – Protecting freedom and security of Europe and its citizens", challenge of the Horizon 2020 Research and Innovation program of the European Union, under grant agreement 787002.

References

1. Abdallah, R., Motii, A., Yakymets, N., Lanusse, A.: Using model driven engineering to support multi-paradigms security analysis. In: International Conference on Model-Driven Engineering and Software Development, pp. 278–292 (2015)
2. Agrafiotis, I., Nurse, J.R., Goldsmith, M., Creese, S., Upton, D.: A taxonomy of cyber-harms: defining the impacts of cyber-attacks and understanding how they propagate. J. Cybersecur. **4**(1), tyy006 (2018)
3. Ashibani, Y., Mahmoud, Q.H.: Cyber physical systems security: analysis, challenges and solutions. Comput. Secur. **68**, 81–97 (2017)
4. Booth, H., Turner, C.: Vulnerability description ontology (vdo): a framework for characterizing vulnerabilities. Technical report, National Institute of Standards and Technology (2016)
5. Choraś, M., Flizikowski, A., Kozik, R., Hołubowicz, W.: Decision aid tool and ontology-based reasoning for critical infrastructure vulnerabilities and threats analysis. In: International Workshop on Critical Information Infrastructures Security, pp. 98–110 (2009)
6. EBIOS: Ebios risk manager - the method. https://www.ssi.gouv.fr/uploads/2019/11/anssi-guide-ebios_risk_manager-en-v1.0.pdf (2019)
7. ENISA: Cyber security and resilience for Smart Hospitals. https://www.enisa.europa.eu/publications/cyber-security-and-resilience-for-smart-hospitals (2016)
8. Fernández-López, M., Gómez-Pérez, A., Juristo, N.: Methontology: from ontological art towards ontological engineering (1997)
9. Horridge, M., Knublauch, H., Rector, A., Stevens, R., Wroe, C.: A practical guide to building owl ontologies using the protégé-owl plugin and co-ode tools edition 1.0. University of Manchester (2004)
10. Ma, M., Liu, L., Lin, Y., Pan, D., Wang, P.: Event description and detection in cyber-physical systems: an ontology-based language and approach. In: 2017 IEEE 23rd International Conference on Parallel and Distributed Systems (ICPADS), pp. 1–8. IEEE (2017)
11. Miller, W.B.: Classifying and cataloging cyber-security incidents within cyber-physical systems (2014)
12. Musen, M.A.: The protégé project: a look back and a look forward. AI Matters **1**(4), 4–12 (2015)
13. Ponemon, I.: Cost of a data breach 2019 report (2019)
14. Syed, Z., Padia, A., Finin, T., Mathews, L., Joshi, A.: UCO: a unified cybersecurity ontology. In: Workshops at the 30th Conference on Artificial Intelligence (2016)

15. Theocharidou, M., Giannopoulos, G.: Risk assessment methodologies for ci protection. part ii: A new approach. Technical report EUR27332 EN (2015)
16. Trucco, P., Petrenj, B., Bouchon, S., Mauro, C.D.: Ontology-based approach to disruption scenario generation for critical infrastructure systems. Int. J. Crit. Infrastruct. **12**(3), 248–272 (2016)

Declarative Process Discovery: Linking Process and Textual Views

Hugo A. López[1,2]([✉])(iD), Rasmus Strømsted[2], Jean-Marie Niyodusenga[3], and Morten Marquard[2]

[1] Software, Data, People and Society Section, Department of Computer Science, Copenhagen University, Copenhagen, Denmark
lopez@di.ku.dk
[2] DCR Solutions, Copenhagen, Denmark
[3] PriceWaterhouseCoopers, Copenhagen, Denmark

Abstract. Business Process models are conceptual representations of work practices. However, a process is more than its model: key information about the rationale of the process is hidden in accompanying documents. We present a framework for business process discovery from process descriptions in texts. We use declarative process models as our target modelling technique. The manual discovery of declarative process models from texts is particularly hard as users have difficulties identifying textual fragments denoting business rules. Our framework combines machine-learning and expert system techniques in order to provide an algorithmic solution to discovery. The combination of the two techniques allows 1) the identification of process components in texts, 2) the enrichment of predictions with semantic information, and 3) the generation of consolidated hybrid models that link text fragments and process elements. Our initial evaluation reports state-of-the-art performance in accuracy against user annotated models, and it has been implemented and adopted by our industrial partner.

Keywords: Declarative process models · Process elicitation · Natural language processing · DCR graphs

1 Introduction

Business process models serve as key artefacts to understand, redesign and optimise organizational work practices. Process models depict *what* activities are important in a process, as well as their dependency relations. However, being *abstractions*, process models hide away important information in favour of understandable representations. Such information is kept in accompanying documents, in *text*. As a result, the understanding of a process requires the integration of multiple artefacts, being textual and graphical representation two of them [2].

Work supported by the Innovation Fund Denmark project *EcoKnow* (7050-00034A).

S. Nurcan and A. Korthaus (Eds.): CAiSE Forum 2021, LNBIP 424, pp. 109–117, 2021.
https://doi.org/10.1007/978-3-030-79108-7_13

This paper focuses on the problems of process discovery and reconciliation of business processes from texts. Process discovery is one of the major areas of research in process mining, where one aims at generating a process model from existing artefacts. Discovering a process model from texts has additional complications as ambiguity is a common denominator. Other aspects complicate discovery. First, there is a risk of lack of generalizability: a discovery method trained in interviews might not work in laws. Second, the writing style can vary and a successful method working in process descriptions will not work when used in normative texts. Finally, texts vary in length, complexity and domain.

The second problem is the reconciliation (i.e. *linking*) of texts and models. When separated, understanding the process from textual and model views require three efforts: first to understand the text, then to understand the model, and finally to understand the relationship between the former two. This last phase is non-trivial as there is no one-to-one correspondence between sentences in the text and elements in the model. A lack of reconciliation might decrease understandability: some users understand texts better than their model views [5], while other users navigate across artefacts to make sense of the process [3].

This paper presents a novel architecture that combines machine learning and heuristic techniques for process discovery and reconciliation from texts. We focus on the discovery of *declarative process models*: those describing events and constraints between them. In comparison to the state of the art in declarative textual process mining [1], our approach includes classification tasks to help to discern which parts of a text corresponds to the process and which is not. Moreover, our approach includes co-reference resolution techniques to decrease the ambiguities generated when the same process element is referred to in multiple ways. Finally, our technique is generalizable to other types of texts and writing styles. This allows for extensions of the framework when new patterns emerge. Generalisation is given via transfer learning using pre-trained language models. To validate our results, we compare predicted process models against user-generated, linked process models. Our results are in pair with state of the art discovery techniques, with a precision score of $F1 = 0.71$.

Related Work. Defining the relations between process models and texts is part of the unsolved challenges for semantic process modelling [13]. We divide related approaches into two categories: discovery techniques of imperative process models and discovery of declarative processes. The discovery for imperative process models include techniques based on taxonomies [10], linguistic information [6], process mining [9] and machine-learning [14]. However, these works are not directly comparable to us as they aim at capturing the flow-based models instead of constraints. Discovery techniques for declarative models is a novel area of research and, to the best of authors' knowledge, only heuristic approaches have been applied [1,12,15]. Despite the difference in languages (Declare for [1], ATDP for [15] and DCR graphs for [11]), we find the formalisms close enough to be used as comparison, and we use parts of their benchmarking to build a external validation experiment in Sect. 5.

Document Structure. In Sect. 2 we introduce our target declarative modelling language. In Sect. 3 we report on the challenges of text-model alignments. In Sect. 4 we introduce the discovery and linking pipeline. Our internal and external validations are presented in Sect. 5. Section 6 concludes.

2 Declarative Process Models as DCR Graphs

DCR graphs is a process modelling notation used in the formalisation and digitalisation of knowledge-intensive processes. Modelling expressiveness in DCR includes multi-perspective dimensions such as time and data constraints [8,16]. In this paper, we only cover the core notation. We introduce DCR graphs via their graphical notation, recalling [7] for its formal semantics.

Figure 1b shows a DCR process model. It contains a set of events (boxes) that describe basic work units and decisions. Each event has a fixed assignment to a label (i.e.: *receives a new claim*). Moreover, we assume a fixed set of roles (i.e.: *insurance company, clerk,* etc.) and a mapping from events to sets of roles. Each event has a state, which is a combination of flags denoting whether the event is currently included in the domain of discourse, it is excluded, it is executed, or it is pending for execution. States can be composed so an event can at the same time be pending and excluded. A DCR graph is a multi-directed graph where edges represent constraints between events. We call edges *relations*, and they can take the following shapes: (1) conditions $e \rightarrow\bullet f$: f cannot be executed until e have executed, or e is excluded. (2) milestones $e \rightarrow\diamond f$: Initially f is included among the possible actions, but if e becomes pending, then f cannot occur until e has occurred. (3) responses $f \leftarrow\bullet e$: When e executes, f must eventually occur or be excluded. (4) dynamic inclusions $f +\leftarrow e$: After executing event e, event f is included among the possible actions to take. Its converse relation is the dynamic exclusion $f \%\leftarrow e$.

3 Challenges in Discovering Annotated Processes

We show some of the challenges in text-model alignments in Fig. 1. The model in Fig. 1b shows a simple model of the textual process descriptions in Fig. 1a, including two documents, one describing the process description, and another with business rules. Aspects in textual alignments will be referred to with numbers (1–10), while model-specific aspects will be referred to with letters (A–G). Different textual fragments describe roles, activities and relations. The correspondence between some fragments and model elements is unique (c.f. annotation (1) and (2)), while other fragments are syntactically different but correspond to the same process element (e.g. annotations (3) and (4) correspond to

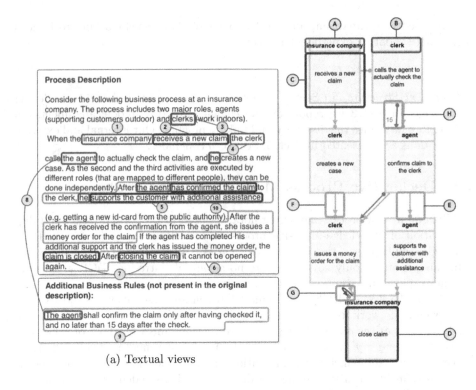

(a) Textual views

(b) Model view as a DCR graph

Fig. 1. Challenges in Text-Model alignments

the role *"clerk"*, and annotations in (7) correspond to activity (D)). Moreover, some fragments are atomic (e.g. the role annotation (1)), and in others cases they denote relations, for instance, the role-attribution relation for activities in annotations (1) and (2). Composition is mandatory in other cases: An annotation describing relations without existing activities lacks meaning, and relations typically involve a pair of activities (e.g. annotation (5)), but they can involve also self-relations (e.g. annotation (6), or one-to-many relations. Finally, multiple perspectives such as time and data can appear in the description, as presented in annotation (9-H). The links between annotations may expand outside the scope of the document itself and can involve multiple documents (e.g. annotation (8)). When discovering a model from texts, the most simple cases refer to 1-to-1 correspondences, for instance, annotations (1-A) and (2-C). However, we can see that it is necessary to link multiple annotations to the same process element as otherwise, we will create false positives unnecessarily. While sometimes syntactic variations are easily solvable ("clerks" and "clerk" come from the same lemma "clerk") in other cases, variations require a deeper analysis of linguistic features such as active/passive voices, or verbal conjugation (e.g. annotations (7-D)).

4   A Discovery and Linking Pipeline

Machine-Learning Components. We use a combination of two instances of BERT's transformer model [4] to extract word-level and sentence-level information using a pre-trained model. We decompose process discovery into a pair of sentence classification problems and a Named Entity Recognition (NER) problem. Algorithm 1 shows an example of the algorithms used for fine-tuning the classification of language models, in this case, for a sentence classification problem. The language models used as inputs are fine-tuned; Binary Classification model (α_1), MultiClass Classification (α_2) and NER (α_3) models.

Algorithm 1: Fine-Tune Sentence Classification($S, \eta, B, b, \mu, \kappa, C$)

---

input : List of sentence-label pairs
$X = (S^1, y^1), ..., (S^n, y^n)$,
language model α
output: language model α
partition X into $X_1, X_2, ..., X_n$;
/* Initialise hyper-parameters */
foreach $X_i \in X$ **do**
  foreach $C_i \in C$ **do**
    if *class* = C_i **then**
      extract features;
      update($\alpha, features$);
  end
end

Model Training. We use the dataset in Sect. 5 for training. Training and benchmarks were done using a BERT$_{BASE}$ model [4]. The dataset was split in a 0.80/0.20 distribution training/validation. The fine-tuning of the model was achieved using self-attention mechanisms in the transformers and it utilises tasks-specific classifications for each classification task. The fine-tuned hyper-parameters used in all models were 1. (η) Learning rate (Adam) of 2^-5,(B) training cycles of 4 epochs, (b) batch size of 32, (K)-fold of 10, and (μ) maximum sentence length of 50.

4.1   Discovery and Linking Algorithm

Algorithm 2 presents our process discovery and reconciliation algorithm. It includes separated phases for pre-processing, relation, activity, role extraction, and co-reference resolution. Generic phrases such as NER combine both expert systems and machine-learning approaches for a given class. The output of the co-reference resolution is added as complementary inputs for the pipeline, while the fine-tuned language models in Algorithm 1 are added as inputs. The algorithm parses the text sequentially, building iteratively roles, events and relations.

Algorithm 2: Discovery Algorithm

---

input : t text;$\alpha_1,\alpha_2,\alpha_3$ language models
output: $\langle G, H \rangle$ where:
    $G = \langle Roles, Events, Relations \rangle$ is a DCR graph
    H is a set of Highlights $\langle PElement, indexRange, PElement? \rangle$

$processedText \leftarrow Preprocess(t)$;
$resolvedText \leftarrow coref(processedText)$;
/* Apply NER (α_3) to identify roles and events, H is updated with new highlights   */
$Roles, H \leftarrow NER(processedText, \alpha_3, null,\text{Class}=Role)$;
$Events, H \leftarrow NER(processedText, \alpha_3, H,\text{Class}=Event)$;
/* Apply relation recognition (α_1 & α_2)and update highlights   */
foreach $sentence \in resolvedText$ **do**
  if $\alpha_1.predict(sentence) \neq Non\text{-}Relation$ **then**
    $Evs \leftarrow NER(sentence, \alpha_3,\text{Class}=Event)$;   /* Ensure that $|Evs| > 1$ */
    $relationsSentence \leftarrow []$;
    if $sentence$ is in passive voice **then**
      for ev_i in $0\ldots|Evs|-1$ **do**
        $r_i \leftarrow$ new Relation$(ev_i, Evs[size(Evs)], \alpha_2.predict(sentence))$;
        $Relations.insert(r_i)$;
        $relationsSentence.insert(r_i)$;
      end
    else
      for ev_i in $1\ldots|Evs|$ **do**
        $r_i \leftarrow$ new Relation$(Evs[0], ev_i], \alpha_2.predict(sentence))$;
        $Relations.insert(r_i)$;
        $relationsSentence.insert(r_i)$;
      end
    end
    $highlightedRanges \leftarrow findOriginalRanges(processedText, sentence)$;
    foreach $r \in relationsSentence$ **do**
      $H.insert(\langle r, highlightedRanges, null \rangle)$;
    end
  end
end

---

5 Validation

We collected a training dataset with 37 process descriptions. The dataset combines four entries from the BPM Academic Initiative, 31 descriptions from interviews and observations done by business process management students at a Danish university. Also, two process excerpts from the Danish Con-

Table 1. Internal Validation Results

Classifier	Type	P	R	F1
Is a relation	False	1.00	1.00	1.00
	True	0.99	0.99	0.99
Total (macro avg)		**0.99**	**1.00**	**0.99**
Semantics	Condition	0.91	0.93	0.93
	Non-Relation	1.00	1.00	1.00
	Response	0.94	0.93	0.93
Total (macro avg)		**0.94**	**0.96**	**0.95**

solidation Act on Social Services were added to enrich variability and mitigate authorship bias. Parts of the dataset were anonymized to hide personal information. A total of 137 roles, 653 activities and 1.526 relations were included. Table 2a summarises the collected dataset.

Table 2. Training dataset: structure and annotations

Modelling language	Models	Roles x̄	Activities x̄	Relations x̄
Linked models				
DCR	16	3,81	17,75	39,44
Expert	4	3,25	10,75	18,50
Student	12	4,00	20,08	46,42
Total linked models	16	3,81	17,75	39,44
Unlinked models				
BPMN	3	2,33	13,00	29,33
Student	3	2,33	13,00	29,33
DCR	18	3,83	18,33	44,83
Student	18	3,83	18,33	44,83
Total unlinked models	21	3,62	17,57	42,62
Total models	37	3,70	17,65	41,24

(a) Dataset structure, x̄ refers to average

Entity type labels	Count	%
Activities	958	50,4%
Roles	621	32,6%
Relations	292	15,6%
Other (Comments, time annotations, data guards, etc.)	29	1,6%
Total	**1.900**	**100%**

(b) Annotation distribution

Internal Validation. A 10-fold cross-validation was performed by randomly splitting the dataset into 10 mutually exclusive subsets of similar size. The classifier is trained on 9 subsets, testing on the last one. This process is repeated 10 times. The results are given in Table 1.

External Validation. We compared precision scores under an external dataset. This dataset was composed of 15 process descriptions not using in the training tasks, including an equal distribution of entries from DECLARE [1], the "Annotated Textual Descriptions of Processes" (ATDP) [15], as well as 5 entries of our own dataset excluded in training. The process descriptions were manually annotated to create a gold standard. We consider a match when there is a process element linked to a textual description, and the predicted fragment corresponds to the manual annotation.

We report the performance of machine learning and expert systems in isolation, as well as in combination. As measurements, we use the standard metrics of (P)recision, (R)ecall, and F1-scores. The results are summarised in Table 3. It is noticeable that for this dataset the contributions of the ML and rule-based approach differ: while ML contribution has a higher recall (suggests more process elements), it also has lower precision (more suggestions are wrong). In contrast, the expert system has a balanced precision/recall rate. Mixing the modes increases precision, but the mode of mixing affects. Surprisingly, role recognition did not benefit from the intersection approach, while activity recognition did. Our performance is slightly better than [15], that for activity recognition scores Precision: 0.75, Recall: 0.68 F1 = 0.70.

116   H. A. López et al.

6   Conclusions

Table 3. External validation: performance over a mixed dataset

Combination modes		P	R	F1
ML only	Roles	0.61	0.81	0.68
	Activities	0.52	0.80	0.61
	Relations	0.69	0.90	0.76
	Average	**0.61**	**0.83**	**0.68**
Expert system only only	Roles	0.49	0.67	0.53
	Activities	0.91	0.75	0.81
	Relations	NA	NA	NA
	Average	**0.70**	**0.71**	**0.67**
Intersection	Roles	0.59	0.54	0.55
	Activities	0.98	0.65	0.71
	Relations	NA	NA	NA
	Average	**0.79**	**0.59**	**0.64**
Best combination roles (ML), Activities (Intersection), Relations (ML)	**Average**	**0.76**	**0.78**	**0.71**

The application of NLP to perform process mining from textual descriptions promises the reduction in the time that process modellers need to use for mapping business processes, which at the moment is a manual, error-prone, repetitive and time-consuming task. We have presented a process discovery and reconciliation technique that generates declarative models and trace their relation with textual artefacts, a task that otherwise need to be established manually. Our proposal allows the inclusion of rules and their extension from patterns mined by existing annotations, making it easier to extend and decouple depending on the precision measures required. Even with a small training dataset, the evaluations suggest a state-of-the-art performance. The discovery algorithm is available at https://github.com/RasmusIven/DCR-Textograph. The discovery pipeline (including training) is integrated with the DCR Process highlighter [11], and it is part of the offering of DCR solutions.

References

1. van der Aa, H., Di Ciccio, C., Leopold, H., Reijers, H.A.: Extracting declarative process models from natural language. In: Giorgini, P., Weber, B. (eds.) CAiSE 2019. LNCS, vol. 11483, pp. 365–382. Springer, Cham (2019). https://doi.org/10.1007/978-3-030-21290-2_23
2. Abbad Andaloussi, A., Buch-Lorentsen, J., López, H.A., Slaats, T., Weber, B.: Exploring the modeling of declarative processes using a hybrid approach. In: Laender, A.H.F., Pernici, B., Lim, E.-P., de Oliveira, J.P.M. (eds.) ER 2019. LNCS, vol. 11788, pp. 162–170. Springer, Cham (2019). https://doi.org/10.1007/978-3-030-33223-5_14
3. Abbad Andaloussi, A., Slaats, T., Burattin, A., Hildebrandt, T.T., Weber, B.: Evaluating the understandability of hybrid process model representations using eye tracking: first insights. In: Daniel, F., Sheng, Q.Z., Motahari, H. (eds.) BPM 2018. LNBIP, vol. 342, pp. 475–481. Springer, Cham (2019). https://doi.org/10.1007/978-3-030-11641-5_37
4. Devlin, J., Chang, M.W., Lee, K., Toutanova, K.: Bert: pre-training of deep bidirectional transformers for language understanding. arXiv preprint arXiv:1810.04805 (2018)
5. Figl, K., Di Ciccio, C., Reijers, H.A.: Do declarative process models help to reduce cognitive biases related to business rules? In: Dobbie, G., Frank, U., Kappel, G., Liddle, S.W., Mayr, H.C. (eds.) ER 2020. LNCS, vol. 12400, pp. 119–133. Springer, Cham (2020). https://doi.org/10.1007/978-3-030-62522-1_9

6. Friedrich, F., Mendling, J., Puhlmann, F.: Process model generation from natural language text. In: Mouratidis, H., Rolland, C. (eds.) CAiSE 2011. LNCS, vol. 6741, pp. 482–496. Springer, Heidelberg (2011). https://doi.org/10.1007/978-3-642-21640-4_36

7. Hildebrandt, T., Mukkamala, R.R.: Declarative event-based workflow as distributed dynamic condition response graphs. PLACES. EPTCS **69**, 59–73 (2010). https://doi.org/10.4204/EPTCS.69.5

8. Hildebrandt, T.T., Mukkamala, R.R., Slaats, T., Zanitti, F.: Contracts for cross-organizational workflows as timed dynamic condition response graphs. JLAMP **82**(5–7), 164–185 (2013)

9. Ivanchikj, A., Serbout, S., Pautasso, C.: From text to visual bpmn process models: design and evaluation. In: MODELS, pp. 229–239. ACM (2020). https://doi.org/10.1145/3365438.3410990

10. Leopold, H., Meilicke, C., Fellmann, M., Pittke, F., Stuckenschmidt, H., Mendling, J.: Towards the automated annotation of process models. In: Zdravkovic, J., Kirikova, M., Johannesson, P. (eds.) CAiSE 2015. LNCS, vol. 9097, pp. 401–416. Springer, Cham (2015). https://doi.org/10.1007/978-3-319-19069-3_25

11. López, H.A., Debois, S., Hildebrandt, T.T., Marquard, M.: The process highlighter: From texts to declarative processes and back. In: BPM (Dissertation/Demos/Industry), vol. 2196, pp. 66–70. CEUR-WS.org (2018)

12. López, H.A., Marquard, M., Muttenthaler, L., Strømsted, R.: Assisted declarative process creation from natural language descriptions. In: EDOC Workshops, pp. 96–99. IEEE (2019)

13. Mendling, J., Leopold, H., Pittke, F.: 25 Challenges of semantic process modeling. IJISEBC **1**(1), 78–94 (2014)

14. Qian, C., Wen, L., Kumar, A., Lin, L., Lin, L., Zong, Z., Li, S., Wang, J.: An approach for process model extraction by multi-grained text classification. In: Dustdar, S., Yu, E., Salinesi, C., Rieu, D., Pant, V. (eds.) CAiSE 2020. LNCS, vol. 12127, pp. 268–282. Springer, Cham (2020). https://doi.org/10.1007/978-3-030-49435-3_17

15. Quishpi, L., Carmona, J., Padró, L.: Extracting annotations from textual descriptions of processes. In: Fahland, D., Ghidini, C., Becker, J., Dumas, M. (eds.) BPM 2020. LNCS, vol. 12168, pp. 184–201. Springer, Cham (2020). https://doi.org/10.1007/978-3-030-58666-9_11

16. Strømsted, R., López, H.A., Debois, S., Marquard, M.: Dynamic evaluation forms using declarative modeling. In: BPM (Dissertation/Demos/Industry), vol. 2196, pp. 172–179. CEUR-WS.org (2018)

A Tool for Computing Probabilistic Trace Alignments

Giacomo Bergami[1]($\boxtimes$)(ID), Fabrizio Maria Maggi[1](ID), Marco Montali[1](ID),
and Rafael Peñaloza[2](ID)

[1] Free University of Bozen-Bolzano, Bolzano, Italy
gibergami@unibz.it, {maggi,montali}@inf.unibz.it
[2] University of Milano-Bicocca, Milan, Italy
rafael.penaloza@unimib.it

Abstract. Alignments pinpoint trace deviations in a process model and quantify their severity. However, approaches based on trace alignments use crisp process models and recent probabilistic conformance checking approaches check the degree of conformance of an event log with respect to a stochastic process model instead of finding trace alignments. In this paper, for the first time, we provide a conformance checking approach based on trace alignments using stochastic Workflow nets. Conceptually, this requires to handle the two possibly contrasting forces of the cost of the alignment on the one hand and the likelihood of the model trace with respect to which the alignment is computed on the other.

Keywords: Stochastic Petri nets · Conformance checking · Alignments

1 Introduction

In the existing literature on conformance checking, a common approach is based on trace alignment [1]. This approach uses crisp process models as reference models. Yet, recently developed probabilistic conformance checking approaches provide a numerical quantification of the degree of conformance of an event log with a stochastic process model by either assessing the distribution discrepancies [7], or by exploiting entropy-based measures [10,11]. As these strategies are not based on trace alignments, they cannot be directly used to repair a given trace with one of the traces generated by a stochastic process model. In this paper, we present, for the first time, a tool for the probabilistic alignment of a trace and a stochastic reference model. The tool provides different alignment options since, conceptually, probabilistic trace alignment requires the analyst to balance between the alignment cost and the likelihood of model traces: an optimal but very unlikely alignment could, in fact, be much less interesting than a slightly worse but very likely alignment.

With reference to Fig. 1, a user might be interested in aligning the log trace ⟨add item, close order, archive order⟩ with one of the two possible model traces ⟨add item, close order, accept order, pay order, archive order⟩ or

© Springer Nature Switzerland AG 2021
S. Nurcan and A. Korthaus (Eds.): CAiSE Forum 2021, LNBIP 424, pp. 118–126, 2021.
https://doi.org/10.1007/978-3-030-79108-7_14

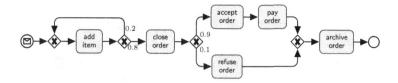

Fig. 1. A simple order management process in BPMN, with choice probabilities.

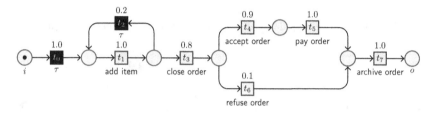

Fig. 2. Encoding of the BPMN diagram in Fig. 1 using a stochastic Workflow net with bounded silence.

⟨add item, close order, refuse order, archive order⟩. The latter model trace provides the least alignment cost, but comes with a very low probability ($0.8 \cdot 0.1 = 0.08$); on the other hand, the former model trace gives a slightly worse alignment cost, but comes with a much higher probability ($0.8 \cdot 0.9 = 0.72$). Depending on the context, analysts might prefer either the former or the latter alignment. In general, finding a portfolio of the "best" k alignments among all the distinct model traces empowers analysts to find their own trade-off between alignment cost and model trace probability.

To achieve this, we frame the probabilistic trace alignment problem into the well-known k-Nearest Neighbors (kNN) problem [2] that refers to finding the k nearest data points to a *query* x from a set $\mathcal{X}$ of *data points* via a distance function defined over $\mathcal{X} \cup \{x\}$. We introduce two ranking strategies. The first one is based on a brute force approach that reuses existing trace aligners [8] requiring to re-compute the alignments for all possible traces in the log. For models generating a large number of model traces, this clearly becomes inefficient. Therefore, we propose a second strategy that produces an approximate ranking where x and $\mathcal{X}$ are represented as numerical vectors via an embedding ϕ. If the embedding ϕ for $\mathcal{X}$ is independent of the query of choice x, this does not require to constantly recompute the numeric vector representation for $\mathcal{X}$. Instead, it is possible to pre-order it to efficiently visit the search space. The developed tool is publicly available[1].

---

[1] https://github.com/jackbergus/approxProbTraceAlign.

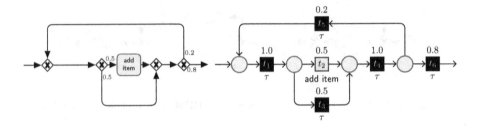

Fig. 3. A process model with a loop accepting fully silent iterations.

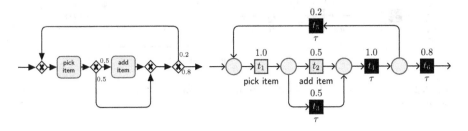

Fig. 4. A process model with a loop accepting iterations with skippable steps.

2   The Process Models

To formalize the kind of processes shown in Fig. 1, we resort to a special class of stochastic Petri nets, following what has been done in the literature [7,11]. We dscribe next the features of the class we consider, and why they lead to an interesting trade-off between expressiveness and amenability to analysis. Figure 2 shows the encoding of the BPMN diagram of Fig. 1 into the Petri net class supported by our conformance checking tool.

Untimed, Stochastic Nets. We focus on stochastic Petri nets with immediate transitions, that is, we do not consider timed aspects such as delays and deadlines, but concentrate on the key feature of having a probability distribution over the enabled transitions. This is achieved by taking a standard Petri net and by assigning weights to its transitions. At each execution step, the probability of firing an enabled transition is then simply computed by dividing its weight by the total weight of all currently enabled transitions.

Workflow Nets. In the whole Petri net spectrum, we focus, as customary in process mining, on Workflow nets with a distinguished pair of input and output places, marking the start and completion of a case in the process. Specifically, a *model run* is a sequence of fireable transitions leading from the initial marking (which assigns one single token to the special input place, while leaving all the other places empty) to the final marking (which assigns one single token to the special output place, while leaving all the other places empty). As usual, the probability of a model run is then computed by multiplying the probabilities of each transition. For example, by considering the net of Fig. 2, we have that $\rho = \langle t_0, t_1, t_3, t_6, t_7 \rangle$ is a model run whose probability is $0.8 \cdot 0.1 = 0.08$.

In our specific setting, focusing on Workflow nets has the advantage that every model run is a maximal sequence of transition firings that cannot be extended into a different model run. This provides a direct way to characterize the (finite-length) runs accepted by the Workflow net and their probabilities, without the need of introducing additional constructs such as the probability of stopping in a marking.

Silent Transitions. To provide support for control-flow gateways, we include silent transitions in the net. More specifically, every transition comes with a label that corresponds either to the name of a (visible) task, or to the special symbol τ (denoting a silent transition). Figure 2 shows how τ-transitions are used to capture the BPMN process of Fig. 1. In particular, silent transition t_2 is used to model that one can loop to add multiple items to the order. Notice that, for simplicity of modeling, we support the possibility of labeling multiple transitions with the same task.

Having silent transitions and repeated labels deeply impacts the obtained framework. In fact, a model run does not directly correspond to a model trace, intended as a "legal" sequence of (visible) tasks according to the process. On the one hand, a model run yields a corresponding trace by extracting, in order, the labels attached to the transitions contained therein, projecting away the invisible ones. For example, model run ρ above yields the model trace $\langle$ add item, close order, archive order $\rangle$. On the other hand, the same model trace may be obtained through distinct model runs, differing from each other in terms of the silent tasks they contain. Hence, in general, to obtain the probability of a model trace, one must sum up the probabilities of *all* (possibly, infinitely many) model runs yielding that trace. This number is guaranteed, by construction, to be between 0 and 1 (since the collective sum of the probabilities of all model runs is indeed 1). In our example, the probability of $\langle$ add item, close order, archive order $\rangle$ is that of the model run ρ (i.e., 0.08), since ρ is the only model run yielding that trace.

Nets with "Bounded Silence". The last requirement we impose over our nets is that of *bounded silence*. This requirement states that the net cannot accept runs containing unboundedly many consecutive silent transitions. Mathematically, this means that there exists an a-priori bound on the maximum number of silent transitions that can be fired between two visible transitions.

In conceptual modeling terms, this requirement imposes that it is not possible to have loops in the process where an entire iteration consists only of visible transitions, that is, where an iteration can be executed without any visible task to witness its existence. We argue that, in this case, executing an entire iteration where all visible transitions are skipped is not different from the situation where the iteration is not executed at all. Consider, for example, the process fragment shown in Fig. 3. There, the trace consisting of three item additions could be produced by infinitely many distinct runs, each containing a different number of silent iterations in the loop.

On the other hand, it is perfectly possible to have loops with skippable tasks, provided that there exists at least one visible transition witnessing that an iteration in the loop has been executed. Figure 4 shows a variant of the process fragment in Fig. 3 where each iteration must be witnessed by (visibly) picking an item, then deciding whether to add it or not (the latter choice resulting in a silent step). This variant has bounded silence, as two consecutive iterations need to contain two distinct executions of the pick item task, with at most one silent transition in between.

In mathematical terms, our untimed, stochastic workflow nets with bounded silence enjoy the following property. Consider a net with a bound b on the maximum number of consecutive silent transitions. Given a model trace of length n, a model run yielding that trace must have a length bounded by $n + (n + 1) \cdot b$. This gives us a direct way to compute the probability of such a model trace:

1. we fetch all model runs of length at most $n + (n + 1) \cdot b$ (which can be easily done with a bounded-depth search strategy over reachable markings);
2. among all such runs, we keep all and only those that yield the model trace of interest;
3. we sum up the probabilities of the so-filtered model runs.

Notice that if the net is bounded in the usual Petri net sense, then we can directly compute this probability by inspecting the reachability graph of the net.

3   The Probabilistic Trace Alignment Tool

Our tool takes as input *(i)* a reference model represented as a BPMN model or an equivalent stochastic Workflow net, *(ii)* a minimum positive probability threshold $\rho \in (0, 1]$ *(iii)* a trace σ of interest, and returns a ranking over all the model traces having a probability greater than or equal to ρ, based on a combined consideration of their probability values and their distance from σ.

Transition Graphs. The model trace probabilities can be directly computed by inspecting the reachability graph of the reference model. Still, graph embedding techniques required to represent traces as data points (e.g., vectors) cannot be directly defined over reachability graphs since they rely on probabilistic *Transition Graphs* [6]. Such Transition Graphs can be computed by shifting the transition labels over graph nodes, and performing τ-closures, while preserving τ-transitions for both start and completion nodes, if required, to preserve trace probabilities. An example of a Transition Graph is shown in Fig. 5.

Alignment Strategies. We frame the probabilistic trace alignment problem into the well-known k-Nearest Neighbors (kNN) problem that refers to finding the k nearest data points to a *query* x from a set $\mathcal{X}$ of *data points* via a distance function d_k defined over $\mathcal{X} \cup \{x\}$. In particular, by exploiting ad-hoc data structures, such as VP-Trees and KD-Trees, we can retrieve the neighborhood of x in $\mathcal{X}$ of size k by pre-ordering (*indexing*) $\mathcal{X}$ via d_k and starting the search from the top-1 alignment.

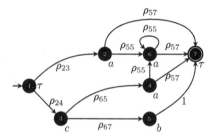

Fig. 5. An example of a Transition Graph.

1) Optimal-Ranking Trace Aligner. One way to probabilistically align traces is to reuse existing trace aligners [1,8], where the distance $d(\sigma, \sigma')$ between model and log traces is the Levenshtein distance. We can then express the ranking score as the product $\mathbb{P}_N(\sigma')d(\sigma, \sigma')$, considering both the alignment cost (given by the distance between the model trace and the trace to be aligned) and the model trace probability. We can represent this weighted distance as a ranking function returning 1 when $\sigma' = \sigma$ and $\mathbb{P}_N(\sigma) = 1$ hold. To this aim, we need to express d as a normalized similarity score $s_d(\sigma, \sigma') := \frac{1}{d(\sigma, \sigma')+1}$. The golden ranking function (i.e., the one producing the optimal ranking) can therefore be represented as $\mathcal{R}(\sigma, \sigma') = \mathbb{P}_N(\sigma')\mathbb{P}_N(\sigma)s_d(\sigma, \sigma')$. Such a function can be exploited to generate the best optimal-ranking trace alignment for a log trace σ, where $\mathcal{R}$ must be computed a-new for all possible σ.

2) Approximate-Ranking Trace Embedder. Ranking optimality comes at the sub-optimal cost of a brute-force recomputation of $\mathcal{R}$ for each novel trace σ to align. Since each embedding ϕ entails an associated similarity metric k_ϕ, and hence an associated distance d_{k_ϕ}, we can compute the embeddings for all the model traces before performing the top-k search ensuring that they are independent of the trace to align, thus avoiding the brute-force cost. This computational gain comes with a loss in precision [3,6] and, in its approximated version, is not able to accurately represent the data using low-dimensional vectors [12]. Our aim is to represent model traces, which might be composed by different valid sequences (paths), as vectors. We are also interested in the intersection of embedding strategies for whole node-labeled graphs with string embedding traces, as we use vectors to compare model traces with log traces.

To obtain our proposed embedding ϕ^g, we hence adapt the embedding strategy ϕ^{tr} from [9] by addressing some shortcomings: we **(a)** propose a weakly-ideal embedding [5], which, differently from current literature, **(b)** exploits an ω factor for preserving probabilities from and to τ transitions. We also **(c)** mitigate the numerical truncation errors induced by trace length and probability distribution skewness through two sub-embedding strategies, ϵ and ν, where the former descends from ϕ^{tr} and the latter approximates the trace similarity via label frequency similarity. Since a model trace embedding, in our tool, requires an intermediate representation G of the model trace, we map each σ' to a pair

Table 1. Projected Transition Graphs associated to model traces with maximum length 4.

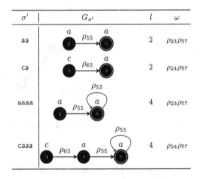

$(G_{\sigma'}, \omega)$, where *(i)* $G_{\sigma'}$ is a transition graph containing all the paths describing σ', where all τ-labeled nodes are removed, while *(ii)* the graph weight ω preserves the weight of the possible initial and final edges that were removed due to the former requirement.

Given the τ-closed Transition Graph in Fig. 5, we assign the probability values $\rho_{23} = 0.8$, $\rho_{24} = 0.2$, $\rho_{55} = \rho_{57} = 0.5$, $\rho_{65} = 0.7$, and $\rho_{67} = 0.3$. The model traces with maximum length 4 are: $\{\langle a, 0.4\rangle, \langle aa, 0.2\rangle, \langle aaa, 0.1\rangle, \langle ca, 0.07\rangle, \langle cb, 0.06\rangle, \langle aaaa, 0.05\rangle, \langle caa, 0.035\rangle, \langle caaa, 0.0175\rangle\}$. Table 1 shows the projected transition graphs associated to such traces, where only the relevant information for embedding them is displayed (e.g., all the τ-labeled nodes are removed).

Our proposed embedding ϕ^g is computed for each pair $(G_{\sigma'}, \omega)$. The goal is to use k_{ϕ^g} for ranking all model traces. To this aim, we extend the embedding ϕ^{tr} [9] by including the trace probabilities, and making the ranking induced by k_{ϕ^g} the inverse of the ranking induced by the sum of the following distances: the transition correlations ϵ and the transition label frequency ν. Therefore, our proposed ϕ^g embedding is defined as follows:

Definition 1 (G-Embedding). *Given a $\overline{G}$ projection over σ' $(\overline{G}_{\sigma'}, \omega)$ and a tuning parameter $t_f \in [0,1] \subseteq \mathbb{R}_0^+$ (that can be inferred from the available data [4]), the G-Embedding ϕ^g exploiting the matrix representation of [6] in ν and ϵ for Transition Graphs is defined as*

$$\phi^g{}_i(\overline{G}_{\sigma'}) = \begin{cases} \omega \dfrac{\epsilon_{ab}(\overline{G}_{\sigma'})}{\|\epsilon\|_2} \, t_f^{|R>0|} & i = \text{ab} \\ \dfrac{\nu_a(\overline{G}_{\sigma'})}{\|\nu\|_2} \, t_f^{|R>0|} & i = \text{a} \end{cases}$$

Here, the kernel function associated to such embedding can be exploited to return the best approximated trace alignment for a log trace represented as G_σ. It can be proven that our embedding performs weakly-ideally. In addition, the proposed embedding is independent of the trace to be aligned. Therefore, it does not have to be recomputed at each alignment for a different σ.

Table 2. Comparison between the ranking induced by the optimal ranking $\mathcal{R}$ and the proposed kernel k_{ϕ^g}: arrows $\downarrow$ remark the column of choice under which we sort the rows.

σ'	$(\mathbb{P}_N(\sigma')$	$,\downarrow s_d(\sigma,\sigma'))$	$= \mathcal{R}(\sigma,\sigma')$	$k_{\phi^g}(\overline{G}_\sigma,\overline{G}_{\sigma'})$	σ'	$\downarrow \mathcal{R}(\sigma,\sigma')$	σ'	$\downarrow k_{\phi^g}(\overline{G}_\sigma,\overline{G}_{\sigma'})$
caa	0.035	0.8333	0.0292	$1.14 \cdot 10^{-40}$	a	0.2500	a	$8.16 \cdot 10^{-21}$
caaa	0.0175	0.8333	0.0145	$9.84 \cdot 10^{-41}$	aa	0.1428	ca	$1.89 \cdot 10^{-24}$
a	0.4	0.6250	0.2500	$8.16 \cdot 10^{-21}$	aaa	0.0714	cb	$7.64 \cdot 10^{-25}$
aaaa	0.05	0.6250	0.0357	$8.44 \cdot 10^{-41}$	ca	0.0500	caa	$1.14 \cdot 10^{-40}$
aa	0.2	0.7142	0.1428	$9.28 \cdot 10^{-41}$	cb	0.0428	caaa	$9.84 \cdot 10^{-41}$
aaa	0.1	0.7142	0.0714	$8.72 \cdot 10^{-41}$	aaaa	0.0357	aa	$9.28 \cdot 10^{-41}$
ca	0.07	0.7142	0.0500	$1.89 \cdot 10^{-24}$	caa	0.0292	aaaa	$8.44 \cdot 10^{-41}$
cb	0.06	0.7142	0.0428	$7.64 \cdot 10^{-25}$	caaa	0.0145	aaa	$8.72 \cdot 10^{-41}$

Table 2 shows the output of our tool. In particular, in the example, the kernel k_{ϕ^g} of model traces of maximum length 4 is provided. From the results, it is possible to see that k_{ϕ^g} approximates the optimal ranking as it tends to rank the transition graphs $\overline{G}_{\sigma'}$ (generated from $\overline{G}$ via projection) similarly to the model traces over $\mathcal{R}$. In the table, the ranking similarities shared between the two different ranking strategies are highlighted in blue, while the most evident ranking discrepancies are marked in red.

Acknowledgments. This research has been partially supported by the project IDEE (FESR1133) funded by the Eur. Reg. Development Fund (ERDF) Investment for Growth and Jobs Programme 2014–2020.

References

1. Adriansyah, A., van Dongen, B.F., van der Aalst, W.M.P.: Conformance checking using cost-based fitness analysis. In: EDOC 2011, pp. 55–64. IEEE (2011)
2. Altman, N.S.: An introduction to kernel and nearest-neighbor nonparametric regression. Am. Stat. **46**(3), 175–185 (1992)
3. Bergami, G., Bertini, F., Montesi, D.: Hierarchical embedding for DAG reachability queries. In: IDEAS, pp. 24:1–24:10. ACM (2020)
4. Driessens, K., Ramon, J., Gärtner, T.: Graph kernels and gaussian processes for relational reinforcement learning. Mach. Learn. **64**(1–3), 91–119 (2006). https://doi.org/10.1007/s10994-006-8258-y
5. Gärtner, T.: A survey of kernels for structured data. SIGKDD **5**(1), 49–58 (2003)
6. Gärtner, T., Flach, P., Wrobel, S.: On graph kernels: hardness results and efficient alternatives. In: Schölkopf, B., Warmuth, M.K. (eds.) COLT-Kernel 2003. LNCS (LNAI), vol. 2777, pp. 129–143. Springer, Heidelberg (2003). https://doi.org/10.1007/978-3-540-45167-9_11
7. Leemans, S.J.J., Syring, A.F., van der Aalst, W.M.P.: Earth movers' stochastic conformance checking. In: Hildebrandt, T., van Dongen, B.F., Röglinger, M., Mendling, J. (eds.) BPM 2019. LNBIP, vol. 360, pp. 127–143. Springer, Cham (2019). https://doi.org/10.1007/978-3-030-26643-1_8
8. de Leoni, M., Marrella, A.: Aligning real process executions and prescriptive process models through automated planning. Expert Syst. Appl. **82**, 162–183 (2017)

9. Lodhi, H., Saunders, C., Shawe-Taylor, J., Cristianini, N., Watkins, C.J.C.H.: Text classification using string kernels. J. Mach. Learn. Res. **2**, 419–444 (2002)
10. Polyvyanyy, A., Kalenkova, A.A.: Monotone conformance checking for partially matching designed and observed processes. In: ICPM, pp. 81–88 (2019)
11. Polyvyanyy, A., Solti, A., Weidlich, M., Di Ciccio, C., Mendling, J.: Monotone precision and recall measures for comparing executions and specifications of dynamic systems. ACM Trans. Softw. Eng. Methodol. **29**(3), 17:1–17:41 (2020)
12. Seshadhri, C., Sharma, A., Stolman, A., Goel, A.: The impossibility of low-rank representations for triangle-rich complex networks. Proc. Natl. Acad. Sci. **117**(11), 5631–5637 (2020)

Innovative Tools and Prototypes

Applied Predictive Process Monitoring and Hyper Parameter Optimization in Camunda

Nico Bartmann, Stefan Hill[(✉)], Carl Corea, Christoph Drodt, and Patrick Delfmann

Institute for Information System Research, University of Koblenz-Landau, Koblenz, Germany
{nbartmann,shill,ccorea,drodt,delfmann}@uni-koblenz.de

Abstract. With the growing amount of data gathered from business processes in recent years, predictive process monitoring (PPM) established as a method to provide valuable insights and make resilient forecasts. However, sophisticated machine learning algorithms and statistical techniques are always equipped with various hyper parameters, which aggravates finding the best configuration for laypeople. Tools like Nirdizati Research (http://research.nirdizati.org/) or apromore (https://apromore.org/) aim to assist in these tasks. Nonetheless these approaches are isolated solutions, which do not integrate into existing productive environments. In this work, a plugin for the widely used workflow and decision automation tool Camunda (https://camunda.com/) is presented which allows creating classifier for the most common operations in PPM. Furthermore, the framework includes a hyper parameter optimization (HPO) and is extensible in prediction types, methods and optimization algorithms.

Keywords: Predictive process monitoring · Hyper parameter optimization · Camunda

1 Introduction

In the last two decades, the digitalization of business processes has equipped companies with substantial new means to investigate the internal company processes. With business processes being executed by workflow management systems that continuously log event data, the availability of big data allows to generate valuable insights into company activities. Here, a wealth of recent research has focused on exploiting such workflow log data for predictive process monitoring, in order to leverage insights to create competitive advantages by means of intelligent predictions (c.f. [5] for an overview). While such results are clearly beneficial for companies, there are unfortunately no user friendly solutions for PPM that integrate seamlessly into existing workflow management systems and guide end-users through the selection of suitable prediction methods. Even though there

© Springer Nature Switzerland AG 2021
S. Nurcan and A. Korthaus (Eds.): CAiSE Forum 2021, LNBIP 424, pp. 129–136, 2021.
https://doi.org/10.1007/978-3-030-79108-7_15

are refined solutions for PPM like for example Nirdizati Research or several ProM-Plugins[1], these are always implemented in an isolated environment. This however impedes a practical usage, as running a workflow engine and analysing tools in parallel can lead to data storage problems such as redundancy and requires extensive employee training for the external tools. Here, methods are needed that integrate PPM with existing workflow management systems in a unified manner, in order to lower the obstacles of adoption.

In this work, we therefore introduce a Camunda plugin[2] which enables an effortless use of machine learning techniques for PPM directly in the running workflow management system. Camunda is an open source workflow management and automation platform which is widely used by a variety of small- to large-scale companies such as Atlassian, Generali and Deutsche Telekom[3]. The presented plugin adds a clean user interface for predictions on single process instances and a detailed configuration panel for administrative tasks. Classifiers may be trained on the basis of the internal Camunda log or with external logs in the common Extensible Event Stream (XES) format. The plugin ships with three available prediction types of next activity, time and risk prediction that can directly be used, however, arbitrary prediction types like forecasting process variables or cost can be added afterwards. Also, the Classifier interface is left generic to allow for an extension with arbitrary prediction algorithms. Out of the box, N-Grams, LSTM neural networks, regression are available inter alia.

While the flexible design allows for a high degree of customization, the wealth of prediction types and prediction algorithms may require extensive background knowledge by end-users to select an optimal prediction method and therefore might hamper the feasibility in practice due to the skill sets of the involved (non-technical) users. Therefore, the core feature of this plugin also includes HPO for combined algorithm search and hyper parameter setting. Classifiers are ranked by an evaluation metric and may be created on the fly. In this way, the optimal classifier type and parameter settings for the company can be determined by the plugin. This is especially useful for the training of predictive models for individual company logs, as the sheer amount of algorithms and hyper parameter settings largely depends on the process definition and the underlying log, which makes it impossible to provide generally suitable parameter settings.

This article will continue with a background section on PPM and optimization. Then, the approach architecture will be introduced in Sect. 3, including data management, different classifier architectures and HPO techniques. Afterwards, the implemented plugin will be demonstrated by showing typical usage examples. To evaluate the feasibility of our approach, results of conducted runtime experiments on real-life datasets will be presented in Sect. 4. Last, the contributions and limitations of this work are concluded in Sect. 5.

---

[1] http://promtools.org/.

[2] https://gitlab.uni-koblenz.de/fg-bks/camunda-ppm-hpo/.

[3] https://camunda.com/case-studies/.

2   Background

As a couple of PPM approaches appeared in the last ten years, there also exist detailed literature reviews [5,11]. [11] illustrates the importance of the research area by showing the growing amount of related publications from 2010 to 2016. Furthermore, from [5], it can be observed that neural networks are frequently used for next activity predictions. Another discovery is that the preponderance of implementations are realized with WEKA [7] or ProM-Tools[4]. Nonetheless, both articles conclude with addressing the need for practical implementations.

2.1   Predictive Process Monitoring

PPM is performed on historic data from process executions, which is usually stored in the XES log standard. An event log $\mathcal{L}$ is a collection of traces $\tau_{0...n}$ from distinct process instances, i.e., possible traversals through a process model. Each trace τ consists of events $e_{1...m}$, such as conducting an activity or receiving a message. Moreover, an event can store additional properties like the assigned employee. In order to make predictions on an event log, the log data has to be encoded to subsequently train a predictive model. Then, depending on its configuration and capabilities, the classifier returns a prediction such as the probability of a task to occur next, the remaining time or the risk to fail. Taylored solutions may also include linear temporal logic business rules [10], alarm based risk models [12] or additional preprocessing steps like clustering [4]. For the actual training process, it is common to split the available data into a training and a validation set. Hence, one can train the classifier on the training set and can calculate a quality metric or a loss function for the validation set.

When training a model, the training process itself often depends on hyper parameters. For instance, neural networks require a variety of parameters such as the number of epochs. Research in machine learning has shown that the outcome of a prediction algorithm may largely depend on its configuration and the underlying data set. Therefore, parameter optimization is an important challenge in the scope of achieving more accurate predictions.

2.2   Hyper Parameter Optimization

The configuration space for a machine learning algorithm $\mathcal{A}$ with N hyper parameters is denoted as $\Lambda = \Lambda_1 \times \Lambda_2 ... \Lambda_N$ where Λ_n is the domain of the n-th hyper parameter. The domain can be real-valued, ordinal, binary or categorical. An instance of $\mathcal{A}$ to a vector of hyper parameters $\lambda \in \Lambda$ is written as $\mathcal{A}_\lambda$. For a given data set D, the optimization problem can be formulated as:

$$\lambda^* = \mathrm{argmin}_{\lambda \in \Lambda} \mathbb{E}_{(\mathcal{D}_{train}, \mathcal{D}_{valid} \sim \mathcal{D})} \mathbf{V}(L, \mathcal{A}_\lambda, \mathcal{D}_{train}, \mathcal{D}_{valid}) \qquad (1)$$

where $\mathbf{V}(L, \mathcal{A}_\lambda, \mathcal{D}_{train}, \mathcal{D}_{valid})$ is the loss the algorithm $\mathcal{A}_\lambda$ trained on $\mathcal{D}_{train}$ and validated on $\mathcal{D}_{valid}$. Typically used loss functions are sum of squared error

---

[4] https://www.promtools.org/doku.php.

or misclassification rate. Vice versa, a quality metric like accuracy can be maximized. For conducting an actual optimization, different strategies such as Grid Search, population-based strategies or bayesian optimization can be applied [6].

Grid Search is the most trivial way to find the minimum of the objective function. It evaluates all permutations of configurations on a finite configuration space and returns the best one. The disadvantage of this simple approach is that the number of executions and the runtime consequently increases dramatically when being applied on a large configuration space. Random Search enhances Grid Search by traversing the configuration space in a random manner for a fixed number of iterations. By design, important parameters are detected faster and evaluated more densely [1].

Population-based strategies like evolutionary algorithms are initialized with a random set of configurations. Thereupon, genetic operations such as crossover, mutation and elitism are applied to generate a new set of configurations. A fixed number of generations or a saturating loss rate forces the algorithm to terminate. The most popular genetic algorithm for HPO is CMA-ES [8], whereas a current genetic algorithm for the PPM domain can be found in [3].

Bayesian Optimization tackles the problem that a configuration space may become infinitely large by creating a model that predicts the best possible configuration. Initially, the model is build on a randomly selected set of configurations considering the observed loss rates. In the following step, the model predicts a configuration that will have a low expected loss rate. Eventually the actual loss rate is evaluated and used to refine the model. The last two steps are replayed iteratively until the loss rate saturates or a maximal number of iterations is reached. The model used for this sequential model based optimization method can be a Gaussian Process [9] or a Tree Parzen Algorithms [2] among others.

A remarkable work in the field of HPO is Auto-WEKA [13], which enables combined selection and HPO for classification algorithms (CASH). Hence, the library is able to find the optimal algorithm with least possible user interaction. Apart from that, the resulting configuration space grows exponentially as WEKA provides 27 base classifier, 10 booster and 2 ensemble learning techniques.

As motivated, HPO is an important aspect in the context of PPM. In the following, we present our developed plugin for applied PPM, allowing for a seamless integration of results from PPM and intuitive HPO in Camunda.

3 Tool Description and Demonstration

The presented plugin is based on a previous plugin (See footnote 2), which equips Camunda with PPM functionalities. While empowering companies with means for PPM may seem beneficial, yet, creating value from a productive plugin for PPM remains a tightrope walk between complexity and usability, as some classifiers depend on a multitude of hyper parameters. Withal, it cannot be assumed that a typical Camunda user disposes of expert knowledge about HPO. Thus, the presented plugin integrates a much needed intuitive HPO functionality to create suitable predictive models.

A new plugin tab in Camunda allows to start a new parameter optimization process, with the goal of finding a) an optimal learning algorithm, and b) the best/suitable parameters for a given process model and the corresponding internal Camunda log. In this way, end-users can be supported in determining optimal algorithms and settings for model training, directly in Camunda.

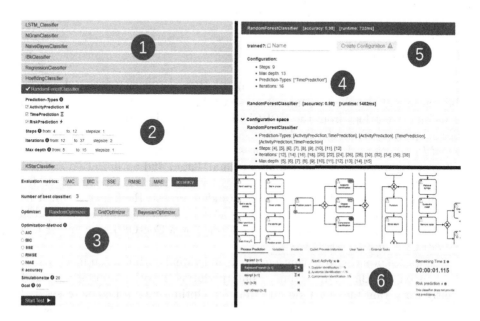

Fig. 1. Steps to find and create the best classifier. Left: Setting configuration space and optimizer. Top right: Selecting and creating a resulting classifier. Bottom right: Prediction in the process view.

Figure 1 shows the user workflow for configuring a new search and deploying the resulting classifier. Different classifier types are included in the search, allowing to compare the suitability of different learning algorithms (1). Note that arbitrary classifiers can be added if needed. Then, for each classifier type, certain ranges for the respective parameters can be specified as a general search space (2). Reasonable ranges for the hyper parameter configurations are provided as a default so that an inexperienced user only has to select which classifier should be included. Regarding the subsequent optimization process, the user may choose and customize the evaluation metrics, as well as the optimization algorithm (3). If the whole configuration space should be tested, the user can use Grid Search. Otherwise, Random Search and Bayesian Optimization offer fast and reliable recommendations after only a few iterations. In the current implementation, the model for Bayesian Optimization may be one of Random Forest, Regression or Naive Bayes. Besides that, own optimization algorithms can be added.

After the parameter optimization has been performed, the user is presented with a comprehensive overview of the best learning algorithms and the best respective parameter settings. The user can browse the n best performing configurations and select a suitable model for deployment (4). Also, the underlying parameters for the model configuration are shown. The user can directly select the "create configuration" option (5), which automatically deploys the selected predictive model in the Camunda PPM environment (6).

4   Evaluation

To investigate the feasibility of applying our plugin in an industrial setting, the runtime of the three optimization algorithms was evaluated with the help of real-life event logs from the BPI Challenge 2020[5]. This dataset includes two logs, namely the *Domestic Declarations* dataset (10.500 traces), and the *International Declarations* dataset (6.449 traces). For each dataset, scenarios with three different configuration spaces (small, medium, large) and optimization methods (Grid Optimizer, Random Optimizer, Bayesian Optimizer) were tested on five classifiers (N-Grams, IBk, Naive Bayes, Random Forest, Hoeffding Tree). A file containing the used configuration setting as well as the runtime results can be found online[6]. The experiments were performed on a CentOS Linux Server with i7-3770 CPU and 16 GB RAM.

Figure 2 shows the total runtime of the individual optimization methods. As can be seen, the Bayesian Optimizer outperforms the other approaches significantly w.r.t. runtime. For Grid and Random Optimizer, runtime increases with growing configuration space. Moreover, Table 1 shows the runtime per classifier. Only classifier with large configuration spaces seem to be found faster by the Bayesian Optimizer. For example, the runtime of N-Grams does not differ a lot per optimization method, whereas a considerable speedup can be observed for Random Forest. Noticeably, the model accuracy while using the prediction-based Bayesian Optimizer does not seem to drop significantly as opposed to a brute-force approach via the Grid Optimizer. Thus, based on our results, the Bayesian Optimizer can be recommended, especially w.r.t. runtime.

Because of a lack of computational power, we were not able to include Regression and LSTM classifiers in our evaluation. Especially for the LSTM with its large configuration space and its massive training effort, it would be interesting to determine the computational speedup. As the capabilities of some classifier increase, difficulties arise when one wants to conduct a comparison objectively. Accordingly, further tests may include larger training logs and more sophisticated prediction types such as risk models.

---

[5] https://data.4tu.nl/collections/BPI_Challenge_2020/5065541.
[6] https://gitlab.uni-koblenz.de/fg-bks/camunda-ppm-hpo/blob/master/Resources/tables.pdf.

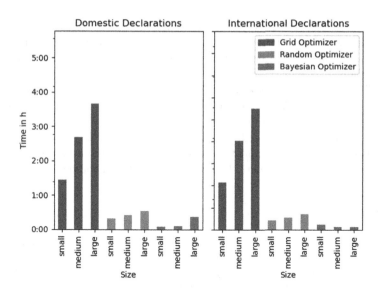

Fig. 2. Runtime evaluation for grouped by dataset, optimizer and size of configuration space.

Table 1. Evaluation of the runtime per classifier. (D: Domestic Declarations, I: International Declarations, G: Grid Optimizer, R: Random Optimizer, B: Bayesian Optimizer, each cell contains runtime in seconds and accuracy in percent)

Data	Opt.	Size	N-Grams	IBk	Naive Bayes	Random Forest	Hoeffding
D	G	Small	.452 s - 98%	685.8 s - 97%	7.79 s - 86%	3705 s - 97%	776.1 s - 91%
D	G	Medium	.565 s - 98%	1042 s - 97%	11.47 s - 87%	7393 s - 97%	1225 s - 91%
D	G	Large	.834 s - 98%	1411 s - 97%	15.07 s - 91%	0272 s - 97%	1495 s - 91%
D	R	Small	.412 s - 98%	667.3 s - 97%	7.462 s - 86%	373.8 s - 97%	83.97 s - 91%
D	R	Medium	.585 s - 98%	1042 s - 97%	11.64 s - 87%	371.1 s - 97%	83.52 s - 91%
D	R	Large	.839 s - 98%	1415 s - 97%	15.58 s - 91%	395.6 s - 97%	83.80 s - 91%
D	B	Small	.408 s - 98%	259.6 s - 97%	7.54 s - 86%	11.20 s - 97%	3.178 s - 91%
D	B	Medium	.568 s - 98%	338.6 s - 97%	3.51 s - 87%	12.87 s - 97%	5.494 s - 91%
D	B	Large	.848 s - 98%	1282 s - 97%	3.85 s - 86%	44.02 s - 97%	3.539 s - 91%
I	G	Small	.634 s - 98%	747.3 s - 96%	11.18 s - 82%	5958 s - 96%	984.2 s - 86%
I	G	Medium	.917 s - 98%	1246 s - 96%	17.53 s - 82%	1702 s - 96%	1557.4 s - 87%
I	G	Large	1.47 s - 98%	168.2 s - 96%	23.03 s - 82%	6218 s - 96%	1881 s - 87%
I	R	Small	.683 s - 98%	762.4 s - 96%	11.11 s - 82%	593.7 s - 96%	108.5 s - 86%
I	R	Medium	.939 s - 98%	1216 s - 96%	17.26 s - 82%	615.9 s - 96%	108.4 s - 87%
I	R	Large	1.47 s - 98%	172.7 s - 96%	22.80 s - 82%	638.5 s - 96%	106.6 s - 87%
I	B	Small	.644 s - 98%	736.3 s - 96%	11.19 s - 82%	21.61 s - 96%	8.46 s - 86%
I	B	Medium	.842 s - 98%	436.9 s - 96%	6.63 s - 82%	15.39 s - 96%	6.44 s - 86%
I	B	Large	1.52 s - 98%	408.9 s - 96%	4.62 s - 82%	18.06 s - 96%	5.25 s - 86%

5   Conclusion

The field of PPM is still developing and solutions for productive environments are still pending. With the introduced plugin, users can effortlessly create powerful and suitable predictive models for immediate predictions, without the need for extensive knowledge on the underlying machine learning algorithms. The direct integration into Camunda promotes a seamless application of predictive process monitoring, without the need for isolated tools and (redundant) data transferals between tools.

Further challenges include the development of additional prediction types like linear temporal logic and further evaluation metrics like Cohen's Kappa. Here again, the trade-off between usability and degrees of freedom must be balanced. Besides, in situations where only little or no training data is available, the results of the HPO are overfitted and thus not meaningful. An integrated simulation environment to create synthetic logs would be useful in these cases.

References

1. Bergstra, J., Bengio, Y.: Random search for hyper-parameter optimization. J. Mach. Learn. Res. **13**(1), 281–305 (2012)
2. Bergstra, J.S., Bardenet, R., Bengio, Y., Kégl, B.: Algorithms for hyper-parameter optimization. In: Advances in Neural Information Processing Systems, pp. 2546–2554 (2011)
3. Di Francescomarino, C., et al.: Genetic algorithms for hyperparameter optimization in predictive business process monitoring. Inf. Syst. **74**, 67–83 (2018)
4. Di Francescomarino, C., Dumas, M., Maggi, F.M., Teinemaa, I.: Clustering-based predictive process monitoring. IEEE Trans. Serv. Comput. **12**, 896–909 (2016)
5. Di Francescomarino, C., Ghidini, C., Maggi, F.M., Milani, F.: Predictive process monitoring methods: which one suits me best? In: Weske, M., Montali, M., Weber, I., vom Brocke, J. (eds.) BPM 2018. LNCS, vol. 11080, pp. 462–479. Springer, Cham (2018). https://doi.org/10.1007/978-3-319-98648-7_27
6. Feurer, M., Hutter, F.: Hyperparameter optimization. In: Hutter, F., Kotthoff, L., Vanschoren, J. (eds.) Automated Machine Learning. TSSCML, pp. 3–33. Springer, Cham (2019). https://doi.org/10.1007/978-3-030-05318-5_1
7. Frank, E., Hall, M.A., Witten, I.H.: The WEKA Workbench. M. Kaufmann (2016)
8. Friedrichs, F., Igel, C.: Evolutionary tuning of multiple SVM parameters. Neurocomputing **64**, 107–117 (2005)
9. Hutter, F., Lücke, J., Schmidt-Thieme, L.: Beyond manual tuning of hyperparameters. KI-Künstliche Intelligenz **29**(4), 329–337 (2015)
10. Maggi, F.M., Di Francescomarino, C., Dumas, M., Ghidini, C.: Predictive monitoring of business processes. In: Jarke, M., et al. (eds.) CAiSE 2014. LNCS, vol. 8484, pp. 457–472. Springer, Cham (2014). https://doi.org/10.1007/978-3-319-07881-6_31
11. Márquez-Chamorro, A.E., Resinas, M., Ruiz-Cortes, A.: Predictive monitoring of business processes: a survey. IEEE Trans. Serv. Comput. **11**(6), 962–977 (2017)
12. Teinemaa, I., Tax, N., de Leoni, M., Dumas, M., Maggi, F.M.: Alarm-based prescriptive process monitoring. In: Weske, M., Montali, M., Weber, I., vom Brocke, J. (eds.) BPM 2018. LNBIP, vol. 329, pp. 91–107. Springer, Cham (2018). https://doi.org/10.1007/978-3-319-98651-7_6
13. Thornton, C., Hutter, F., Hoos, H.H., Leyton-Brown, K.: Auto-WEKA: combined selection and hyperparameter optimization of classification algorithms. In: Proceedings of the 19th ACM SIGKDD International Conference on Knowledge Discovery and Data Mining, pp. 847–855 (2013)

SmartRPA: A Tool to Reactively Synthesize Software Robots from User Interface Logs

Simone Agostinelli$^{(\boxtimes)}$, Marco Lupia, Andrea Marrella, and Massimo Mecella

Sapienza Universitá di Roma, Rome, Italy
{agostinelli,marrella,mecella}@diag.uniroma1.it,
lupia.1694700@studenti.uniroma1.it

Abstract. Robotic Process Automation (RPA) is an emerging technology that automates intensive routine tasks (or simply *routines*) previously performed by a human user on the User Interface (UI) of a computer system, by means of a software (SW) robot. To date, RPA tools available in the market strongly relies on the ability of human experts to manually implement the routines to automate. Being the current practice time-consuming and error-prone, in this paper we present SmartRPA, a cross-platform software tool that tackles such issues by exploiting UI logs keeping track of many routine executions to generate executable RPA scripts that automate the routines enactment by SW robots.

1 Introduction

Robotic Process Automation (RPA) is an automation technology that operates on the user interface (UI) of software applications and replicates, by means of a software (SW) robot, mouse and keyboard interactions to remove high-volume routine tasks (a.k.a. *routines*) [3]. To take full advantage of this technology in the early stages of the RPA life-cycle, organizations leverage the support of skilled human experts to:

1. identify the candidate routines to automate by means of interviews and observation of workers conducting their daily work;
2. record the interactions that take place during routines' enactment on the UI of SW applications into dedicated *UI logs*, which are mainly used for debugging purposes only;
3. manually specify their conceptual and technical structure (often in form of flowchart diagrams), which will drive the development of dedicated *RPA scripts* reflecting the behavior of SW robots.

While this approach has proven to be effective to execute rule-based and well-structured routines [5], it becomes time-consuming and error-prone in presence of routines that are less deterministic and require decisions [7].

In this paper, we tackle the above issue by presenting SmartRPA, an open-source software tool that is able to reason over the UI logs keeping track of many

S. Nurcan and A. Korthaus (Eds.): CAiSE Forum 2021, LNBIP 424, pp. 137–145, 2021.
https://doi.org/10.1007/978-3-030-79108-7_16

routine executions (cf. step 2), and to automatically synthesize SW robots that emulate the most suitable routine variant for any specific intermediate user input that is required during the routine execution, thus skipping completely the manual modeling activity of the flowchart diagrams (cf. step 3). SmartRPA implements the approach presented in [2] and is available for download at https://github.com/bpm-diag/smartRPA/.

The rest of the paper is organized as follows. Section 2 introduces a running example. Section 3 presents the tool architecture and the technical aspects of SmartRPA. Section 4 discusses some experiments performed to evaluate the robustness and feasibility of the tool. Finally, Sect. 5 concludes the paper.

2   Running Example

Below, we introduce a real-life scenario used to explain the functioning of our tool. The example is inspired by the work performed by the Administration Office of the Department of Computer, Control and Management Engineering (DIAG) of Sapienza Università di Roma, which consists of filling the travel authorization request form made by the personnel of DIAG for travel requiring prior approval. We specifically consider the task of filling a well-structured Excel spreadsheet (cf. Fig. 1(a)), manually performed by a request applicant that provides some personal information together with further information related to the travel. Then, the spreadsheet is sent via email to an employee of the Administration Office of DIAG, which is in charge of processing the request: for each row in the spreadsheet, the employee manually copies every cell in that row and pastes that into the corresponding text field in a dedicated Google form (cf. Fig. 1(b)). In addition, if the request applicant declares the need to use a personal car as one of the means of transport for the travel (by filling the dedicated row labeled with "Car" in the spreadsheet), then the employee has to activate the request on the Google form (in this case, a dialog box labeled "Own car request" appears on the UI, cf. Fig. 1(b)) and then accept or reject the personal car request. When the data transfer for a given travel authorization request has been completed, the employee presses the "Submit" button to confirm data and submit them into an internal database. Finally, a confirmation email is sent automatically to the applicant when data are submitted.

The above routine procedure (in the following, we will denote it as R) is usually performed manually, it is tedious (as it must be repeated for any new travel request) and prone to errors. A proper execution of R requires a path on the UI made by the following user actions:[1]

- loginMail, to access the client email;
- accessMail, to access the specific email with the travel request;
- downloadAttachment, to download the Excel file including the travel request;
- openWorkbook, to open the Excel spreadsheet;

---

[1] Note that the user actions recorded in a UI log can have a finer granularity than the high-level ones used here just with the purpose of describing the routine's behaviour.

(a) Excel spreadsheet   (b) Google form

Fig. 1. UIs involved in the running example

- openGoogleForm, to access the Google Form to be filled;
- getExcelCell, to select the cell in the i-th row of the Excel spreadsheet;
- copy, to copy the content of the selected cell;
- clickGoogleFormTextField, to select the specific text field of the Google form;
- paste, to paste the content of the cell into a text field of the Google form;
- activateCarRequest, to activate in the Google form the dialog box for approving or rejecting the car request;
- accept, to press the button on the Google form that approves the request;
- reject, to press the button on the Google form that rejects the request;
- formSubmit, to finally submit the Google form to the internal database.

The user actions openWorkbook and openGoogleForm can be performed in any order. Moreover, the sequence of actions ⟨getCell, copy, clickTextField, paste⟩ can be repeated for any travel information to be moved from the Excel spreadsheet to the Google form. Finally, in case of a car request to be evaluated (action activateCarRequest), the execution of accept or reject is exclusive.

3   SmartRPA Architecture

In this section, we give a detailed description of the architecture of SmartRPA (see Fig. 2) that consists in five main SW components implemented in Python.

The first SW component of the architecture is an **Action Logger** able to record different types of UI actions from multiple SW applications during the enactment of the routine under study. Specifically, a training session in which several users perform the routine to be automated is required to record the UI actions involved in its execution. The Action Logger provides a Graphical User

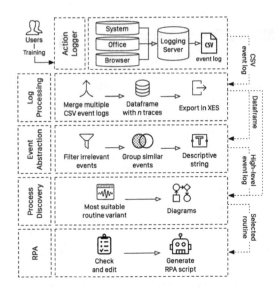

Fig. 2. SmartRPA architecture

Interface (GUI) that allows a user to select which SW applications s/he wants to record UI actions on (cf. Fig. 3). The Action Logger provides three different types of logging modules: *(i)* a *System Logger* able to detect those UI actions not related to specific SW applications, *(ii)* an *Office Logger* able to detect the UI actions performed within Microsoft Office applications, and *(iii)* a *Browser Logger* able to detect the UI actions on web browsers.

The UI actions recorded by the logging modules are sent to a Logging Server, implemented with the *Flask* framework,[2] in charge to store and organize them as *events* into several CSV event logs, i.e., the UI logs.

The exact steps to correctly perform R (cf. Sect. 2) are the following ones:

1. Open the Action Logger, tick the checkboxes related to Excel, Clipboard and the browser installed on the applicant's PC/MAC, and click *"Start logger"*.
2. Open the Excel spreadsheet containing the information about the travel.
3. Open the Google form.
4. Copy and paste each value from the Excel spreadsheet to the Google form.
5. Accept or reject the personal car request (if required).
6. Submit the form. Once done, a confirmation email is sent to the applicant.
7. Push the *"Stop logger"* button to stop the Action Logger.

It is worth noticing that multiple users can run the Action Logger on their computer system many times performing R in different training sessions. Each CSV event log contains exactly one long trace of UI actions performed in a single training session by a single user. Technically speaking, *(i)* system events are

---

[2] https://palletsprojects.com/p/flask.

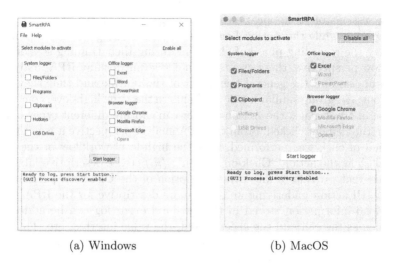

(a) Windows   (b) MacOS

Fig. 3. GUI of SmartRPA both on Windows and MacOS

captured using *PythonCOM* (for Windows APIs and COM objects) and *MacF-SEvents* (for MacOS); *(ii)* events generated by Microsoft Office applications are captured using the Office JavaScript APIs; and *(iii)* browser events are captured using JavaScript web extensions developed for each supported web browser.

The second SW component of the architecture is the **Log Processing** tool that is triggered when any training session is considered as completed. Specifically, after n training sessions, the Logging Server will deliver the n created CSV event logs to the Log Processing component, in charge of import them into a single Pandas dataframe.[3] A dataframe is a two-dimensional size-mutable and heterogeneous tabular data structure with labeled axes, which is used as the main artifact to represent event logs in SmartRPA. The dataframe created by the Log Processing component consists of low-level events with fine granularity associated one-by-one to a recorded UI action, including several columns representing the payload of the recorded event, i.e.: the timestamp, the application that generated the event, the resources involved, etc. SmartRPA is also able to produce a XES[4] (eXtensible Event Stream) version of the datastream that will contain exactly n traces, one for each recorded CSV event log and can be inspected using the most popular process mining tools, such as *ProM*,[5] or *Disco*[6].

The third SW component is an **Event Abstraction** engine used to produce a high-level event log from the low-level one with the goal to: *(i)* filter out noise and irrelevant events for the routine execution. For example, during several

---

[3] https://pandas.pydata.org/.

[4] XES is the standard for the storage, interchange, and analysis of event logs.

[5] http://www.promtools.org/.

[6] https://fluxicon.com/disco/.

training sessions of R, applications related to the operating system may start in background while the Action Logger is being recording the UI log, and they may dirty the recording phase of the users during their training session. From a workflow perspective, these events are not relevant for any RPA analyst that aims to understand the general behaviour of the routine and thus they can be filtered out; *(ii)* group similar low-level events to the same high-level concept. For example, in a web page, the Action Logger can capture different types of clicks, based on the element clicked. From the RPA analyst perspective it is not relevant what kind of click was performed, thus the high-level workflow of the routine may just show the action "Click on button"; *(iii)* create descriptive labels. Any recorded event provides a low-level description of the UI action performed. To make the UI action underlying an event more descriptive for the RPA analyst, the payload information stored in the low-level event log can be added to its label, such as the cell and the sheet edited, the value inserted, etc. This allows us to create a more descriptive label for any event in the high-level event log, e.g., *"Edit cell B2 on Sheet 'Request' with value 'Full Professor'"*.

At this point, the **Process Discovery** component exploits the high-level event log to derive the underlying high-level workflow as a Directly-Follows Graph (DFG), by applying the heuristic miner (the decision to employ the heuristic miner has been driven by its ability to discover highly understandable flowcharts from a BPM analyst perspective [1]) implemented in PM4PY [4]. In addition, the knowledge of the workflow underlying the routine, coupled with the low-level version of the dataframe-based event log, will be used to support the identification of different *variation points*, thus leading to the detection of the most suitable routine variant according to intermediate user inputs observed in the low-level dataframe-based event log. A variation point is a point in the routine execution where a user choice needs to be made between multiple possible variants. For example, the routine under analysis in Sect. 2 consists of one variation point that contains three different user inputs that can led to three different routine variants of R: *(i)* the user performs the UI action `activateCarRequest` by clicking 'No' on the Google form, *(ii)* the user first performs the UI action `activateCarRequest` and then the UI action `accept`, *(iii)* the user first performs the UI action `activateCarRequest` and then the UI action `reject`.

Once the routine variant to automatize is selected, before its enactment with a SW robot, it is possible for an RPA analyst to personalize the values stored in its events, thanks to the **Script Generation** component. SmartRPA automatically detects the events that can be edited, such as pasting a text or editing an Excel cell, and let the RPA analyst editing them. After confirmation, the low-level dataframe-based event log is updated. Finally, the Python executable script based on the selected routine variant and updated with the RPA analyst's edits, is generated by scanning the recorded low-level events in the dataframe-based log and converting them into executable pieces of SW code in Python. The script generation component relies on *Automagica*[7] and *Selenium*,[8] a popu-

---

[7] https://github.com/automagica/automagica.
[8] https://www.selenium.dev/.

Table 1. Experimental results for the *synthetic* case study for logs with 1000 routine executions. The time (in *milliseconds*) is the average per trace.

Event size: 40	Time				
Trace size	1	2	3	4	5
25	0.453	0.452	0.53	0.409	0.423
50	0.417	0.433	0.417	0.425	0.419
75	0.439	0.511	0.424	0.43	0.431
100	0.454	0.416	0.421	0.424	0.431
Event size: 80	Time				
Trace size	1	2	3	4	5
25	0.422	0.428	0.43	0.413	0.412
50	0.427	0.425	0.444	0.417	0.428
75	0.42	0.428	0.553	0.422	0.437
100	0.442	0.434	0.428	0.438	0.432
Event size: 120	Time				
Trace size	1	2	3	4	5
25	0.413	0.507	0.421	0.416	0.421
50	0.421	0.412	0.417	0.42	0.421
75	0.425	0.433	0.438	0.451	0.429
100	0.437	0.433	0.428	0.532	0.523

lar suite of tools for process and web browsers automation. Note that the Script Generation component considers only the platform where the SW robot is going to be run regardless of the operating system used to record the log, thus achieving cross-platform compatibility. SmartRPA is also able to generate RPA scripts compatible with the commercial tool *UiPath Studio*.[9]

4   Evaluation

SmartRPA has been tested using synthetic experiments employing UI logs of increasing complexity. We generated 240 different UI logs (containing in total 150.000 different routine executions), in a way that each UI log was characterized through a unique configuration obtained by varying the following input settings:

- *log_size*: number of routine executions in the UI log (250/500/750/1000);
- *trace_size*: number of events in each routine execution (25/50/75/100);
- *events_size*: number of possible different events to be considered for the creation of a trace (40/80/120);
- *variation_points*: number of variation points in the UI log (1/2/3/4/5).

---

[9] https://www.uipath.com/product/studio.

The amount of possible decisions to be taken in a variation point was generated randomly, ranging from 2 to 10 possible outgoing decisions. The synthetic UI logs generated for the test are available at: https://github.com/bpm-diag/smartRPA/. The target was to investigate if the amount and anatomy of variation points discovered by SmartRPA is the same that was syntetically introduced in the sample routine executions recorded in the UI logs (i.e., *robustness*), and to measure the performance of the tool to generate a SW robot by solely using the UI logs (i.e., *feasibility*). Concerning the robustness of the tool, for all the 240 tested logs the tool was able to always discover the correct variation points to be considered for the synthesis of SW robots. Concerning the feasibility, it was measured in terms of the computation time required to generate a SW robot starting from UI logs of growing complexity. The results, which are summarized in Table 1,[10] indicate that the tool scales well in case of an increasing number of variation points and routine executions/alphabet of events of growing size.

5   Concluding Remarks

SmartRPA offers an innovative contribution to RPA technology with the goal of mitigating some of its core downsides related to the implementation of SW robots made by expert users. Close to SmartRPA there is Robidium [6], a tool that generates RPA scripts based on the *most frequent* routine variant observed in the UI log. Conversely, SmartRPA enables to generate the *best observed* routine variant, employing the input conditions available before the routine enactment. The main weakness of SmartRPA is correlated with the quality of information recorded in real-world UI logs. Since a UI log is fine-grained, routines executed with many different strategies may potentially affect the robustness of our tool to the detection of variation points. For this reason, as a future work, we are going to perform a robust evaluation of the tool on real-world case studies including heterogeneous UI logs obtained from different application domains.

Acknowledgments. This work has been supported by the "Dipartimento di Eccellenza" grant, the H2020 project DataCloud and the Sapienza grant BPbots.

References

1. Agostinelli, S., Maggi, F.M., Marrella, A., Milani, F.: A user evaluation of process discovery algorithms in a software engineering company. In: EDOC (2019)
2. Agostinelli, S., Lupia, M., Marrella, A., Mecella, M.: Automated generation of executable RPA scripts from user interface logs. In: Asatiani, A., et al. (eds.) BPM 2020. LNBIP, vol. 393, pp. 116–131. Springer, Cham (2020). https://doi.org/10.1007/978-3-030-58779-6_8

---

[10] For the sake of space, the table includes only the results related to UI logs containing 1000 routine executions.

3. Agostinelli, S., Marrella, A., Mecella, M.: Research challenges for intelligent robotic process automation. In: Di Francescomarino, C., Dijkman, R., Zdun, U. (eds.) BPM 2019. LNBIP, vol. 362, pp. 12–18. Springer, Cham (2019). https://doi.org/10.1007/978-3-030-37453-2_2
4. Berti, A., van Zelst, S.J., van der Aalst, W.: Process Mining for Python (PM4Py): Bridging the Gap Between Process and Data Science (2019)
5. Jimenez-Ramirez, A., Reijers, H.A., Barba, I., Del Valle, C.: A method to improve the early stages of the robotic process automation lifecycle. In: Giorgini, P., Weber, B. (eds.) CAiSE 2019. LNCS, vol. 11483, pp. 446–461. Springer, Cham (2019). https://doi.org/10.1007/978-3-030-21290-2_28
6. Leno, V., Deviatykh, S., Polyvyanyy, A., La Rosa, M., Dumas, M., Maggi, F.M.: Robidium: automated synthesis of robotic process automation scripts from UI logs. In: BPM Demonstration Track (2020)
7. Marrella, A., Mecella, M., Sardiña, S.: Supporting adaptiveness of cyber-physical processes through action-based formalisms. AI Commun. **31**(1), 47–74 (2018)

PatternLens: Inferring evolutive patterns from web API usage logs

Rediana Koçi[✉], Xavier Franch[✉], Petar Jovanovic[✉], and Alberto Abelló[✉]

Universitat Politècnica de Catalunya, BarcelonaTech, Barcelona, Spain
{koci,franch,petar,aabello}@essi.upc.edu

Abstract. The use of web Application Programming Interfaces (WAPIs) has experienced a boost in recent years. Developers (i.e., WAPI consumers) are continuously relying on third-party WAPIs to incorporate certain features into their applications. Consequently, WAPI evolution becomes more challenging in terms of the service provided according to consumers' needs. When deciding on which changes to perform, besides several dynamic business requirements (from the organization whose data are exposed), WAPI providers should take into account the way consumers use the WAPI. While consumers may report various bugs or may request new endpoints, their feedback may be partial and biased (based on the specific endpoints they use). Alternatively, WAPI providers could exploit the interaction between consumers and WAPIs, which is recorded in the WAPI usage logs, generated while consumers access the WAPI. In this direction, this paper presents PatternLens, a tool with the aim of supporting providers in planning the changes by analyzing WAPI usage logs. With the use of process mining techniques, this tool infers from the logs a set of usage patterns (e.g., endpoints that are frequently called one after the other), whose occurrences imply the need for potential changes (e.g., merging the two endpoints). The WAPI providers can accept or reject the suggested patterns, which will be displayed together with informative metrics. These metrics will help providers in the decision-making, by giving them information about the consequences of accepting/rejecting the suggestions.

Keywords: Web API evolution · Pattern detection · Process mining · Web API change

1 Introduction

As the use of web Application Programming Interfaces (WAPIs) is increasingly growing, their evolution becomes more challenging in terms of the service provided according to consumers' needs. While a lot of effort is put in analyzing consumers' struggles when WAPIs change [4,5,7], little is known about providers' burdens: what, how, and when to evolve [1]. When deciding on which changes to perform, besides several business requirements (from the organization whose data are exposed), providers should take into account the way consumers use

S. Nurcan and A. Korthaus (Eds.): CAiSE Forum 2021, LNBIP 424, pp. 146–153, 2021.
https://doi.org/10.1007/978-3-030-79108-7_17

the WAPI. Moreover, knowing the impact that changes usually cause to the consumers, they have to strike a balance between not imposing irrelevant, unexpected, frequent changes and providing an up-to-date, maintainable, bug-free WAPI, that fulfills their needs [3].

While consumers may report various bugs or may request new endpoints (i.e., URLs to access WAPIs resources), their feedback may be partial and biased (based on the specific endpoints they use), as well as difficult to gather and interpret at scale [9]. Alternatively, WAPI providers could exploit the interaction between consumers and WAPIs, which is recorded in the WAPI usage logs, generated while consumers access the WAPI. Every time a consumer application makes a request, a log entry is generated and stored in the usage log file. Therefore, consumers' behavior is recorded in these logs, and their analysis can obliquely reveal consumers' needs for new features hidden under several workarounds (solutions found by WAPI users that allow them to get data, functionality, or features they need, but that are not yet implemented by providers), or find room for potential improvements.

As applications are the actual WAPI consumers, we should consider the different ways they consume WAPIs over their own lifecycle. Basically, applications interact with the WAPIs during design time and runtime, over both of which they manifest different aspects of their behavior. Following on from this, we distinguish two types of logs: (i) development logs, generated while developers build and test their applications and (ii) production logs, generated while applications are being used by end users, meaning that the WAPI requests are predetermined by the implemented functionalities of the applications. We make this distinction as each of these log types, even though provide useful information about WAPI consumption, can be analyzed in different ways. But how much are these logs used and analyzed, beyond the typical traffic monitoring? Several works [2,8] suggest analyzing development logs to measure the usability of WAPIs and thus perform changes that increase the perceived usability from consumers point of view. In addition, there are various WAPI monitoring tools available that take as input the WAPI usage logs, but they are mostly oriented toward providing reporting dashboards or automatic alerting in case of WAPI failure [10]. Providers have all this potentially insightful, large volume of data that is being generated, but not enough proactively used for evolution.

To address the problem of understanding consumers' needs, we present PatternLens, a tool that aims to support providers in planning the changes by analyzing consumers behavior recorded in the WAPI usage logs. We make use of process mining techniques and compute from the logs a set of metrics regarding the real consumption of WAPI endpoints by consumers, like the calling frequency of the endpoints, the frequency of a sequence of endpoints, etc. Using these metrics and a pre-defined set of patterns, we detect from the logs all the patterns, whose occurrences imply the need for potential changes (e.g., merging two endpoints called always one after the other). The WAPI providers can accept or reject the suggested patterns, which will be displayed together with informative metrics, helping providers in the decision-making.

2   Background: Process Mining in the WAPI Context

Process mining is a process-oriented data mining discipline that uses event logs to extract process-related knowledge. We give the definition of some fundamental concepts of process mining, as presented by Van der Aalst [6], adapt them to the WAPI domain, and use them to give the definition of concepts referred in the rest of the paper:

- *Activity* - a specific step in the process. For WAPIs, activities are calls to the endpoints, i.e., the WAPI resources URL.
- *Case* - a process instance. We refer as a case to a set of requests that an application is submitting to the WAPI during a certain time period, commonly referred as session.
- *Event* - an activity occurrence. An event refers to an activity and belongs to a specific case. We refer to WAPI requests as events, and identify them by activity names (request method like GET, POST, and the endpoint).
- *Event log* - a set of cases. A WAPI usage log contains all the requests (i.e., events) that consumers (i.e., applications) make against the WAPI.

Using these concepts, we define a sequence as an ordered occurrence of events within a case, and a pattern as a frequent sequence that when fulfilling some pre-defined conditions, indicates the need for a specific change.

In order to apply process mining, an event log should have at least three attributes: (i) case identifier that identifies the case to whom each event belongs, (ii) activity name that identifies each event, and (iii) timestamp that indicates the time when an event occurs. The presence of these three attributes allows to infer process insights from the event log. Certainly, other attributes that might store additional information about the events (e.g., device IP, application ID, status code), whenever available, add value to the analysis.

In the WAPI context, process discovery consists on creating a graph-based process model from the event log, where nodes represent the endpoints being called, and edges the calling sequence of two endpoints. Even though we do not visualize the process model, we aim at gathering statistical information about it (e.g., the frequency of calling one endpoint after another).

3   PatternLens Overview

PatternLens takes as input the usage log file (i.e., event log) containing all the WAPI calls from several consumers' applications. We assume that the logs are already cleaned and prepared, meaning that (i) every event (i.e., request) belongs to one case (i.e., session), (ii) every event has a distinct timestamp, making able to build the right sequence of calls, and (iii) the activities' names are precise enough to identify each process step, so that no two different process steps to appear with the same activity name, and at the same time no the same process step to appear with different activity names.

Based on process mining concepts, the tool first computes a set of metrics for each WAPI endpoint and sequence of endpoints as appearing in the file. Then, using a pre-defined set of patterns and the computed metrics, it detects and displays to the users all the patterns, of different types. Along each pattern, the users are presented with the suggested changes that the patterns imply, as well as various metrics that might help them in selecting the patterns that better fit their interest. The users are given the possibility to accept the patterns that are interesting to them (i.e., the implied changes are feasible from the providers point of view and would really improve the WAPI with regard to consumers' needs), reject the ones that do not seem interesting, or ignore the ones for whom they are neutral or do not have any conscious thought. We want to note that PatternLens is designed to be used by WAPI providers in analyzing consumers' behavior. As such, we assume that its users (i.e., providers) have a strong prior knowledge of the WAPI, needed in order to proper accept/reject patterns and the recommended changes. In the following, we introduce and explain two main parts of the tool: the metrics calculator and the patterns detector (see Fig. 1).

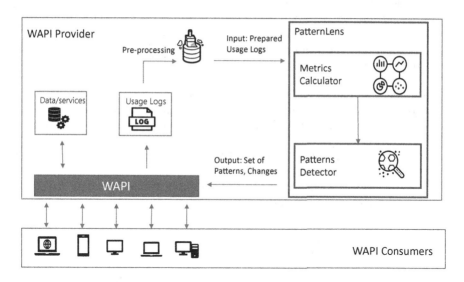

Fig. 1. PatternLens in the full context of WAPI - consumers interaction

3.1   Metrics Calculator

PatternLens considers the interaction between consumers and WAPI as a process. As such, to build the process model, we refer to the process activities (calling method and endpoint) as nodes, and to the order two endpoints are being called by the consumers, as edges. Before detecting the patterns, PatternLens defines all the nodes and edges, by extracting for each of them a set of attributes and computing some metrics (Fig. 2).

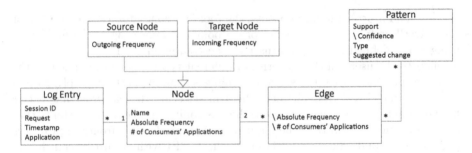

Fig. 2. PatternLens: class diagram

For the nodes we compute and make use of the following metrics:

– *Absolute frequency:* total number of times that an endpoint was called.
– *Incoming frequency* (for target nodes): total number of times that an endpoint was called after other endpoints.
– *Outgoing frequency* (for source nodes): total number of times that an endpoint was called before other endpoints.
– *# Consumers' application:* the number of applications that have called the endpoint in study.

Each edge combines two nodes: a source node (i.e., the first called endpoint in a two-node sequence), and a target node (the second called endpoint in a two-node sequence). We define the edges by the following derived metrics:

– *Absolute frequency:* total number of times that a sequence of endpoints was followed.
– *# Consumers' application:* the number of applications that have called the sequence of endpoints in study.

3.2   Patterns Detector

Instead of visualizing the process map with all the sequences of calls, we filter only those parts of the process, where we see a specific behavior of the way consumers use the WAPI. We pre-define the set of patterns, whose occurrence may imply the need for potential changes, rather than extracting all the frequent patterns from the model to redundantly display them to WAPI providers without giving any hints on the behavior these patterns manifest.

To measure the effectiveness of the patterns, we use two basic concepts from association rules, namely the support and confidence metrics, and adapt them in the context of our approach. We refer as *support* to the number of times a pattern appears in the log file. We give the users the possibility to enter the desired minimum support, based on the size of the file they upload and how specific or general they want the patterns to be. We refer as *confidence* to the relative frequency of the patterns, regarding the source and the target node. As such, if a pattern has a high support (i.e., high absolute frequency: it appears too often in the log file), but this frequency is too low comparing with the absolute frequency of the source and the target nodes, then the pattern will have a low confidence. The tool presents the patterns to the users in a tabular form as in Fig. 3.

Confidence ↑	Type	Source	Target	Affected consumers	Accept/Ignore
0.99	Type 4: Split	GET api/system/tasks/EVENT_IMPORT	GET api/system/tasks/EVENT_IMPORT	5	☑ ✕
0.98	Type 4: Split	GET api/system/tasks/ANALYTICSTABLE_UPDATE	GET api/system/tasks/ANALYTICSTABLE_UPDATE	5	☑ ✕
0.94	Type 4: Split	GET api/system/tasks/ANALYTICS_TABLE	GET api/system/tasks/ANALYTICS_TABLE	5	☑ ✕
0.92	Type 4: Split	GET api/dataElementOperands	GET api/dataElementOperands	8	☑ ✕
0.92	Type 1: Merge	GET api/programIndicators	GET api/programRules	10	☑ ✕
0.92	Type 1: Merge	GET dhis-web-commons/security/login.action	GET api/system/tasks/DATAVALUE_IMPORT	1	☑ ✕
0.91	Type 4: Split	GET api/dataElements/ID	GET api/dataElements/ID	2	☑ ✕

« Previous 1 2 3 4 5 .. 67 Next »

Fig. 3. PatternLens: application interface

We add to each pattern the metrics related to the pattern or the source/target nodes (e.g., confidence, absolute frequency, number of applications where the pattern appears), to better inform the users about the occurrence of the pattern and help them in better understanding consumers' behavior. Along to the patterns, we give a short description of the implied changes (e.g., merging the two endpoints, creating a new attribute).

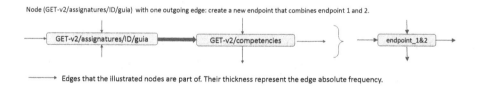

Fig. 4. The pattern and the change it implies

Figure 4 gives an example of a pattern that the tool is able to detect. Figure 5 depicts how PatternLens displays the pattern. As seen from the Fig. 4, the GET-v2/assignatures/ID/guia endpoint, responsible to get data about specific courses in university (source node), has one outgoing edge, the one toward

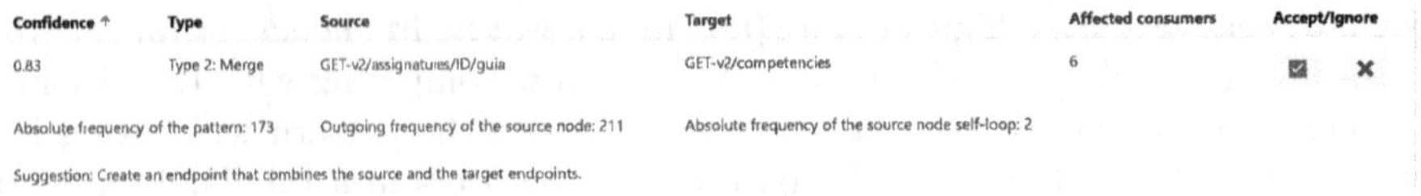

Confidence ↑	Type	Source	Target	Affected consumers	Accept/Ignore
0.83	Type 2: Merge	GET-v2/assignatures/ID/guia	GET-v2/competencies	6	☑ ✖

Absolute frequency of the pattern: 173   Outgoing frequency of the source node: 211   Absolute frequency of the source node self-loop: 2

Suggestion: Create an endpoint that combines the source and the target endpoints.

Fig. 5. The pattern as displayed in PatternLens

GET-v2/competencies, responsible to get data about the required competencies to take a course (target node). This means that after getting information about a specific subject, consumers always call the endpoint for the competencies of the course. For this reason, we suggest merging these two endpoints in one, that combines the data from both of them, reducing this way the number of calls consumers have to submit to get the desired data. PatternLens is able to detect this type of pattern, and displays it as in Fig. 5. Along the pattern, that is defined by the source and target node, the user is informed about the confidence of the pattern ($confidence = \frac{edge\_abs\_freq}{out\_freq_s - self\_freq_s} = \frac{173}{211-2} = 0.83$), the pattern absolute frequency, the outgoing frequency of the source node, the frequency of the source node self-loop, and the change implied by the pattern. The shown metrics are different for every type of pattern, as the tool presents the most relevant ones depending on the way the pattern is being detected.

4 Onsite Demonstration

In the onsite demonstration, we will present the functionality of PatternLens using log files from two real world examples of different domain, namely health and education. The first log file comes from the District Health Information Software 2 (DHIS2) WAPI. DHIS2 is an open source, web-based health management information system platform used worldwide from various institutions and NGOs for data entry, data quality checks and reporting. It has an open REST WAPI, used by more than 60 native applications. The second log file belongs to WAPI of the Barcelona School of Informatics at the Polytechnic University of Catalonia (Facultat d'Informàtica de Barcelona, FIB, UPC). It is built under REST architecture and is mainly being used by the FIB website, monitoring systems, school news' screen, and several applications created for academic purpose. The API provides a set of endpoints for extracting data about departments, courses, exams, rooms reservations, etc. With these two examples, we aim to show that PatternLens performs the same, despite the domain of the WAPI.

Currently, PatternLens is able to detect four different pattern types. As we assume that the users of the tool should have prior knowledge of the WAPI to decide on accepting or rejecting a pattern, and as the demo participants are not expected to be familiar with our examples, we will encourage the participants to evaluate the usability of the tool. Nevertheless, all the elements of the tool and the examples, will be well-explained, so that non WAPI experts can assess the potential of PatternLens in supporting providers in planning WAPI evolution.

5   Future Work

We aim to further extend the PatternLens features in the following directions:

- Provide the users with more types of patterns.
- Quantify the impact that the suggested changes may cause, if the providers decide to implement them. We plan to measure the effectiveness of the changes by predicting the excepted behavior of the consumers.
- Improve the tool according to historic data about users selections. Currently PatternLens stores information about the metrics of the patterns that users select or reject. We aim to improve the way the information is presented to them, based on their feedback.

Acknowledgment. This work is supported by GENESIS project, funded by the Spanish Ministerio de Ciencia e Innovación under project TIN2016-79269-R.

References

1. Abelló, A., Ayala, C., Farré, C., Gómez, C., Oriol, M., Romero, O.: A data-driven approach to improve the process of data-intensive API creation and evolution. In: Proceedings of the 29th International Conference on Advanced Information Systems Engineering (CAiSE 2017), pp. 1–8. CEUR-WS. org (2017)
2. Macvean, A., Church, L., Daughtry, J., Citro, C.: API usability at scale. In: PPIG (2016)
3. Koçi, R., Franch, X., Jovanovic, P., Abelló, A.: Classification of changes in API evolution. In: 2019 IEEE 23rd International Enterprise Distributed Object Computing Conference (EDOC), pp. 243–249. IEEE (2019)
4. Wang, S., Keivanloo, I., Zou, Y.: How do developers react to RESTful API evolution? In: Franch, X., Ghose, A.K., Lewis, G.A., Bhiri, S. (eds.) ICSOC 2014. LNCS, vol. 8831, pp. 245–259. Springer, Heidelberg (2014). https://doi.org/10.1007/978-3-662-45391-9_17
5. Li, J., Xiong, Y., Liu, X., Zhang, L.: How does web service API evolution affect clients?. In: 2013 IEEE 20th International Conference on Web Services, pp. 300–307. IEEE (2013)
6. Van der Aalst, W.: Data science in action. In: van der Aalst, W. (ed.) Process Mining, pp. 3–23. Springer, Heidelberg (2016). https://doi.org/10.1007/978-3-662-49851-4_1
7. Espinha, T., Zaidman, A., Gross, H.-G.: Web API growing pains: loosely coupled yet strongly tied. J. Syst. Softw. **100**, 27–43 (2015)
8. Koçi, R., Franch, X., Jovanovic, P., Abelló, A.: A data-driven approach to measure the usability of web APIs. In: 2020 46th Euromicro Conference on Software Engineering and Advanced Applications (SEAA), pp. 64–71. IEEE (2020)
9. Zhang, T., Hartmann, B., Kim, M., Glassman, E.L.: Enabling data-driven API design with community usage data: a need-finding study. In: Proceedings of the 2020 CHI Conference on Human Factors in Computing Systems, pp. 1–13 (2020)
10. Doerrfeld, B.: 10+ API Monitoring Tools. https://nordicapis.com/10-api-monitoring-tools

Designing a Self-service Analytics System for Supply Base Optimization

Sven Michalczyk[1]([✉]), Mario Nadj[1], Harald Beier[2], and Alexander Maedche[1]

[1] Institute of Information Systems and Marketing (IISM), Karlsruhe Institute of Technology (KIT), Karlsruhe, Germany
{sven.michalczyk,mario.nadj,alexander.maedche}@kit.edu
[2] Robert Bosch GmbH, Stuttgart, Germany
harald.beier@de.bosch.com

Abstract. Reducing the number of suppliers – a process known as supply base optimization – is crucial for organizations to achieve better quality, higher service levels, and lower prices. The buyers in the role of the business analyst in corporate purchasing departments are responsible for this process and usually consider various selection criteria. Their decisions rely on accessing and analyzing large amounts of data from different source systems, but typically, they lack the necessary technological and analytical knowledge, as well as adequate tools, to do this effectively. In this paper, we present the design and evaluation of a self-service analytics (SSA) system that helps business analysts manage the maintenance, repair, and operations (MRO) supply base. The system recommends shifting purchasing volume between suppliers based on a machine learning (ML) algorithm. The results demonstrate the potential of SSA systems in facilitating ML model consumption by business analysts to perform supply base optimization more effectively.

Keywords: Supply base optimization · Self-service analytics · Machine learning · Maintenance, repair and operations

1 Introduction

Globalized competition leads organizations to establish highly responsive supply chains [1], a complex and challenging process because an interwoven network of relationships needs to be managed [2]. A relevant decision in designing a supply chain refers to the number of suppliers and the underlying relationships an organization needs to maintain for a product or service – the so-called supply base [3]. Supply base optimization (SBO) is defined as a "strategic option (…) to effectively manage their supply chains (…) reducing number of suppliers, (…) reconfiguring existing supply base by selecting new high-performance suppliers excluding underperforming suppliers" [4].

In the last two decades, SBO evolved into an important topic in academia and industry [5–7]. For instance, Singh [6] proposed an algorithm that prioritizes suppliers and allocates demands among them. Other studies showed that SBO results in stronger buyer-supplier relationships, leading to better quality, higher service levels, and lower prices

© Springer Nature Switzerland AG 2021
S. Nurcan and A. Korthaus (Eds.): CAiSE Forum 2021, LNBIP 424, pp. 154–161, 2021.
https://doi.org/10.1007/978-3-030-79108-7_18

[5, 8, 9]. Additional positive downstream effects were reported for the lead time for product development and suppliers' planning of their production efforts [10].

However, SBO is a complex endeavor for organizations because business analysts – buyers who manage the supply base – need to choose the best suppliers considering multiple selection criteria (e.g., the supplier's coverage of demand or overlap to other suppliers) from different source systems. These business analysts must be capable of accessing and analyzing large amounts of data, but they typically lack the required technological and analytical knowledge or adequate tools to do this effectively [11].

Against this backdrop, developing an SSA system for business analysts based on machine learning (ML) is a promising approach to tackle this problem, since SSA systems enable business analysts to prepare and analyze data on their own, with nominal IT support and are typically described as easy-to-use [12]. ML is suitable in this context because many decision criteria for SBO exist and need to be applied to large amounts of data. Following this approach, we collaborated with the industry to design and evaluate an SSA system for MRO in order to address two research questions: *(1) Which ML approach is suitable to identify overlapping demand in large supply bases? (2) How to design an SSA system for business analysts to consume ML models for SBO?*

We conducted semi-structured interviews with six corporate business analysts (CBAs) to elicit the underlying requirements. For the ML evaluation, we constructed null classifiers and calculated the accuracies to compare our models. Lastly, we evaluated our SSA system using a think-aloud session [13] with two CBAs. In summary, we developed and evaluated (1) an ML approach for SBO and (2) an SSA system, which facilitate the consumption of the trained ML models by business analysts in order to better manage the supply base of their organization with an easy-to-use interface. In the remainder of this article, we describe the related work, the usage scenarios, and the user groups involved. Subsequently, we introduce our ML approach and the user interface (UI), followed by an evaluation and a conclusion.

2   Supply Base Optimization

Research distinguishes between individual, integrated, and emerging models for supplier selection and evaluation [14]. The data envelopment analysis (DEA) is an established individual model that simultaneously considers various input (e.g., price index, delivery performance, and distance) and output criteria (e.g., supply variety, quality) [15] to measure supplier performance. In turn, integrated models, combine individual models. A prominent integrated model refers to the AHP (analytical hierarchy process), which can be combined with DEA [16] or specific ML models, such as artificial neural networks [17]. The AHP aims at selecting inhomogeneous suppliers with missing input or output values. Lastly, models that mitigate risks are emerging. For instance, Micheli et al. [18] suggest a risk-efficiency-based supplier selection approach.

However, most of these models assist in selecting new suppliers but not in identifying reduction potentials in existing supply bases. In this direction, Talluri and Narasimhan [4] developed a quantitative methodology, one of the first attempts to evaluate new suppliers against an existing supply base. However, this method is also not directly resulting in a reduction of the supply base. Furthermore, all models presented assume that products or services are directly comparable between suppliers, which is usually not true for real-world cases (as in the case of our industry partner) due to data quality issues such as poor item descriptions and incorrectly assigned material fields. Material fields cluster similar items into groups to organize purchasing departments. Against this backdrop, we trained an ML model to make items comparable and suggest an optimal number of suppliers for existing supply bases. Thereby, we considered various criteria for our system based on requirements received from our industry partner.

3 Self-service Analytics Prototype

3.1 Usage Scenarios and User Groups

A first analysis of the industry partner's supply base revealed that suppliers' purchasing volume distribution showed a large tail-end area. Tail-end suppliers accounted for only 20% of the purchasing volume, but for 80% of the number of suppliers, resulting in high relationship management effort and limited saving potentials. Thus, suppliers in the tail end were prime candidates for SBO. However, not all of those suppliers were fitting as they, for instance, sold niche products or were strategic partners. Thus, suppliers were manually flagged with "preferred" for suppliers to retain or "non-preferred" to consolidate.

At the industry partner, SBO refers to a process performed along three hierarchy levels of user groups. First, a bundling team manager set the target for the SBO (e.g., the number of suppliers to be reduced). Next, the CBAs need to achieve the specified target and determine in which material fields and regions suppliers are to be substituted, usually with a high bundling potential. From this information, the CBA can derive which regional business analyst (RBA) comes into question. Each RBA is responsible for a material field in a region and knows the demands that need to be covered. RBAs carry out the bundling by replacing existing suppliers or eliminating suppliers.

Our interview results revealed that business analysts in the MRO domain need to consider several selection criteria in this process: First, it is crucial to study whether the supplier has purchasing volume in other sub material fields and regions. Thereby, the regional availability of the supplier must be considered. Second, one needs to analyze whether parts from a supplier are in stock, and third, if the supplier delivers expendables or spare parts. If the criteria apply, a reduction could lead to difficulties in the production chain. Fourth, it is important to check whether the supplier is a preferred supplier, as elaborated above. Fifth, it is important to see if the supplier is a distributor or manufacture. Especially for small demands in the tail-end, distributers are favored because they can consolidate demands from different manufacturers. Sixth, it must also be investigated whether a supplier provides products or services since services are typically much harder to substitute and difficult to compare. Seventh, the hierarchy must be considered because if a supplier belongs to a hierarchy, all suppliers in that hierarchy are affected. Eighth, it must be investigated whether the preferred suppliers can substitute the demand of the targeted supplier. The latter requires the comparison of a huge set of purchase items.

3.2   Machine Learning Approach

We used supervised ML to fit a model to all tuples described by predictor variables to their respondent classes [19]. In our case, a tuple is an item, predictors are tokens constructed from item descriptions, and the respondent class is the supplier where the order was placed. We trained the model on preferred suppliers and made predictions with items of the non-preferred suppliers. In this way, we achieved a reallocation of ordered items from preferred to non-preferred suppliers and, on the supplier-level, a reallocation of non-preferred to one or more preferred suppliers. Our pipeline for data and natural language processing consisted of the following steps: First, we separated items by preferred suppliers, non-preferred suppliers, and material fields to train models for each material field independently. This was necessary to properly account for the individual characteristics in each material field. Second, we kept only alphanumeric characters and converted the item descriptions to lower characters. Third, we removed standard stop words and self-defined stop words such as "shipping, position, DHL" and applied a stemmer. Fourth, we performed unigram tokenization because items were shortly described and did not contain complete sentences. Fifth, we generated a document-term-matrix (DTM). A document was an item in this matrix (a row), and TF-IDF-weighted term counts served as the predictor variables (columns). TF-IDF stands for term frequency-inverse document frequency and is a measure for the originality of a term. We did not remove infrequent terms because they are already sparsely described. The processed DTMs were sparse as most variables occurred in only a few items. Sixth, we chose a memory-efficient version of a multinomial logistic regression as our matrixes were very large and sparse. This maximum entropy classifier estimated a probability model p for the classes (suppliers) represented by the short item texts' features. The principle of maximum entropy, as the name suggests, is to choose a distribution that maximizes entropy and adheres to the facts known in the data. Compared to a Naïve Bayes classifier, the features are not assumed to be statistically independent [20].

3.3   User Interface

The first view (see Fig. 1) supports CBAs. To facilitate data understanding, we chose the following visualizations: A histogram shows the distribution of the supplier volume with the reduction candidates marked as red bars to create a sense of urgency for business analysts (4). Red suppliers are flagged as non-preferred and fall below the volume threshold defined in the sidebar. Below, a heat map breaks down the reduction potential into sub material fields and regions (5). Lastly, we provide a table that allows for sorting by reduction potential (6). The reduction potential is calculated by multiplying the normalized purchasing volume and the share of substitutable items given the sidebar's probability threshold. With the heat map and the table, CBAs can quickly identify responsible RBAs.

The UI aims to make the result of the ML models easily accessible for business analysts, namely CBAs and RBAs. It consists of two views and a fixed sidebar on the left side. The sidebar has the following global filters: In the two dropdowns, the material fields can be selected (see 1 in Fig. 1). The first slider determines how confident the reallocations should be in terms of a probability measure (2). This measure makes the ML model accessible to business analysts, promoting an understanding of the reallocation possibilities. It ensures that only those items are reallocated that match the preferred suppliers well enough. With the next slider, business analysts can define a volume threshold to determine supplier candidates for reduction (3).

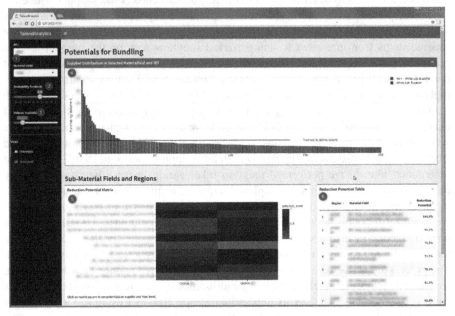

Fig. 1. View for Corporate Business Analyst (CBA)

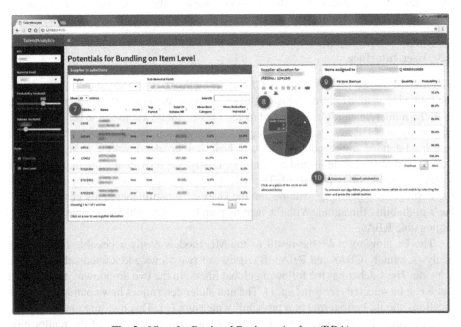

Fig. 2. View for Regional Business Analyst (RBA)

The second view (see Fig. 2) can be accessed through a drill-down either by clicking at a heat map cell, at a row in the table or through the sidebar. Because an RBA needs detailed information, we relied mostly on tables. The left table "suppliers to substitute" is ordered by the selection criteria described in the usage scenario above (7). The reallocation results can be explored by clicking at rows representing a reduction candidate. Subsequently, a pie chart shows the item reallocation to preferred suppliers (8). We chose a pie chart because it supports the understanding that items are potentially shifted to several preferred suppliers. Hence, a pie segment represents a matched preferred supplier. Dependent on the probability threshold setting in the sidebar, items might not be matching to any of the preferred suppliers because the association is not strong enough. They fall into a "rest category" that is displayed as a segment in the pie chart and as a column in the table. To drill down, the RBA can click on a segment to show the reallocated items. The items are displayed page-wise in a table to avoid overwhelming the user (9). Below this table, we integrated two buttons, one for downloading the set of items and one to submit a voting whether the items can be reallocated (10). This line of thinking is further supported by our usage scenario that requires different business analyst types to interact at different levels of hierarchy to perform SBO. Moreover, for shifting demands, business analysts need to contact suppliers and might initiate negotiations. In this regard, we integrated a link to the supplier's contact information.

4   Evaluation

4.1   Machine Learning Approach

We trained maximum entropy classifiers for each material field by performing grid searches with 4-fold cross-validation to tune the L1 and L2 regularizer and to assess whether stochastic gradient descent should be used to approximate the functions. The regularizers prevented the models from overfitting. We compared the results with null classifiers that predicted the largest preferred supplier per material field. We achieved reasonably high accuracies between 70 and 97% with holdout data, outperforming the null classifiers. Table 1 shows a sample of the results due to page limitations.

Table 1. A sample of material field accuracies

Material field	Accuracy null model	Accuracy model
A1	0.2834974	0.8951894
B3	0.2415432	0.8851104
B6	0.3571477	0.8321878
C1	0.5806726	0.9632521

4.2 User Interface

We have evaluated the UI in a think-aloud session [13] with two CBAs. Hereby, we asked them to identify high potential material fields and recommend suppliers for reduction to RBAs. In general, both CBAs have confirmed the usefulness of our solution and the importance of the SSA system's selection criteria. In particular, CBA 1 was positively surprised and stated that "*usually, we have to wait for 2-3 h to get this data*". However, both CBAs argued that the most significant impediment referred to the understanding of the ML related selection criteria "rest category" and "probability threshold". They played around with the probability slider in the sidebar, and CBA 2 concluded, "*this is the probability that this product can be shifted*". On this basis, both CBAs agreed on the measures' usefulness but requested a dedicated explanation, for instance, by relying on tooltips. Furthermore, the UI visualizations helped both CBs to explore the reduction potential and judge the output of the ML models. One exception was the heat map where they faced difficulties to spot areas of high reduction potential. The main reason for the difficulties referred to the overreliance on dark colors, such as "blue" or "violet". For the future, we plan to adjust the color coding of the heat map with a gradient from light to dark. In turn, both CBAs understood the tabular data on a fast level as they are familiar with tabular data in their daily work with Microsoft Excel. Lastly, both CBAs used the drill-down anywhere functionality extensively, and CBA 1 stated that "*the tool is working with a good structure*" (CBA 1). They naturally clicked on segments in the plots or rows in the tables to drill down, especially to investigate which items will be reallocated.

5 Conclusion

In this article, we (1) developed and evaluated an ML approach for SBO and (2) an SSA system, which facilitate the consumption of the trained ML models by business analysts who manage the supply base of their organization with an easy-to-use interface. We conducted semi-structured interviews with six CBAs in the MRO domain and derived several selection criteria for SBO. Through initial discussions with two experienced purchasing teams from other areas (e.g., office supplies), we consider the generalizability of these selection criteria to be possible. Nevertheless, future studies must verify this initial support. For the ML evaluation, we constructed null classifiers and calculated the accuracies to compare our models. We achieved reasonably high accuracies between 70 and 97% with holdout data for different material fields, outperforming the null classifiers. Finally, we performed a think-aloud session with two CBAs from our industry partner to evaluate the UI. For future work, we plan to incorporate the feedback from the think-aloud session to further improve our system towards a production-ready solution. From the ML perspective, we plan to apply association rules mining to achieve optimal allocations to preferred suppliers [21].

References

1. Park, J.H., Lee, J.K., Yoo, J.S.: A framework for designing the balanced supply chain scorecard. Eur. J. Inf. Syst. **14**, 335–346 (2005)

2. Stock, J.R., Boyer, S.L.: Developing a consensus definition of supply chain management: a qualitative study. Int. J. Phys. Distrib. Logist. Manag. **39**, 690–711 (2009)
3. Choi, T.Y., Krause, D.R.: The supply base and its complexity: implications for transaction costs, risks, responsiveness, and innovation. J. Oper. Manag. **24**, 637–652 (2006)
4. Talluri, S., Narasimhan, R.: A note on "A methodology for supply base optimization." IEEE Trans. Eng. Manag. **52**, 130–139 (2005)
5. Ogden, J.A., Carter, P.L.: The supply base reduction process: an empirical investigation. Int. J. Logist. Manag. **19**, 5–28 (2008)
6. Singh, A.: Supplier evaluation and demand allocation among suppliers in a supply chain. J. Purch. Supply Manag. **20**, 167–176 (2014)
7. Stump, R.L., Sriram, V.: Employing information technology in purchasing: buyer-supplier relationships and size of the supplier base. Ind. Mark. Manag. **26**, 127–136 (1997)
8. Hartley, J.L., Choi, T.Y.: Supplier development: customers as a catalyst of process change. Bus. Horiz. **39**, 37–44 (1996)
9. Hingley, M.K.: Power to all our friends? Living with imbalance in supplier-retailer relationships. Ind. Mark. Manag. **34**, 848–858 (2005)
10. Cormican, K., Cunningham, M.: Supplier performance evaluation: lessons from a large multinational organisation. J. Manuf. Technol. Manag. **18**, 352–366 (2007)
11. Michalczyk, S., Nadj, M., Maedche, A., Christoph, G.: A state-of-the-art overview and future research avenues of self-service business intelligence analytics. In: ECIS 2020 Research Paper, pp. 1–18 (2020)
12. Lennerholt, C., van Laere, J., Söderström, E.: Implementation challenges of self service business intelligence: a literature review. In: Proceedings of the 51st Hawaii International Conference on System Sciences (HCISS), pp. 5055–5063. Hawaii International Conference on System Sciences (2018)
13. Solomon, P.: The think aloud method (1995)
14. Ocampo, L.A., Abad, G.K.M., Cabusas, K.G.L., Padon, M.L.A., Sevilla, N.C.: Recent approaches to supplier selection: a review of literature within 2006–2016. Int. J. Integr. Supply Manag. **12**, 22–68 (2018)
15. Liu, J., Ding, F.-Y., Lall, V.: Using data envelopment analysis to compare suppliers for supplier selection and performance improvement. Supply Chain Manag. **5**, 143–150 (2000)
16. Farzipoor Sean, R.: A new mathematical approach for suppliers selection: accounting for non-homogeneity is important. Appl. Math. Comput. **185**, 84–95 (2007)
17. Ha, S.H., Krishnan, R.: A hybrid approach to supplier selection for the maintenance of a competitive supply chain. Expert Syst. Appl. **34**, 1303–1311 (2008)
18. Micheli, G.J.L., Cagno, E., Giulio, A.D.: Reducing the total cost of supply through risk-efficiency-based supplier selection in the EPC industry. J. Purch. Supply Manag. **15**(15), 1478–4092 (2009)
19. Gareth, J., Witten, D., Hastie, T., Tibshirani, R.: An Introduction to Statistical Learning with Applications in R, vol. 618. Springer, Heidelberg (2013)
20. Pang, B., Lee, L., Vaithyanathan, S.: Thumbs up? Sentiment classification using machine learning techniques. In: Proceedings of the 2002 Conference on Empirical Methods in Natural Language Processing (EMNLP 2002), pp. 79–86. Association for Computational Linguistics (ACL) (2002)
21. Lin, R.-H.: Potential use of FP-growth algorithm for identifying competitive suppliers in SCM. J. Oper. Res. Soc. **60**, 1135–1141 (2009)

Author Index

Printed in the United States
by Baker & Taylor Publisher Services